MAITREYA'S MISSION

BENJAMIN CREME

MAITREYA'S MISSION

BENJAMIN CREME

SHARE INTERNATIONAL FOUNDATION
Amsterdam, London, Los Angeles

First published in the Netherlands,

by Share International Foundation;

P.O. Box 41877, 1009 DB, Amsterdam

ISBN 90-71484-02-5

Manufactured in the United States of America
by GRT Book Printing, Inc., Oakland, CA

The painting reproduced on the cover was painted by Benjamin Creme in 1973/4. It represents the spiritual heart centre in man which is seen against the even-armed cross of Aquarius.

Dedicated to my revered Master
with profound gratitude
for His shared Wisdom and limitless patience
with my endless questioning.

ACKNOWLEDGEMENTS

I am grateful to the members of the San Francisco Bay Area Transmission Meditation groups and Tara Center for their invaluable help in transcribing, typing and proof-reading, often at short notice, the manuscript of this book. In particular, I am indebted to Michiko Ishikawa for her help in editing, organizing and arranging the material in the present form.

Note to Reader: The articles and questions and answers were published in *Share International* over the period from January 1982 to September 1986. In the present work, for ease of reading, they have been arranged according to subject with the result that they do not appear in the original order. The original date of publication is also given at the end of each question. Questions without dates were either newly transcribed from tapes and/or will be printed in forthcoming issues of *Share International*.

CONTENTS

INTRODUCTION

Since the publication of *The Reappearance of the Christ and the Masters of Wisdom* in 1980 I have been asked continually when I would be writing a sequel. My answer was always that I had no intention of writing another such book. What more could I say than I had said?

As my contribution to *Share International* magazine (apart from that of Editor) has evolved to include not only articles but a regular section of "Questions and Answers," a large body of material has gradually been formed which, we believe, supplies the long-awaited sequel to the Reappearance book. Since many other people simultaneously had the same idea, it would appear to answer a genuine need. This book then is a complilation of my articles and questions and answers published in Share International up to now (September 1986).

Certainly, in inspiring me to answer the many questions sent to *Share International*, my Master has illumined large areas of esoteric knowledge, some for the first time, others more deeply than was hitherto the case. This is particularly so in connection with the Seven Rays. A large body of information is presented, much of it entirely new, which should lead to new insights and deeper study of these energies which so condition our lives.

Transmission Meditation is also dealt with at length, together with reincarnation, karma, the after-life states, initiation, service and other subjects. In the interests of readability, rearranging the material into book form has necessitated a considerable degree of editing to keep the repetitions to a minimum. This is especially the case in the first chapter on the Emergence of Maitreya. During the 'waiting' period from May 1982 until now, I answered so many questions, many rather similar, on 'the state of play' and the media's role, action and non-action, that a decision had to be made between strict historical chronology—with the inevitable lengthy repetition—and readability. I have opted for the latter and have supplied a summary, only, of the events since May 1982. The original questions and answers, after all, are still available for their historical interest in back issues of Share International. I hope readers will agree with this judgement.

As usual, this has been very much a group endeavour, and my deep gratitude goes to the many people, on different continents, whose co-operative work has made this book possible.

Benjamin Creme

London 1986

CHAPTER I

MAITREYA AND THE PROCESS OF EMERGENCE

The Media and the Emergence

Maitreya, the Christ, has been in London since July 1977. He lives as an ordinary man concerned with modern problems—political, economic and social. Since March 1978, He has been emerging as a spokesman for the Pakistani-Indian community there. He is not a religious leader but an educator in the broadest sense, pointing the way out of the present world crisis.

He comes as the head of that group of enlightened men known as the Spiritual Hierarchy of Masters. The existence of such a group was first made public in the writings of H. P. Blavatsky and later Alice A. Bailey, whose book, *The Reappearance of the Christ* describes the events which are now unfolding.

In every age great teachers have emerged from the Spiritual Hierarchy to guide humanity through its next evolutionary step. We know Them historically as (among others) Shankaracharya, Krishna, the Buddha, the Christ and, later, Mohammed.

All the great religions posit the idea of a further revelation to be given by a future Teacher. Christians hope for the return of the Christ, the Buddhists look for the coming of another Buddha (the Lord Maitreya), while Moslems await the appearance of the Imam Mahdi, the Hindus a reincarnation of Krishna, and the Jews the Messiah. Students of the esoteric tradition know these as different names for one and the same individual, the World Teacher, the head of the Spiritual Hierarchy of Masters, and they look for His imminent return now.

According to esoteric teaching, the Christ manifested Himself 2,000 years ago in Palestine by 'overshadowing' His disciple Jesus, now the Master Jesus. This time Maitreya (the personal name of the Christ) comes Himself, as World Teacher for the Aquarian Age. From an astronomical viewpoint, we are now in the transitional phase between the Age of Pisces and that of Aquarius. To guide us safely through this difficult period, Maitreya has taken the extraordinary step of entering the modern world.

In July 1977, He emerged from His centre, a valley in the Himalayas, when least expected. As He foretold, He came "like a thief in the night" to take up His role as the World Teacher to help us transform our world. Maitreya took up residence in the East End of London, in a large, poor community of Pakistani-Indian immigrants.

Hierarchy had hoped that Maitreya, emerging as a community leader, would become first nationally, and then internationally, known. The British media, however, take little interest in the activities of the minority communities. The result was that public knowledge of Maitreya's activities remained confined to the immigrant community.

Because of this situation, as part of a contingency plan, I publicly disclosed the whereabouts of the Christ at a well-attended press conference in Los Angeles, U.S.A., on 14 May, 1982. This conference was intended not only to focus attention on London but also to galvanize the press into action. It was their responsibility, as representatives of the public, to search for the Christ and invite Him to speak to the world. It was hoped that the media would respond to my information at a level which would allow Him to come forward to them.

This hope, however, was not fulfilled. While the media did show an interest in the reappearance story, it did not go so far as to actually get involved in searching for Maitreya. The lack of interest shown by the British media after the press conference was partly explained by the Falkland crisis which at the time was commanding the almost exclusive attention of the British public. Only by the end of June 1982 did a few journalists, working independently, make any effort to find Maitreya.

The search did not prove easy. The community Maitreya was living in did not welcome the inquiries of curious Americans and Europeans. For fundamentalist Moslems, the idea of the coming of the Mahdi in this way was as much a heresy as the reappearance story is to the fundamentalist Christians.

For three years, my colleagues and I sought to inspire the media to take this information sufficiently seriously to become involved, thus enabling Maitreya to emerge into public life without the infringement of our free will—a major law governing His emergence. An invitation to Him from the world's media networks, representing humanity, to come forward and prove His true status was not only necessary, but a sign that humanity was ready for His guidance.

In the meantime, I was told that Maitreya intended to make His presence rather more obvious. He did so to a South American woman journalist who co-ordinated the 'search' for Him. Dining with another journalist in the Indian community one evening, and sitting with her back to the window of the restaurant, she suddenly felt that someone was watching her. Turning round, she saw looking at her a tall Asian figure, dressed in white from head to toe. She knew it was Maitreya, not only from His authority, dignity, loving smile, and the waves of energy which overwhelmed her, but also because she recognized Him. She had seen His face before—superimposed on my face and radiating brilliant light—during His overshadowing of myself while giving His Message at one of my lectures in January 1982. (This is an often-seen phenomenon at these lectures.) Her impulse was to run after Him when He moved away from the window but she was too moved by the event to think clearly—and no doubt He would not wish to be followed. *The Sunday Times* of 2 December 1984 carried an article on this story illustrating it with a drawing made under her direction by an artist friend.

At long last, in the summer of 1985, mainly through the persistent efforts of this free-lance journalist, an internationally representative group of 22 journalists from America, Europe and Japan gathered together at a rendezvous point—the same restaurant—in Brick Lane, East London, at 8 pm on 31 July, 1985. They met in the hope of being contacted by an envoy of Maitreya or even by Maitreya Himself. The date of the meeting was chosen by the journalists on purely practical considerations: the availability at the venue of a long-awaited American network owner assigned by NBC and of various British journalists returning from, or about to go on, holiday.

Despite the lack of media involvement since 1982, the passing of time allowed Maitreya to take steps towards discovery. The equation—Law of free will in relation to energy expended—was gradually fulfilled by the lapse of time and the presence of media representatives. For several months in 1984, the above-mentioned free-lance journalist organized such gatherings of media representatives. In this way, the needed expenditure of energy in 'searching' was gradually made. This large gathering of influential and representative members of the media led to high hopes that a contact would be made. The contact was planned but in the event had to be postponed. The following explanation was given by my Master:

The advent of a Being of the stature of the Christ is an event of planetary and even cosmic importance and is governed by certain laws. Inevitably, it also inspires the opposition of those materialistic forces, seen and unseen, planetary and cosmic, who stand to lose the power which has kept humanity in thrall for untold ages. On July 31, beginning about 12 noon, an initiative was launched by these forces which took the total attention of Maitreya and His Brotherhood of Light to contain. This containment was not achieved until about 3 am. The unanimous advice of the Masters was to postpone the contact. This decision was finally made about 9 pm. It was decided that the reception through the news media channels would not be of the best, evoking more disbelief, opposition and fear than was desirable.

In relation to Maitreya's advent, all influences and energies have to be at their most beneficial, and according to my Master the timing was not right. Even the fact that 31 July was a full moon (which we had thought auspicious) was, in the event, counterproductive.

Of course, all of us who had worked so hard to bring this gathering of journalists about were disappointed. From the viewpoint of the Christ, however, the evening was a great success. For thc first time, a truly representative group of the world's media, East and West, made themselves available to be contacted. This represented a symbolic invitation from humanity to come forward, and immeasurably freed Maitreya's hand to act directly Himself. In the long run, the media still have to make Maitreya known to the world but the work of getting them involved had now been done.

This symbolic action allowed Him to make His own approach to the media without infringing our free will. He had to wait until all signs and influences were at their most favourable for the communication of His presence and His message. This favourable period began about 8 December 1985. Maitreya took advantage of this and made His approach to major media in England and through them, in the world. As I understand it, the media contacted had little difficulty in seeing Him as a most remarkable, probably very holy teacher from the East, but found an initial difficulty in seeing Him as the Christ, and had an understandable reluctance to 'promote' Him as such. This was resolved, at least to a degree, and a 'modus operandi' evolved by which to present Him to the world without actually claiming Him as the Christ.

They (the media) agreed to issue a statement to the effect that a man claiming to be the Christ lives in London; that he is a member of the Pakistani community but presents himself as a World Teacher for all groups, religious and otherwise; that he wishes an opportunity to meet members of the press and media from all lands and peoples in order to establish his credentials; that if invited to do so he would welcome an opportunity to address all mankind through the linked TV channels in a way that will convince the world of his true status. This announcement will lead, through such an international press conference, to the Day of Declaration.

I don't understand how the TV controllers would come to decide to broadcast Maitreya on Declaration Day. Would they not have to have received a profound experience first? (Mar. '86)

Yes. They would have to be very sure that Maitreya was indeed the World Teacher, Christ or Messiah before they would invite Him to address the world. This would require some profound experience of His stature first. We can assume that Maitreya is able to provide such an experience.

If these media people announce that Maitreya merely *claims* to be the Christ, won't the other media think He is another of the false Christs? (Apr. '86)

Some may be very sceptical but the fact that the announcement will come from such high media sources will lend weight to the probable authenticity of the claim.

If Maitreya or any of the other Masters were not able to make contact in Brick Lane in July, could they not have sent an envoy either to explain or arrange another day? (Oct. '85)

The plan was that Maitreya Himself would make the contact, hence the weight of the initiative against its happening. It was not simply a physical contact being prevented, but an interference in the reception that such a contact would have had in the world. More opposition, fear and distortion, it was calculated, would have occurred than was acceptable to Maitreya and His plans for emergence. Any kind of contact would have undergone the same distortion. The really important result is that Maitreya is now able to act directly in a way not possible before.

You have said that Maitreya could not walk into the BBC, say, and announce Himself, because they would tell Him "to go and see a doctor." Now you say He can do so because after the journalists' meeting (on 31 July) He would not be infringing our free will. But why do you think the reaction would be different now? (Oct. '85)

I have not said the reaction would be different now, but that He is free to make a more direct approach. Also, I have not said that He will approach the BBC but that that is one of His options. Nor would He simply go to the reception desk and announce Himself. If He were to approach the BBC, for instance, it would be to the highest level, where decisions can be taken in relation to His general announcement. This is now possible to Him for the first time because of the action of the media on 31 July.

There have been many reports from Ireland that the figure of the Christ appeared on television during a report on the moving statue of Ballinspittle. Have you any information on this? (Oct. '85)

It is interesting to note that this image of the Christ appeared on Irish television during a report on the moving statue of Mary at Ballinspittle on the 9 pm news on 31 July. It was at 9 pm on that evening that the planned contact with the media was abandoned, for reasons previously given. The image seen was, in fact, of the Master Jesus (much closer to the thought-form of the Christ held by all Christians than the figure of Maitreya would be).

It has been five months since Maitreya made His approach to the British media, but they have not yet announced His presence? Why? (June '86)

It has been difficult for the media to make the full connection between Him and their concept of the Christ. This has proved an ongoing source of worry for them and has delayed their taking action. (They would have no interest in giving publicity to yet another Eastern 'guru.' He has to be the Christ.) Maitreya had further meetings with them in an attempt to encourage them to go ahead with their announcement as planned. They are, apparently, divided between those who are prepared to make a statement now and those who counsel caution (perhaps in the hope that somehow, as time goes by, they will know better what to do).

There is another factor which has recently arisen. The media in London have informed the authorities and certain representatives of religious and governmental bodies, with a view to ascertaining their reactions to an announcement of Maitreya's presence. In each case the response has been rather negative, and in some cases hostile. In this way, an atmosphere not conducive to bold action has been generated and a policy of 'wait and see' has developed. How long this can be maintained is difficult to say. It depends very much on which faction within the media involved has its way. Maitreya has not set a time-limit but has strongly impressed on the individuals contacted the need for immediate action to tackle the many and formidable problems which call for His attention and aid.

The media for their part have assured Him of their readiness to cooperate. The Masters are in no doubt about the eventual successful outcome of this delicate situation, and counsel a positive and hopeful attitude as we await events.

The major media contacted by Maitreya seem to be in no hurry to make His presence known. If they continue to be silent has Maitreya other plans? (July/Aug. '86)

Yes. As readers will know from the June issue of *Share International*, the media contacted are divided over whether to make an announcement now about Maitreya (despite their assurances of co-operation). It is certainly a difficult decision for them, for even the most guarded announcement from such a highly influential source and level is tantamount to a statement that the Christ is indeed in London.

Unless they are *absolutely* sure that Maitreya is 'the Christ' in their meaning of the term (and without an esoteric background this is difficult), their reluctance to speak out is understandable. However, if they take too long to act, Maitreya will seek again to 'chivvy' (nudge) them. Should this continue to fail, He will put into effect plans for a discreet emergence on His own, thus engaging normal media attention. He has been reluctant to do this as it means a degree of infringement of humanity's free will.

In what way would Maitreya's activity be limited if He were to come forward uninvited by the world's media?

Maitreya appears now, actually ahead of schedule, as the Agent of Divine Intervention, to mitigate the effects of earthquakes which have been mounting in frequency and intensity throughout the world over the past 150 years. If He were to come before the world, uninvited, He would infringe, to some degree, human free will. This He is reluctant to do (and would do only as a last resort) because it would limit, to some extent, His ability to act as Agent of Divine Intervention. The result would be greater human suffering from earthquake activities.

The energy He may use on our behalf is related to the invocative appeal we make to Him. The more, the more. (The more energy used by humanity to invoke Him, the more energy He may use on our behalf.)

You have said in the past that humanity is on an "upward wave of response to the outflow of energies"—does this still hold? (Nov. '82)

Yes, this still holds. We are on that upward wave of response which the Christ utilized in His emergence in 1977. He took advantage of the fact that humanity's response to the spiritual outflow from Hierarchy is, as it is to everything, cyclic in nature, and luckily we are still within that upward flow. I believe this will last several more years. ([*1986 update*] Although time is obviously shortening we still have a few more years in hand.)

Delay of Maitreya's Emergence

Since Maitreya has been working in London for five years now, haven't many people recognized Him? (July '82)

He Himself has said that while there are those in the group in which He dwells who do know His true status, He is withholding His identity for the time being so that He can appeal to us simply as an ordinary man. He did say very pointedly in Message No. 61: "Nothing which I do will seem extraordinary, nothing which I say will be bizarre or strange, simple indeed will be My approach."

So He will not do miracles, except on the Day of Declaration, when obviously the ability to speak telepathically to the whole of humanity at one time and to perform hundreds of thousands of instantaneous cures throughout the world, is a major miracle. But it is clear that He will do nothing which will set Him apart, and that is what makes locating Him rather difficult.

Does the delay in the Day of Declaration mean that humanity is not really ready for the transformations Maitreya is advocating? (July '82)

Humanity has invoked Maitreya into the world in a broad sense; His decision to reappear was made between 1936 and 1945. But He still has to be invoked into the general arena of the world. The fact that the media, who represent the people, are not really responding to the hypothesis of His presence means that humanity is not either. This is governing His emergence. He must see the non-response of the media as a sign of the non-responsiveness of humanity to His presence.

Whether this means that humanity is not ready for the transformations when He does come before them is another matter. I would think humanity is ready. Obviously in my work I have tended to create the most hopeful picture which could galvanize human response and hope and expectancy. It may well be that His problems are greater than I envisage, but I do not think any delay in His declaration to the world will effect the speed of our response. Maitreya Himself said: "All else failing I shall emerge into a world ready, but unprepared, a world which knows not yet that I am among you. Far better would it be for Me to come before you as the expected one."

So Maitreya knows that humanity is ready.

Could not your Master, in his beautiful and inspiring articles, give us some specific information about the Emergence? (May '83)

The request has been passed on—but it is my belief that the Master, and Maitreya Himself, do not know exactly when He will be discovered and therefore when the Declaration can take place. As far as They are concerned, the Day of Declaration will occur when humanity, through its representatives the media, invites Him to speak to mankind.

(This question makes reference to the articles written by my Master for *Share International* and published as *A Master Speaks.*)

In 1982, near the original time for the Day of Declaration, the Falkland war broke out. Now that Maitreya's emergence is again imminent, the business with Libya, America and terrorism intensifies. Is there any connection?

Yes. Those with most to lose by Maitreya's emergence, that is the forces of materiality, the forces of evil, do everything in their power to prevent it. War, terrorism, tension, fear, chaos are their main weapons. Many world leaders play right into their hands, not because they are evil, but because they are often ignorant, dogmatic and chauvinistic, lacking in a world view.

Events Regarding the Day of Declaration

What exactly will happen on Declaration Day? (May '86)

The Christ will come on the world's television channels, linked together by satellite. All those with access to television will see Him but He will not speak. He will establish a *telepathic* rapport with *all* humanity simultaneously. This rapport will take place on three levels: (1) mentally, as an overshadowing of the minds of all peoples, so that they will hear His words inwardly in their own language; (2) as an outflow of the Christ Principle (the energy which He embodies) through the hearts of all humanity, invoking their intuitive and heartfelt response; and (3) as a mass healing—many hundreds of thousands of spontaneous 'miracle' cures will take place simultaneously.

These are the ways, on Declaration Day, in which Maitreya will convince the world of His true status as the Christ,

Maitreya Buddha, Imam Mahdi, Krishna, Messiah, Miroku Bosatsu, Messenger and Representative of God, World Teacher and Avatar for the Aquarian Age. This will be a repetition, only now on a world scale, of the true happenings of Pentecost, 2,000 years ago. It will also foreshadow *our* future ability to communicate telepathically, at will, over any distance. In celebration of this event, Pentecost will become one of the major festivals of the New World Religion which, eventually, Maitreya will inaugurate.

What criteria will be used to determine who will be healed or cured on Declaration Day?

Karma and faith. Those whose karma permits and whose faith opens them to the energy of the Christ Principle as it flows from Maitreya will be healed.

You have said that the communications satellites are there so that the Christ may speak to the world. Could you elaborate on this please? Are any of the people at the "top" of the process of putting them into orbit aware of this? (July/Aug. '84)

Until now, every Teacher who has come to the world has given His teaching to a small group. It has then taken centuries for the Teaching to be disseminated—and in the process distortions and discolorations of the original teaching have crept in. For the first time in our history the Teacher can speak directly to all through the linked media networks—and can be seen by all simultaneously on Declaration Day. The communications technology is inspired by Hierarchy for this purpose. (It is not really so that we can all watch World Cup Soccer.) The people involved in this process, "top" or otherwise, are not aware of this.

How is it possible for the Christ to connect with us telepathically (on the Day of Declaration) when most of us are restless and have 'broken' mental microphones? Is not this chronic condition only cured by regular and deep meditation? (Oct. '84)

Yes, I agree that most of us do not have the inner mental focus or magnetic aura that makes conscious telepathy possible, but the Day of Declaration must be seen as a unique event and situation for the Christ. For Him, there is no separation. He is omniscient and omnipresent. He will overshadow the minds of humanity in such a way as to make us—*temporarily*—open to His message.

On the Day of Declaration will the one-third of the world who will be sleeping hear the Christ and experience the overshadowing? (Oct. '82)

Not unless they wake up! Everyone will know beforehand the date and time arranged for the Christ's 'broadcast,' so, if they have any sense, whatever the time of day or night in any particular country, they would be well advised to miss some sleep for that unique event!

On Declaration Day you say we will hear Him (the Christ) telepathically while we see His face on TV. Is He going to speak into a microphone for those with only radio? (Mar. '86)

No. It will be the same telepathic rapport which he will establish with all humanity. The radios will alert people to the timing of the event.

What do you think would happen if the people of the world fail to recognize the Christ or if they reject Him? (July/Aug. '84)

If that were to happen then I believe we would destroy ourselves—and all life on this planet. However, the Christ Himself has said: "have no fear that mankind will reject Me. My plans are safe in your hands." (Message No. 65)

Doesn't a worldwide telepathic overshadowing imply that a large part of humanity forcibly has to accept the occurrence of "miracles?" Would this change of world concept not be too quick? Can we conclude from this that Declaration Day will not take place? (Mar. '84)

For nearly nine years I have stated as strongly as I know how that Declaration Day will take place, and through a telepathic rapport established between Maitreya and humanity. I have learned nothing to make me change that information given to me by my Master, a Master of the Wisdom and a close disciple of Maitreya. The question implies an understanding of the need for preparation of humanity before D-Day. That preparation—the creation of the climate of expectancy and an awareness of the mode of appearance—is precisely what I and all those working with me have been engaged in all these years. I really do not see that the overshadowing of humanity on D-Day forces "a large part of humanity to accept miracles." People can accept it or reject it, just as today many reject the evidence of their eyes and mind experience, for example, in questions of survival after death, or ESP, etc. The really important thing is whether people accept and act on the appeal of Maitreya made in this extraordinary way. I believe the majority will.

Could you not have got it slightly wrong and the real Declaration Day occurred with the Live Aid Concert showing human unity? (Sept. '85)

The Live Aid Concert was a fine manifestation of the aspiration for human solidarity and unity shared by millions around the planet. But let us not exaggerate its importance or effect. It cannot be said to have galvanized the world into accepting the principle of sharing. The aim of Maitreya on the Day of Declaration will be to do just that.

How are efforts such as Band-Aid, Live-Aid, USA for Africa affecting the reappearance of the Christ? (May '86)

Not at all. His reappearance takes place according to its own laws. These Aid manifestations, however, are a direct result of His energy which pours daily into the world, and are a sign that His teaching (about the need for sharing) is finding response.

Why was there not telepathic communication with all of mankind at the last coming of Christ? (Oct. '84)

The world was too fragmented until now for telepathic contact to take place in such a way as to avoid infringing human free will—by preparation in advance. Every Teacher who has come up until now, including the Christ in Palestine, has given His teaching to one small group in one country, and it has taken centuries for the Teaching to be disseminated, leading to its distortion. Because of world-wide communications, today is the first time that the Teacher can speak simultaneously and directly to the whole world.

Maitreya's Life in the Asian Community

Why did Maitreya choose to emerge in London? (July '82)

Many people have asked me "why London," with a certain degree of envy; I mean what is wrong with New York for instance? Yes, quite so; as I said in Los Angeles, if I had been Maitreya I would have picked Laguna Beach or the Côte d'Azur. It is a question of the work of the disciples in preparing the way for Him. He would come into that arena in which the disciples, along the line of His work, mainly in the economic/political field, have been most successful. The disciples working in the United Kingdom have been rather more successful in their work than in other parts of the world. That is His major reason for coming to London. Of course the more obvious reason is that, coming from the Himalayas as He does, and descending as He did into Pakistan, He can come as a visitor into this country for a few years and lose Himself in the Pakistani/Indian community—which He has been able to do rather well, in fact rather too successfully for our liking.

Was it of astrological importance that the Christ chose to come to London? (Oct. '85)

No. That had no significance.

Would it not have been more suitable if He had appeared in the Eastern world, where He would have been more easily recognized? (Oct. '85)

I do not think we can be sure that He would be more easily recognized in the East. Nor do many Eastern countries have the media facilities and influence which He needs to be accepted. Is there any media network in the world which has the reputation for sober judgement and truth of the BBC, for example? Besides that, there are other reasons (with which I have dealt in previous questions) for His choice of London.

After Declaration Day, or even before, will Maitreya immediately relinquish all affiliation with the British Asian Community? (Jan. '82)

After Declaration Day He will immediately belong to all humanity. No one nation or people will be able to claim Him as theirs alone. That He will continue to identify Himself with persecuted and impoverished minorities I have no doubt, but I imagine that no formal affiliation with the London Asian community will be kept.

Is it possible that Maitreya is no longer in London? (Aug. '82)

Maitreya is still in London. He has not left. However, it may be useful to point out that His public meetings are not limited to the Brick Lane area. He speaks publicly in various parts of London, but always in areas where it is most natural for Him to be—in Asian communities.

Has Maitreya appeared in any way outside the U.K.? If so, when and where? (June '86)

No. So far, He has confined His public activities to the Asian community in Britain.

While in India this February we heard a rumour that Maitreya had returned to Pakistan. Can you comment on this? (Sept. '83)

I wonder who starts these rumours off on their journey. Some wish-fulfilling fundamentalist or reactionary politician perhaps? Or even some old-ager in new age clothing who does not want Him around? Or simply a pessimist? Needless to say, there is no truth at all in this rumour. Maitreya has taken a one-way ticket into the modern world.

If I went to London would I have a chance to meet the man who calls himself the Christ? (Oct. '84)

No. He does not call Himself the Christ or Maitreya, but is living for the time being as an ordinary member of the Asian Community using a common Moslem name.

What are his daily activities? Does Maitreya ever attend, for example, morning prayers at the local mosque? (July/Aug. '83)

He has occasionally done so in order to become known and seen as one of the community—an ordinary man.

Does He meet and discuss community issues and problems with local community leaders? (July/Aug. '83)

He has met with and does meet and discuss with people of the community. But none of this takes place on a formal basis or 'officially.' He takes part in discussions and meetings, and puts forward His opinions and suggestions just as anyone might do, simply as a matter of his personal judgement.

Does He ever, for instance, advise the community on racial issues? (July/Aug. '83)

As a member of that community how could He avoid discussing racial issues? However He would be unlikely to make that a separate or sectarian focus of His work. He helps all who ask His help. He is a wise guide, friend and counselor to all in need. He makes Himself available to the people. He serves them. He helps in ways they request and know about, and He works in ways of which they are quite unaware.

We are told that the Christ is visiting His community. Is this only the Asian community in London or does it include New Age communities all over the world? Has He personally visited communities in the U.S.A.? (Oct. '84)

His contacts have been restricted to the Asian community in London. After the Day of Declaration He will make an itinerary around the world visiting most countries.

Is the Christ necessarily confining Himself to personal contacts within the Asian community only, since London contains so many other opportunities for contact, perhaps influence, both individually and socially? (July/Aug. '83)

So far, yes. He is at pains to emerge as a spokesman of the Asian community, identified with them and their problems, which are symptomatic of underprivileged humanity everywhere. He is therefore reluctant to spread the area of His activity beyond the group of which He is now a part. In this way, He can emerge as "a man among men," one of the people, emerging from their midst.

If the Christ is here where may a devotee go to see and be with Him? (Jan. '86)

The last thing the Christ wants is a group of devotees around Him. Those who see Him in that kind of guru relationship are, I believe, mistaken. He is a teacher, an educator, an executive, and comes to help humanity to right the wrongs of society rather than to sit devotedly at His lotus feet.

Does Maitreya ever allow people to visit Him? (Apr. '84)

Apparently, yes, but only those who would have good reason to do so—that is, His co-workers and intimates. I have known His address and the name He uses for a long time but have not been allowed to visit Him. It would appear that it is better for me, from the karmic point of view, that I continue my work of preparation without the final, absolute confirmation and proof which a physical meeting would bring. In this way, despite the many subjective experiences which make me convinced of His presence, I still work with a small degree of faith.

Presumably He does not need sleep—surely, those with whom He lives must realize that while in one way He truly is a man of the people, He is in no way ordinary? Do they know that He is the Christ, or the Mahdi? Are they sworn to secrecy, for the present? (July/Aug. '83)

Those with whom He lives know Who He is and are sworn to secrecy. They are close disciples.

Does Maitreya eat food? Is He vegetarian? If so, what is His diet? Does He consume any alcohol? (Jan. '86)

Maitreya does not need to eat but can do so if required to for social purposes. In that case he would eat only vegetarian food in small amounts. He never drinks alcohol.

Does He heal? Has He gained a reputation as a healer? (July/Aug. '83)

He performs healing all the time, but He is not known as a healer. None of the healing He carries out would call any attention to Him. It is as unsensational as possible. The people healed do not even realize, necessarily, that they are receiving healing from Him. He visits the sick in the hospital. While there, He heals others in the hospital without anyone being aware of it at all.

Is Maitreya 'employed' in some capacity by the local community? (July/Aug. '83)

No, He is not employed. But that does not mean He is ever idle. He never ceases His work.

Does Maitreya always wear the little Moslem crochet cap which the journalist described? What clothes does He wear? (July/Aug. '85)

No. He varies His headgear and clothes to suit the occasion, sometimes Moslem, sometimes Western. I understand He frequently wears 'local' Moslem costume.

Does Maitreya have another 'standard' name by which He is known by close associates, or does He go by the name "Lord Maitreya" exclusively? (Dec. '85)

He is known by the Masters and higher initiates of the Hierarchy as Maitreya. In the Asian community of London, however, as I have said earlier, He uses a common Moslem name.

Did Maitreya choose His own name? (Apr. '84)

No. It was given to Him by His Master long, long ago, in mid-Atlantean times, when He took the second initiation. It means The Happy One, The One Who brings Joy or Gladness.

You have said that He has played various musical instruments at Asian concerts and meetings. Which instruments does He play? (July/Aug. '85)

He occasionally plays at gatherings but is not a professional musician. He plays the flute, tabla, vina and several other instruments.

How does the Christ get to the various venues at which He presently speaks? Public transport or car? Could He materialize and dematerialize without being found out? (Feb. '83)

He could, no doubt, materialize and dematerialize at will without being found out, but I understand He does not employ these magical methods. He is living very much as an ordinary man, one of us. My information is that He travels to the meetings occasionally by car but usually by public transport.

When Maitreya entered London did He pass through customs? (Nov. '83)

Yes, in the usual way. (I do not know what He answered when asked: "Have you anything to declare?")

What occupation was listed on His passport? (Nov. '83)

Teacher.

Did He enter as an individual or as part of a group or family? (Nov. '83)

As an individual.

Are the close disciples He lives with known to those who have studied the teachings? (Feb. '83)

No.

Why is the Christ in an Indian body? (Nov. '85)

He is not in an Indian body. He has lived in the Himalayas for thousands of years and has really no nationality. The body in which He now appears is self-created—as a thoughtform of Himself—and is not specifically Indian, although he does live in the Asian community in London, and came through Pakistan to London.

Does the Christ ever record His instructions by His own handwriting or His own voice ? (Oct. '84)

No. His "instructions" go only to the higher initiates and the normal mode of contact between Them is telepathy.

Has the group around Maitreya published anything in English? (Feb. '84)

No. So far the only articles presented by those around Maitreya have been in the Indian languages. That group consists of those close to Maitreya and also those who are simply responding to His ideas. ([*1986 update*] There have now been several pamphlets issued in English by Pakistanis responding to His teaching.)

Would it generally be possible to recognize the Christ's voice on radio or TV, for example, purely by the similarity between that voice and your (Creme's) recorded voice

during the mental overshadowing in the Messages from Maitreya? (Feb. '83)

No. The voice on the tapes of Messages, however changed in timbre and pitch by the overshadowing energy, is mine. There is no reason to suppose that Maitreya's voice is remotely like this.

Does Maitreya need to be in seclusion or undisturbed meditation when sending His blessing through you? If so, do His close co-workers or disciples co-operate in ensuring this? (Sept.'84)

No, absolutely not. He can divide His consciousness into thousands of separate areas of attention and probably only a minuscule part of His consciousness is used to overshadow me.

Have you ever attended any of Maitreya's lectures? Are you allowed to attend them? (Aug. '82)

I have never attended any of His lectures. Since most of the meeting is in Bengali or Urdu, I would not have understood much, either. I might add I have been asked not to attend even if I know the venue in advance.

The Christ mentions several times (in the Messages) that His face is becoming widely known among His brothers—is that the inner group at His Centre who know who He really is? (May '84)

Not necessarily. I believe He means that He is becoming more widely known in various parts of the Asian community as He visits their different community meetings every week.

Does the drawing of the Lord Maitreya by David Anrias in his book, *Through the Eyes of the Masters*, correspond to the physical form which the World Teacher has adopted in His return? If so, would this be a help in trying to locate Him? (July/Aug. '83)

To my eyes, the drawing bears no resemblance to the Lord Maitreya and would therefore be of no help in discovering Him. It cannot have escaped people's notice that all the drawings are very alike, whereas the Masters are as individual and distinct as we are.

Is Maitreya still giving talks in the Asian community on a regular basis? (Dec. '85)

Yes indeed. The normal thing is for Him to turn up—as an ordinary member of the community—at one or other of the community gatherings which take place, all over London, each weekend. During the course of the meeting—He may stay for the whole evening or only for a short time—He will speak on His concerns, the need for justice, sharing, co-operation. These talks may last for five, ten, twenty, thirty, sometimes forty-five minutes, but in a quite informal manner, not as a "lecture." The gatherings, too, may be small or of several hundred people, in halls or private houses.

Very recently, an Asian gentleman who has attended my London lectures several times was taken by friends to such a meeting in a large house in east London. The meeting was held in a very large room which was not completely filled. There they listened to a man who spoke for about five minutes or so. "He spoke very quietly and simply, in perfect English, never repeating a phrase or sentence," said my informant. "And his words seemed to penetrate your mind, your whole body, so that you believed them, you knew he was speaking the truth—you didn't have to ask any questions. He talked about just what you talk about at your lectures: the need to change our direction, our ways of living, the need for co-operation, justice. And the Masters—He talked about the Masters and how they bring enlightenment to humanity. He said that soon the world's leaders would be saying what he was saying."

"There was a group around him who tried to keep people away from him. When we asked them who this man was, where he came from, where he lived, they would tell us nothing. We asked when we could hear him again and they said: 'Look in your local papers, it will be advertised.' I managed to get near him and asked him if he knew anything about Maitreya. He answered: 'Ask yourself.' (*B.C.*:In other words, use your intuition.) Then the group around him bundled him out into a motor car. He was extraordinary, like us and yet not like anyone I have ever seen. He had an extraordinary calm about him. We all agreed that he was most remarkable; he had the same effect on my friends."

A week later my informant went again to the house in east London and there met one of the group around this man. "Who is the man who spoke last week, I asked. 'We believe he is the one they are looking for. There is a whole movement which grows all the time. I am new to it, only this year, so I don't know too much, but some have been in it for some years now. We try to carry out his teaching, to change society. Some who have been in this for a long time have had extraordinary experiences. They have seen many strange things but when they try to talk about them they forget, their minds go blank. We write letters and pamphlets and send them to institutions, showing what changes are needed. He talks not only in London, but also in other cities like Leicester and Birmingham.'"

The Asian gentleman who gave me this information described 'the man' in very similar terms to the journalist who saw Maitreya at a Brick Lane restaurant last year: tall, slim, dressed in white Pakistani clothes, broad-shouldered, long face, long nose, high cheekbones. There was one striking difference—the eyes. Whereas the journalist saw his eyes as "large, dark, very luminous," this man's eyes were curiously dull, hollow, empty. When he smiled, they did not twinkle. My experience of Maitreya is that His eyes are extraordinarily bright. Does this prove that 'the man' cannot be Maitreya? Not at all. The simple explanation would be that, assuming he *was* Maitreya (my informant is convinced he was—and so am I) He was 'out of the body' while talking at the meeting; really only a shadow of Himself was present while He was engaged on a thousand other tasks and levels. (Apparently this dull-eyed phenomenon is frequently seen in Sai Baba whose eyes are usually very luminous.) The information that He talks in cities other than London is new to me. Checking this with my Master, it seems that a 'counterpart' body does visit these places, while He remains in His centre, London.

Making Known the Story of the Reappearance

Why are you looking for another spiritual teacher to appear? Do we not already know from the great teachers who have already demonstrated that we are spiritual beings and have all (God) the Father within us? But when we are not consciously aware of it we live like a branch cut off from the vine. (Jan. '86)

I am not looking for another spiritual teacher. I am simply making known the fact that, *according to cyclic law*, another Great One has come. The great teachers of the past may well have demonstrated *in themselves* that we are spiritual beings and have innate divinity, but where is the expression of that divinity in humanity—when millions starve in a world of plenty; when the world stands on a knife-edge of peace or war; when the poor get poorer and the rich richer? It obviously takes a great spiritual teacher to inspire humanity to *reveal* the divinity we so glibly claim to have within.

According to the Master D.K., Maitreya cannot return before 2025. Can you give an explanation or can Maitreya? (May '82)

First of all, with respect, the Master D.K. did *not* write that the Christ cannot return until 2025. In His very first book, *Initiation Human and Solar*, published in 1922, He said (on page 61) that we could look for the return of the Christ sometime towards the middle or close of this present century. In *The Reappearance of the Christ*, published in 1948, the Master D.K. said that the time is known only to the few, but that They "are ready to move at any time." He also revealed in *The Externalisation of the Hierarchy* that it was hoped that the Christ might return around 1950. This was not to be. The experience of the war, however harrowing, had not been sufficient to change mankind's attitudes. The world quickly returned to the old ways. Barriers were thrown up again and the Cold War began. The date of the Christ's return was put back until later. If it was thought that 1950 was a possible date how much more possible is His return now?

Nowhere in all the works of the Master D.K. does He say that the Christ *cannot* return until 2025, but it was thought in the early days that the preparation of humanity and of the Masters Themselves would probably take that time. Many groups believe that it is impossible for the Christ to return before 2025 because the necessary changes as outlined by the Master D.K. do not appear to have taken place. But as far as Hierarchy is concerned mankind is inwardly—mentally and emotionally—ready. Humanity has accepted the principles necessary to bring the Christ into the everyday world. What is now required is the outer manifestation of this inner reality.

The Christ is in the world now, actually ahead of the planned date (which is not 2025) for three main reasons. One is to speed up the process of change and so save from certain death and starvation countless millions. He also mitigates, by His physical presence in the everyday world, the effects of disasters in the form of earthquakes. Another important reason for His return now is that humanity is at present on an upward wave of response to the energies pouring into the planet and directed by the Hierarchy. The Christ is here now to take advantage of this fact while it lasts.

In the news articles which came out several years ago it was stated that "soon the Christ will acknowledge His identity and *within the next two months* will speak to humanity through a worldwide television and radio broadcast. His message will be heard inwardly, telepathically, by all the people in their own language." Well, two months (and more) have gone by, and I've yet to see anything which would suggest that this prophecy has been fulfilled. Should I consider this a false prophecy or a 'postponed' one? There were about 333 prophecies in the Old Testament which predicted the arrival of 'the Christ' 2,000 years ago, all fulfilled perfectly. If Maitreya *is* the Christ shouldn't the same hold true today? (Dec. '85)

The full-page advertisements of April, 1982, referred to in the question were placed by myself and my colleagues as a last major attempt to alert the world to the Christ's presence before 30 May 1982 (the date chosen by Maitreya as the *earliest* possible time by which humanity would be ready to respond to His appeal. The precise date of 30 May—the festival of Pentecost—was chosen for symbolic reasons). The statement in the full-page advertisements was not, therefore, a mystical or psychical 'prophecy' but the release of information about a plan to prepare humanity for the event. The non-response of the media to my announcement—at a press conference in Los Angeles on 14 May, 1982—that Maitreya was in London, and that the media were invited to approach Him in the Asian community there, led to the postponement of the Day of Declaration.

Many people have a rather naive view of events like the appearance of an Avatar or World Teacher, believing—through prophecies often centuries old—that they are scheduled for some exact day in some particular year and in some particular manner. (Some people believe the date of the Christ's reappearance is to be found in the mathematics of the Great Pyramid, for example.) This is not so. Of course, there is a general time period, cosmically determined, but the exact timing of such events depends on humanity's readiness and ability to respond. I do not know how many prophecies there are in the Old Testament concerning the coming of the Christ in Palestine, but even had there been 3,333 the facts are that the *timing* of His appearance through Jesus was not involved in them—nor did the people of the time respond to Him; only the few recognized Him. The others, interpreting the prophecies through their religious and nationalistic hopes, fears and prejudices, rejected Him. It has been my work these last 11 years, therefore, to prepare the way for Him by creating the climate of hope and expectancy—and by presenting His return and concerns in such a way as to *ensure* His recognition.

Humans relate to actions! Defending the existence of the Christ seems to be counterproductive action. Wouldn't humankind be better served by *showing* that the Christ is here and ready to be accepted? (May '86)

(1) I am not 'defending' the existence of the Christ but making it known, releasing the information. (2) I do not believe this activity to be counterproductive. On the contrary, the number of people alerted to this event grows daily—thus my work gets done. (3) If I had Him in my pocket I would most certainly show Him.

How are we to know for certain that Lord Maitreya is not the false Christ? (Oct. '82)

There is not only one 'false Christ.' There are several well-known teachers who believe themselves, or are believed by their followers, to be the Christ, and from my personal experience alone I know scores of deluded people who are convinced that they are the Christ. Discrimination and Spiritual Recognition are the key. I suggest that on the Day of Declaration, by the overshadowing and telepathic rapport which He will establish with all humanity simultaneously, you will have no doubts about His true status. A tree is known by its fruits and it is by His love, wisdom, spiritual potency and work for humanity that you will recognize Maitreya and know Him for what He is.

Why is there no other messenger in public to tell the story of the Christ's return? Is one messenger not too little for such a large-scale plan? (July/Aug. '84)

In my book *The Reappearance of the Christ and the Masters of Wisdom*, and frequently at lectures, I have said that five disciples, one in each of the five major Spiritual Centres—New York, London, Geneva, Darjeeling and Tokyo—were given the task of making the initial approach to the public about the Reappearance, so creating a climate of hope and expectancy. I am the only one of these five to work publicly, openly. Had the other four also done so I have no doubt that the media response to this information would have been altogether more open-minded and dynamic. It would appear that these four do not have the close moment-to-moment contact with their Masters which I enjoy, so perhaps lack the conviction (and therefore the confidence) to take a public stand in affirming the Christ's presence.

Do you know if any of the four disciples have now started to speak openly? (Apr. '86)

It appears that some of them at least are a little more active, albeit still with their own interpretation of what is meant by 'the return of the Christ.' For example, the one in New York (who apparently has attended my lectures but does not believe my information) is somewhat more open than before, but still sees the 'return' in terms of the Christ Principle in humanity. The one in Geneva is a little more active but still along 'Christ Principle' lines. The one in Darjeeling is still asleep, while the one in Tokyo, though active, can hardly be recognized as talking about the Christ or World Teacher at all.

Has the method of relaying communications or messages through a disciple *before* the advent of the Avatar, such as in your case, ever been employed by previous avatars? If so can you name the individuals? (July/Aug. '83)

I understand that this is a method which has often been used in the past. The only one we know of historically is John the Baptist, although many of the Prophets performed a similar function.

I don't understand the hostility you have encountered. The things you have said are sensible and loving. But I can understand why the Christ has not revealed Himself yet. Given the hostile environment, He would not live two minutes. Don't you agree? (May '86)

Any hostility I have encountered has come from two sources: the Christian fundamentalist groups and certain esoteric groups—and for the same reason: they are both defending territory. They are, both of them, the prisoners of their own dogmas.

It is not a hostile environment, however, which has delayed Maitreya's emergence but the non-response of humanity—through its representatives, the media, to the information that He has awaited discovery in London since May 1982. As for His safety, that is assured. He is invulnerable.

Are you discouraged by the fundamentalist resistance to your message? (May '86)

No, not at all. Nor am I surprised by it, since my information shakes their dogmas to the core.

What might become of the fundamentalist leaders of all religions once Maitreya has established Himself openly?

I am sure there are some who will never change but many, I believe, will be offering their services—perhaps for a small love-offering!

What was the reason for Him to give the last Message in May 1982—was it because it had been hoped that the Day of Declaration would be in June that year? And why, when that was not possible, do you suppose that there have been no more Messages from the Christ? (May '84)

The Day of Declaration was planned to take place on 30 May 1982. I suppose that the last Message was given in May 1982 because Hierarchy expected that He would soon be discovered and revealed to the world. They could be given again at any time—the overshadowing of myself by Maitreya continues at every meeting—but presumably it is thought that the 140 already given are sufficient to evoke a response from any open-minded person. They contain the essence of His concerns.

Why does Maitreya refer only to brothers in His Messages? (Oct. '82)

The fact is, if you read the Messages as a whole, that He does not refer only to "brothers," but quite often to "brothers and sisters." Every Message has a very definite rhythm and mantric effect and is therefore pruned of all unnecessary words. One of the striking things about the Messages, to my mind, is precisely their economy of means, the sheerness and austerity of the language and yet density of meaning conveyed so simply.

Do you think that the delay in the 'discovery' of the Christ has caused people to lose interest? (Aug. '82)

Everyone is, naturally, disappointed that the media has not yet revealed the Christ to the world and no doubt the delay has disheartened some people. On the other hand, there continues to be persistent hope and conviction on the part of many, many individuals that they will shortly see the Christ. What I believe the delay has done is to allow enough time for the idea and the possibility of thc Christ's presence to 'filter through' to more people. It is extraordinary, but we are still receiving requests for information prompted by the full-page statements placed in approximately twenty newspapers around the world in April. So people are still responding to the information and interest is actually growing. (This continues to be the case in 1986.)

How far can we go in telling people about the Christ? We don't know how evolved people are so we don't know how much information they can take. For how long can we insist? (Apr. '83)

The point in evolution is not important. People are hungry for information at all levels. It is important not to be dogmatic. This turns people away. Simply tell people about the Christ's return for as long as they want to hear. If the soil is fertile the seeds you plant will grow.

If we have lost faith, lost the previous enthusiasm about the reappearance, what can we do? (Sept. '84)

It is perfectly natural that in this waiting period—for Maitreya's emergence—many have lost their early enthusiasm—especially if their belief has an emotional rather than a mental or intuitive basis. The best thing is to continue to act *as if* it is true and spread the word nevertheless. This helps to uphold the spirit and hope of a despairing humanity and speeds the process of transformation.

Historical Perspective

1875 Formation of Theosophical Society by H. P. Blavatsky and colleagues under stimulus of Masters Morya and Koot Hoomi.
1875-1890 Publication of *Isis Unveiled* and *The Secret Doctrine* by H. P. Blavatsky.
1919-1949 Publication of *Alice Bailey Teachings* given through her by the Master Djwhal Khul.
1924-1939 Publication of *Agni Yoga Teachings*, by Helena Roerich, given through her mainly by the Master Morya.
1945 Announcement of Maitreya's decision to return to the world with the Hierarchy of Masters.

The Emergence of Maitreya

1977

8 July: Maitreya leaves His centre in the Himalayas.
19 July: Arrival by aeroplane in His 'centre' somewhere in a modern country.
22 July: The actual beginning of Maitreya's mission.
6 September: First Message from Maitreya during a public lecture given by Benjamin Creme in London via a process of mental overshadowing.

1978

3 April: Beginning of the gradual emergence of Maitreya into the open. During the course of 1978 a TV film is made of Maitreya and the Asian Community of the Brick Lane area of London but is never shown.

1979

16 January: In Message No. 57 Maitreya announces a new phase in His work.
In 1979 Maitreya gave 4 public talks, in March, in July, on 21 September and 8 December, all within the Asian community.

1980

14 February: Maitreya announces in Message No. 95 that the first phase of His emergence is almost over.

16 February: Maitreya's 5th public talk to an audience of 1,000 people.

19 April: 6th public talk to an audience of approximately 800. For the first time a representative of the local press is present. At subsequent public meetings; on 31 May, 5 July, 10 August and 13 September there is evidence of increasing interest from the local press.

26 November: In Message No. 113 Maitreya announces that His "phase of approach" is nearly completed and that the "phase of broader sight" will begin in 1981.

1981

7 February: Second public lecture in 1981 (1 January was the first). Maitreya is interviewed (as an ordinary member of the Asian Community) for radio for the first time.

19 July: Creme announces that a television programme featuring Maitreya (of course, incognito) has been broadcast. The tempo of Maitreya's public meetings has increased to one in every two weeks.

21 October: Broadcast of a radio interview with Maitreya (incognito).

7 November: Maitreya's public talks are now once a week, i.e. November 7, 14, 21, 28, etc.

November 1981-April 1982

The plan was that through media coverage of Maitreya's participation in the (by then) weekly meetings He would become known first nationally and later internationally.

April 1982

Creme and colleagues mount a worldwide publicity campaign with full-page advertisements in 19 of the world's major newspapers announcing the Christ's presence.

14 May 1982

Creme holds a press conference in Los Angeles and is allowed to disclose for the first time that the Christ has been living and working within the Asian community of London since 1977. The media is called upon to find the Christ and invite Him to address the world.

1982-1985

Between 1982 and 1985 various journalists and people connected with the media joined for brief periods in efforts to 'find' the Christ.

1984

A freelance journalist began contacting other journalists in an effort to bring together a group which might be such as to evoke contact with the Christ.

1985

31 July 1985: 22 influential journalists representing media in East and West meet in the East End of London hoping for contact with Maitreya or envoy.

July 1985-July 1986

The Christ is now free to act directly. It remains for Him to take the necessary steps to bring about His acceptance by the world's media leading subsequently to the Day of Declaration. This step He has now taken. The major media in London (and to some extent abroad) *know* that Maitreya is here, and have agreed to make a statement.

CHAPTER II

THE TEACHINGS AND WORK OF THE CHRIST IN THE NEW AGE

The Teachings of the Christ

The Master D.K. has outlined for us the teachings of the Christ which, we shall find, are the teachings which we all inherently know and accept to be true: right human relations are at the basis of our lives, and to create such right relations we come into incarnation again and again. He will reiterate the need, and show again the way, to implement them.

The first step in the creation of right human relations is the transformation of our political, economic and social structures. The spiritual crisis through which mankind is passing is focused today through these fields, and at the core of the economic problem is the problem of distribution and redistribution. Right human relations is the next, divinely ordained, achievement of humanity. It is not possible to stand in right relationship to our brothers and sisters in the Third World when we live in luxury and waste while they starve and die in their millions.

The solution is obvious: sharing the resources of this plentiful world is the essential first step into right relationship. The Christ will make this clear and inspire humanity to act towards this end. His call for sharing and justice as the only way to true peace (and therefore to the continuance of the race and the saving of the world) is essentially a call for the establishment of right human relations and the renunciation of the manifestly wrong relationships in the world today: the competition and greed, individually, nationally, and internationally; the hatred and violence, world-wide and potent as never before; the separativeness and exclusiveness, the fanatical adherence to one's own ideal; all the bitterness and distrust which has brought us to the edge of self-destruction.

The potency of His energy of Love—the 'sword of cleavage'—has produced the polarization which now exists, and will show clearly the way forward for humanity. Around Him will gather all those who stand for inclusiveness and love, justice and freedom of the human spirit. Those who stand for separativeness and exploitation, competition and greed will likewise stand revealed, and the choice before humanity will be crystal clear: between love and hate, between sharing and greed, peace and war, life and death. The Christ has said (in Message No. 11, January 1978) "My heart tells Me your answer, your choice, and is glad." Responding to His Love energy, people in every country (it is already happening) will form themselves into groups demanding justice and peace and right relations. Soon these groups will become the largest and most potent force in the world, ushering in the new era of peace and goodwill.

In the recognition and understanding of the Law of Rebirth lies the key to right human relations and the solution of humanity's problems. It has been almost totally ignored in the West (although this is now changing), while in the East its passive acceptance and misinterpretation has resulted in stagnation of effort. The Christ will show its total relevance to our long evolutionary journey to perfection, and this doctrine will become one of the keynotes of the new world religion.

Where this law is accepted in the West today, the emphasis is almost exclusively on the recovery of past lives, with all the glamours and delusions to which that activity is open. The Christ will show the true functioning of this law as the process of perfectionment of the soul in incarnation. It is the soul (in all forms) which incarnates, gradually bringing its successive vehicles to the point where it can express its nature in the three worlds of human living—physical, emotional, and mental.

He will show the relation of the Law of Rebirth to the Law of Cause and Effect (the Law of Karma in the East). Through the correct understanding of this relationship, humanity will come to see the necessity for harmlessness in all its activities. Souls incarnate in groups, cyclically, to achieve right relations with each other and with their source. The responsibility and obligations inherent in this fact will be understood, and the necessity for, and practicality of, right relations will be made abundantly clear.

The reappearance of the Christ today is the reappearance also, into outer manifestation, of the Spiritual Hierarchy of which He is the Head. For the first time since Atlantean days the Hierarchy of Masters and initiates will work openly in the world, known to us for what They are.

They are the custodians of the ancient Mysteries which contain the key to the evolutionary process, hidden in numbers, ritual and symbol, and the key to the Divine Science, which will unlock for mankind the secrets of life itself and place within our hands the energies of the universe. These ancient Mysteries will be revealed, the fact of the soul will be proved, and man's essential immortality will be known.

The esoteric process of initiation is the conscious experience of thousands of initiates today. In this coming age it will become the exoteric experience of millions more. Essentially, initiation is the result of, and leads to, an expansion of conscious awareness, a refinement of the instrument of perception and reception of higher values and spiritual understanding. Through this expansion of consciousness the initiate becomes aware of levels of divine existence and states of consciousness from which he was hitherto cut off. This experience enhances his radiatory capacity and equips him for greater service to the world. He becomes a knower.

Of these Mysteries of Initiation the Christ will teach. As the Hierophant at the first two initiations, He will guide humanity into the Kingdom of God—the Hierarchy of which He is the Head. Through this experience, men will come to realize themselves as the gods they are.

The majority of humanity today are still largely Atlantean in consciousness, that is, polarized on the emotional plane, which remains their normal, everyday seat of consciousness. They are lost in the maze of the delusions of that plane—hence the present world turmoil and problem. To quote the Master D.K., "The greatest service a man can render his fellow men is to free himself from the control of that plane (the emotional) by himself directing its energies through the power of the Christ within," and, "The moment that the hearts of men are active, that moment sees the termination of emotional, solar plexus activity." It is through the heart that men respond to the call of the Christ. By this stimulation of the love aspect, the Christ can work through all to change the world and at the same time lift us out of our delusions, our ignorance and fears. Through the greater livingness which His energy bestows, He will lead us into the light and a truer manifestation of our divinity. (July '82)

The Work of the Christ

The decision to return to full physical plane work and living was not, we can be sure, lightly or easily taken by the Christ. The Master D.K. in *The Reappearance of the Christ*, through Alice A. Bailey, tells us that it took nine years—from June 1936 to June 1945—for the decision to be made. The Hierarchy is still working in the state of tension engendered by that momentous decision which culminated in His entry into the modern world on 19 July 1977.

His decision to reappear had profound occult repercussions: as a result of it, He was granted the right to use—for the first time—the great mantram or prayer known as the Great Invocation, and to give it out to humanity. Not a day has passed since June 1945 without His sounding it forth for the benefit of the world. It is hoped that one day this prayer or invocation will become the world prayer, sounded alike by all peoples, and a potent keynote of the new world religion which it will be one of the Christ's major tasks to inaugurate—when we have set to rights the world.

His decision led, also, to His becoming the recipient and channel of certain great divine energies which, in His work for humanity in this new age, will enhance and potentize all He does. The Spirit of Peace or Equilibrium overshadowed Him in a way very similar to that whereby He overshadowed the disciple Jesus in Palestine. Working closely with the Law of Action and Reaction, the effect of this cosmic Entity's work through Maitreya will be to produce a reaction to the present chaotic and violent conditions and usher in an era of peace and emotional calm commensurate to the hatred and violence today.

He became the Embodiment, in an altogether new and potent way, of the energy that we call the Christ Principle or Christ Consciousness—the energy of evolution, per se. Flowing from Him into the world, this energy has re-oriented humanity to the spiritual (not necessarily religious) life and prepared us to recognize and follow Him now and to accept the principle of sharing. Millions are responding to this potent energy today, and as it awakens us to the spiritual basis of life, one of the Christ's modes of appearance is fulfilled—in the hearts of men.

A great cosmic Being, the Avatar of Synthesis, entered, through the Christ, our planetary life. He embodies the energies of Will, Love and Intelligence, plus another energy for which we have as yet no name. This Entity can come only as low as the mental plane, and from that level He pours His fourfold energy through the Christ and thus into the world. Together with the Buddha, Who brings in the Wisdom energy from cosmic levels, these great Beings form a triangle whose energies the Christ channels to us. In this coming time the Christ will be known as the Point within the Triangle. The

Will of the Avatar of Synthesis, the Love of the Spirit of Peace or Equilibrium, and the Wisdom of the Buddha, all focused through the Christ, will transform—are now transforming—this world. Thus one of the major works of the Christ, as the transmitter of energies, will proceed.

"I come that men may have life and that life more abundantly." As the Dispenser of the Waters of Life of Aquarius, Maitreya will perform one of His major tasks in the new time ahead. As He so eloquently puts it in Message No. 42:

> "Many times have you heard Me say that My coming means change.
> Specifically, the greatest change will be in the hearts and minds of men, for My return among you is a sign that men are ready to receive New Life.
> That New Life for men do I bring in abundance.
> On all the planes this Life will flow, reaching the hearts and souls and bodies of men, bringing them nearer to the Source of life Itself.
> My task will be to channel these Waters of Life through you.
> I am the Water Carrier.
> I am the Vessel of Truth.
> That Truth shall I reveal to you and lift you into your true nature.
> I am the River.
> Through Me flows the new stream of God-given life, and this shall I bestow on you.
> Thus shall we together walk through My Garden, smell the perfume of My Flowers, and know the joy of closeness to God.
> My friends, these things are not dreams.
> All of this will be yours.
> My Mission will vouchsafe this to you."

His is the task to transmit these Waters of Life: as physical life, nourishing the very cells of our bodies; as a new livingness—love and light within our hearts; and as life more abundant—love, light and power within and above the head of the disciples of the Christ, enabling them to co-operate more fully with the Plan issuing from Shamballa.

As the Hierophant at the first two initiations, Maitreya's work will be to take the masses of humanity into the Kingdom of God—the Hierarchy—through the portals of initiation. Many stand now on the threshold. One of His most important roles will be as the "Nourisher of the little ones." Who are these "little ones?" They are those who have taken the first two initiations and who stand ready for that experience of Transfiguration, the third initiation, which is the first demonstration of true divinity. By the nourishing, the stimulation of their spiritual life, He will bring them, as He so often says in the Messages, to "the feet of God," "before the Throne," that is, before Sanat Kumara, the Lord of the World on Shamballa, the Hierophant at the third and subsequent initiations.

Contrary to the average Christian's belief that the Christ comes exclusively for them, He comes as the World Teacher, for all humanity. With the help of His Brother, the Buddha, He will unite East and West, and in particular the different approaches to God of the East and of the West. Notwithstanding the Christ's teaching in Palestine that God is within, the general approach to God in the West has been to see Him as transcendent, above and beyond His creation, essentially unknowable by that creation, only to be worshiped from afar. The approach of the East, on the other hand, is to see God as immanent, in man and all creation, "closer than hand or foot, closer even than the breath." He will synthesize these two approaches in the new world religion. The Christ is the great exponent and expression of Love, while the Buddha is the Embodiment of Wisdom. In this coming time, the Christ will fuse and blend these two divine energies and answer the call of the East as well as of the West for succour and guidance. He will be in truth the World Teacher, come to inaugurate the new age of synthesis and brotherhood, based on the establishment of right human relations.

No Avatar has been so equipped for His task as the Christ now is. Fusing and blending in Himself the energies of Will, Love and Wisdom, overshadowed by the Spirit of Peace and of Equilibrium, aided and supported by the Avatar of Synthesis and the Buddha, and focusing through Himself the sum total of the energies of the last two thousand years of Pisces and of the coming potencies of Aquarius, He is a mighty Avatar, equal to His daunting task. That task is to create harmony out of chaos, to awaken humanity to its true nature and destiny, and to guide and inspire the building of the new civilization. He will be with us for the next two thousand five hundred years—the whole of the age of Aquarius. As we come into incarnation time and time again during that period we will find the Christ, Maitreya, at the centre of our planetary life.

Then His work for humanity will be over and, having trained and prepared His successor, He will then go on to higher work on the Way of the Higher Evolution. His path, the Path of Absolute Sonship, will take Him away from this earth, to return, as foretold by H. P. Blavatsky, as the Cosmic Christ, the Cosmic Maitreya, at the end of the last, the seventh, world cycle.(Sept. '82)

[These two articles are a summary of the teachings on the subject by the Master D.K. in *The Reappearance of the Christ*, by Alice A. Bailey. Readers are referred to that work for a deeper and more detailed account of the Christ's future work and teachings.]

What is the essence of Christ's teaching for the new age? (Oct. '84)

His teaching will be released in phases, each phase being relevant to the needs of humanity at each stage over the next 2,350 years or so. In the first place, we will find that He will lay the emphasis on the oneness of humanity, on the fact of the human soul, and on the need for sharing and right relationships. He will teach, again, the Law of Cause and Effect and its relation to the Law of Rebirth, showing the need for harmlessness in all relationships.

When these ideas have permeated society and brought about the changes in our political, economic and social structures, He will set about the inauguration of the new world religion, bringing together the approaches to God of the East and the West, God immanent and God transcendent. He will teach the Mysteries of the Path of Initiation, the scientific path to God. Initiation will be central to the new world religion. Above all, He will reveal a new aspect of God. This is the New Revelation which He brings.

What will Maitreya's initial task be? (Sept. '82)

In the first place, He will be concerned with inspiring humanity to create the conditions in which world peace can be guaranteed. He will show that this requires, above all, the acceptance of the principle of sharing. This will insure a harmonizing of the imbalance caused today by the tremendous discrepancies in the living standards of the developed and the developing nations.

His immediate proposal will be to launch a crash programme of aid to save the starving millions in the Third World. Then, over the next few years, the restructuring of society along more just lines will gradually form the basis for a new civilization. He will inspire humanity to create the new world. His initial task is really one of reconstruction.

Since He is the World Teacher, does that mean He will be more involved in certain fields of human endeavor than in others? (Sept. '82)

Many people, particularly Christians, see Him as the head of the Christian Church, but in fact this is not the case; the Master Jesus is the head of the Christian Churches. The World Teacher is the stimulus behind a whole range of activities, not only religion. He is as much the stimulus behind the scientific discoveries and the educational concepts which are today engaging men's minds as He is with religious matters.

He will inaugurate the new world religion which will engage a large part of His energy, but He is the recipient and transmitter of a great rainbow of energies from various sources which stimulate many different facets of our life. One of His major tasks will be the synthesizing of humanity through the energy of the Avatar of Synthesis and the energies of Aquarius, and through galvanizing the United Nations Assembly, bringing the world together and filling it with a sense of its wholeness. That is a great and continuing task, which will be spread over a good many years. When we have really set the world to rights He will begin to inaugurate the new world religion.

Which of the world's major religions, if any, do you expect will disappear first, once Maitreya begins His work openly?

None of them. It is not Maitreya's task to stimulate the destruction of any of the major religions—quite the contrary. His main work, in the first place, will be to stimulate economic, political, and social change. When He does eventually inaugurate the new world religion based on initiation, its adherents will be drawn, as is already the case, from all religions.

Could you expand on the work of the New Group of World Servers, whom you mentioned before as being sensitive to the energy of the Avatar of Synthesis? (Oct. '82)

When He came before in Palestine, the Christ found that there were not enough servers, disciples, in the world through whom He could work, who could have prepared the way for Him, and through whom He could construct the new civilization of the time. Also, He had not yet that deeper relationship and at-one-ment with the Will aspect of God—which in the last two thousand years He has achieved—necessary for Him to complete His task. He is now an Embodiment of the Will as well as the Love aspect of God.

In 1922, therefore, He inaugurated the New Group of World Servers, which is the most important group existing in the world, although it has no outer form or organization. Each member of it is related subjectively (i.e. on the inner, soul level) to Hierarchy; they know and understand the Plan and their part in it. On the outer plane there are two groups: one large group, unaware of their subjective link with Hierarchy and working only under impression from the Masters; the other, a small inner nucleus which works consciously on the outer plane under the direct supervision of the Masters.

Made up of men and women of all levels of society, the New Group of World Servers has members in every country in the world, without exception. Since 1922, apart from the war years, they have been active in placing before humanity the very principles which will govern our lives in the future—principles of right relationship, sharing and justice. They are to be found in the educational, political, economic and scientific fields. They are the forerunners of the Christ, the vanguard, sent ahead to prepare the way. From their understanding of the Plan, from their altruistic love of humanity, from their desire to serve, they are the guarantee of the correct working out of the Plan of the Hierarchy of which they are also a part. So in this way, the work of Hierarchy does not infringe human free will. The New Group of World Servers forms a bridging group between humanity and Hierarchy. It is several million strong today.

Presumably the Christ's role and tasks will change over the years? (Oct. '82)

His tasks will change and therefore His role will change. He is, above all, the galvanizer and inspirer of humanity. He has to show humanity the nature of the Reality we call God, take humanity into closer relationship with that Reality, and invoke a deeper and more meaningful response to life. This is an enormous task, one which only someone of His stature could accomplish.

I have read that Buddha brought Light, Christ brought Love, and that the next Avatar will bring Power. Is this the aspect which the Christ Maitreya is attempting to bring forth at this time, or is there yet another Avatar to come? (Dec. '84)

The Christ does indeed bring the Power or Will aspect of God into the world. In the last two thousand years since His Advent in Palestine through Jesus, He has become the Embodiment of the Will, as well as the Love and Light, of God. Through His advocacy, humanity's little separate self-will will come into correct alignment with the Will of God for the first time. As far as the individual disciple is concerned, this Will aspect only makes itself felt around the time of the third initiation. Its energy comes from the Monad or Divine Spark, whereas the energies of Love and Light come from the Soul. To the purist, of course, all three aspects come from the Monad, but at-one-ment with the soul alone brings in Light and Love alone.

Quite apart from this, of course, there will be many further Avatars in humanity's long evolution to perfection.

Will the Christ have a long ministry compared to the three years Jesus had? (May '86)

Yes. The whole of the Age of Aquarius.

What will be some of the attributes or characteristics of the Aquarian Age? (Oct. '84)

The outstanding quality of the energy of Aquarius is synthesis, hence the result of its action will be a blending and fusing of the present divided and separative humanity into a whole. A new sense of oneness (with all creation) will replace the present sense of separation. In the social and political sphere this will demonstrate as brotherhood, justice and sharing. The present fear and confusion will give way to a new freedom and sense of meaning and purpose in life. It will be an age in which humanity—for the first time as a whole—realizes and manifests its inherent divinity. Co-operation will replace competition; tolerance and goodwill will supersede division and hate.

Why did Maitreya elect to fulfill the office of the Christ for two cycles—the Piscean and the Aquarian? (Feb. '84)

For a number of reasons: to complete His work of service vis-a-vis humanity (His mission in Palestine was largely prophetic); humanity, then, was ready for little more. He returns now to continue and fulfill that which He set in motion then. At the end of the Aquarian Age His work with humanity will be over and He will go on to higher work. This will lead Him and the Masters onto the Way of the Higher Evolution (seven paths of service of which we can know little or nothing), such being the primary reason for His return to the everyday world now. He is also the one most fitted, by evolutionary attainment, to hold the office of the World Teacher and to embody the Christ Principle.

Who held Maitreya's office in Egyptian times? (June '86)

In one cycle, His Brother, the Buddha, as Memnon.

Is the invocation of the Christ today directly stimulating the birth of the Christ Principle in individuals? (June '84)

Very much so. Maitreya embodies that principle for us, and its manifestation in millions of humanity today is, simultaneously, one of His threefold ways of return (the others being the mental overshadowing of the disciples open to this stimulus, and His direct physical presence). That Christ Principle invokes the esoteric Hierarchy into the world, and it is the guarantee of the success of His mission through us.

Why does the Avatar have to be personified by one human individual? (Nov. '85)

This question, I think, arises from the mistaken idea that an Avatar (in this case the Christ) is some kind of abstract Principle which might embody itself in many individuals simultaneously. Many people see the Christ in this sense, separating the man—Maitreya—from the Christ Principle which He embodies, and looking for a multiple manifestation of the Christ. The Christ Principle does indeed manifest through millions today, but this is only one of the three ways in which Maitreya promised to appear—on mental, astral and dense physical levels. My submission is that all three forms of His manifestation have taken place.

Don't you think we have advanced enough for the (Christ) Principle without needing the form (the man)? (July/Aug. '86)

Take a look at the world and decide for yourself. How do you think we are doing with the Christ Principle, given the nuclear confrontation between East and West, the starving millions, the thousand-million poor? We are indeed fortunate that, for the love of humanity, the man, the Son of Man, has graced us with His presence.

Furthermore, the primary reason for His physical return is to lead His group, the Spiritual Hierarchy of Masters, back into the world.

Is it not possible that Sai Baba is Maitreya, and that the man in London waiting to be recognized as Christ is the Master Jesus Who, you say, won't show Himself to the public until Maitreya—the Cosmic Christ—has done so? I am a firm believer in Sai Baba as the Cosmic Christ. (June '86)

If I thought it possible that Sai Baba is Maitreya then, of course, I would have said so. I believe Sai Baba to be a cosmic Avatar Who works in close relation to Maitreya and His mission. I have never said that Maitreya is the Cosmic Christ, but that He is rather the planetary expression of the Christ Principle. It is my understanding that the Master Jesus is at present living in the suburbs of Rome awaiting the Declaration of Maitreya in London.

There does seem to exist one great difference between the new teachings and the old teachings of the Christ in Palestine. The latter were centered so much on repentance—a word I have not noticed once in the new Messages from Maitreya, the Christ; and 'faith' is also seemingly omitted. The fundamentalists such as Billy Graham and Luis Pilau still base their campaigns upon these values and get many 'converts.' Might one assume that such teachings are still valid and useful for younger egos who still require external discipline as younger chil-

dren do, and that it is they who are drawn to these doctrines? (May '85)

By 'the new teachings' I assume the questioner means the Messages from Maitreya given through me. I think it is necessary to make clear that no claim is made that the Messages represent the new teachings of the Christ, but simply that they contain fragments of His teaching and show the various areas of His concern. I doubt that they were meant to do more than that. The new teachings will come directly from Maitreya Himself.

What I think is very evident in them is a shift in emphasis from personal salvation to group responsibility and action. This is entirely in line with the change in evolutionary expression from Piscean individualism—and its accompanying separatism—to Aquarian group consciousness and unity. I doubt very much that the Christ did or will lay such emphasis on 'sin' as do the Churches, nor on 'repentance' except as the action needed to undo wrong action consciously recognized and accepted. For the Masters, 'sin' is simply imperfection.

I do agree that the success of fundamentalists like Billy Graham, basing their appeal on sin and repentance, is with younger, unsophisticated egos for whom such emotionally-charged concepts have great meaning. Faith is something else again—an inner or intuitive recognition and continuous communion, and not a simple belief in this or that doctrine or dogma.

Is it true that Maitreya has been enlisting people to serve and help Him over the last several (twenty or more) years? (Nov. '83)

It depends on what is meant by 'enlisting.' If it means, has He been inspiring people to help Him in altruistic service to humanity (e.g. by His reiterated appeals for help in the Messages from Maitreya, the Christ), the answer is yes. If, on the other hand, it means by direct physical-plane enlisting, as into the army, the answer is a definite no, He has not.

If Maitreya can divide His consciousness into thousands of separate areas of attention, is He indeed present at the moment of consecration in the Roman Catholic and Anglican Masses, and does His blessing remain in the consecrated Host which is revered in the Roman Catholic Churches? Or, since the Master Jesus is in charge of the Christian religion, is it rather His presence in this ritual? (May '85)

It is always the energy and blessing of Maitreya which consecrates the Host at this ritual. This is the most valid and authentic part of the Christian Church service. Of course, the wafer and the wine are not turned into the 'body and blood' of the Christ. This is a symbolic act in memory of Him. The energy transmission, however, is indeed real.

When one feels very strong energies how can one tell whether it is from the soul, a Master, or, dare I hope, Maitreya? For instance, this always happens when I read the Messages from Maitreya. (July '85)

It is impossible to read the Messages from Maitreya, especially aloud, without invoking His energy. That is one reason why they were given. The first part of the question is more difficult to answer—it really is a matter of experience and discrimination. It is usually more correct to assume that the energy is from one's soul.

Does Maitreya use any of the many statues of Him to transmit His energies through? (Sept. '85)

Yes, most certainly. One example is a famous statue in wood in the Koryuji Temple in Kyoto, Japan, dating from the 6-7th centuries. For centuries it has been known as "the statue of the golden light" because of the radiance which is sometimes seen to emanate from it.

Is it possible for ordinary people, longing to see Him, to make contact with Maitreya inwardly? (May '85)

It depends on what is meant by 'make contact.' If it means can 'ordinary' people receive communications, messages, enlightenment, guidance, from Maitreya, then the answer is no. He does not make that kind of contact. I know that many people claim such contact—and often send me the results—but my information is that these claims are mistaken, and the nature of the received material bears this out.

If it means can people invoke His energy, His love, then the answer is, assuredly, yes. He Himself has said: "My help is yours to command. You have only to ask." (Message No. 49)

Have many people told you that they have 'seen' Maitreya, i.e. not in London, but as a vision appearing before them? (May '86)

Not many, but a few have related such experiences.

Can the Christ come to us in a sleep state to aid us? (May '86)

Yes, He frequently uses this form of contact.

I believe that coming with Maitreya are certain great devas or angels. Can you tell us anything about them and the significance of this for humanity now? (Dec. '82)

The Christ was called, by both Gautama Buddha and St Paul, "the Teacher alike of angels and of men," and that is precisely what He is. He is as much a teacher for the devas as He is for the human evolution. As the Master D.K. has shown (in the books of Alice A. Bailey), He will bring—in fact, has brought—into the world, certain great devas who will work closely with humanity and teach us many aspects of the art of living.

(1) Is Maitreya without sin? (2) Was He born of a virgin? (Nov. '84)

(1) Maitreya is totally perfected in a planetary sense. Even in a systemic sense He is without that sense of separation which we call sin.

(2) No. He is a Resurrected and Ascended Master. In His present manifestation in the modern world (London), He is in a self- created body—a mayavirupa.

Was the Christ responsible for the appearance of the 'eye-in-the-triangle' on the USA $1 bill, announcing the 'new order of the ages?' (Apr. '84)

No.

Is Maitreya inspiring the now-world-wide use of the triangle or 'delta' symbols as business and association logos? (Apr. '84)

No.

Does Maitreya have an esoteric group known as the Triangle Forces (world-wide) that wear red and blue clothes as signs of their membership? (Apr. '84)

No.

Does the name 'Tara' have roots in Buddhism, and if so, how does it relate to the present work of Tara Center? (Jan. '84)

'Tara' is the Buddhist name (taken over from Hinduism) for the Mother Goddess, the Mother of the World, the Female Origin. One of Her manifestations was the Hindu Kali, her aspect as the destroyer. She was also Isis and Ishtar. Mary, mother of Jesus, is Her symbol. The coming age of Aquarius, the age of Maitreya, is also the age in which the female, nurturing aspect regains expression. The age of Maitreya, therefore, is the age of Tara.

Is the Holy Trinity masculine? (July/Aug. '84)

The Holy Trinity combines the masculine (spirit) and the feminine (matter) aspects and the relation between spirit and matter—the Christ aspect. It is in this sense that the Christ is the Son of God—Father-Mother God.

What has Maitreya told you about His physical immortality? I mean, He seems to have lived in the Himalayas for a very long time. (Mar. '86)

Maitreya has lived in His retreat high in the Himalayas (at about 17,500 feet) for the last 2,000 years in a 'body of light,' that is, the resurrected and ascended body of a perfected Master of high degree. That body is now 'at rest,' as He has termed it—a state of suspended animation. The body in which He now lives and works in London is self-created especially for this mission and will remain as it is today for the next two and a half thousand years.

The Christ is formless, but He is also centred within His mayavirupa body in London, and His light-body lies asleep in the Himalayas. Where is His centre, His focal point of

existence? Does He meditate from His light-body? (Mar. '83)

The Christ is not formless but, of course, the energy He embodies, the Love energy, the energy which we call the Christ Principle, is formless. His consciousness is centred in the mayavirupa (self-created body). He meditates and lives and works as a normal man, in the mayavirupa, which is a completely real body.

Now that He lives in London, will the Christ (Maitreya) still function as Head of the Hierarchy, e.g. during the May Wesak Festival and, if so, will He then make use of His 'body of light' now resting in His Himalayan centre? (June '84)

He does and will still function as Head of the Hierarchy while physically present with us, and also during the Wesak Festival which takes place in May in a remote valley in the Himalayas. During that ancient festival, in which the Buddha makes His close contact with humanity, Maitreya functions in the mayavirupa in which He lives now in London. He does not leave London in order to do this, but is present in both places simultaneously.

Could you explain how Maitreya built His body? How do its atoms differ from ours? (Oct. '85)

I am afraid there is little I may say about the creation of His body of manifestation except that the process of its manufacture (by an act of will) is without parallel in the history of the world, by a quite different method from that used by the Masters in creating Their mayavirupas. This body allows Maitreya to carry out His duties as the World Teacher while at the same time living among us as an ordinary man, something never before possible. What I can say is that the atomic structure is such that He can move from the highest spiritual level to the densest physical without effort. The atoms of His body have the necessary resilience to accommodate either pole.

During the five to six years before 7 July 1977, Maitreya slowly brought together the necessary matter (mental, astral and physical) into which His consciousness could 'incarnate.' He tested each level out in the world until He was satisfied that it had the necessary qualities of resilience and sensitivity. When He was sure that all was 'well-fashioned,' to use His own phrase, He finally 'donned' it, as He put it, on 7 July 1977.

Considering what humanity has done in the name of Christ in the past, what does the Christ plan to do in the future to avoid this? (Apr. '84)

Mainly, be present. One could give a lecture on the Christ's plans, teachings and work in the coming time to inspire humanity into making a change of direction, but the great difference this time is the fact that He has promised to stay with us to the end of the Aquarian Age, i.e. approximately 2,500 years. No theologians or priests will be necessary, therefore, to interpret (or misinterpret) His teachings.

Maitreya's Activity after the Day of Declaration

How much in evidence will Maitreya be? Will we be able to see and hear Him regularly on radio, TV, read about Him in the press? Will He have an official mouthpiece—a newspaper or a magazine? (Oct. '82)

There will not be an official 'mouthpiece,' an official magazine, or whatever, for Maitreya. As He is an Advisor, a Teacher, He will appear often (I do not know how regularly) on radio and TV; He will be quoted in newspapers and so on. His Teaching will be mainly through television and radio. This is the Revelatory phase—prophesied by the Master D.K. through Alice Bailey to begin after 1975.

Surely people will take up the work of collecting His lectures, His words, His proposals, etc., and compiling books, articles, tapes, films, videos? (Oct. '82)

Yes, I have no doubt that all this will be collected and made available in some form for study, for gradual assimilation and for general education. But, of course, that is our work, not His.

Will the Christ travel to all countries of the world? Will the Masters also travel around the world? (Oct. '82)

Some will and some will not. Certain Masters have been designated for particular posts in specific centres—the five major spiritual centres and two minor ones. However, the Christ will make a journey—I do not know how soon after the Day of Declaration—to all countries of the world, so that all of us will have the opportunity to see Him more personally.

Will His journeys be similar in style to those of the present Pope? Will He be more or less accessible? (Oct. '82)

The sheer logistics, the technical problems, make that a difficult question to answer. I would think that His tours would be similar to those of the Pope but, naturally, on a far larger scale. The Pope attracts mainly Roman Catholics and other interested people, but the Christ will attract the attention of millions, even billions, of people of all faiths and of no religious background at all. I am sure He will attempt to make Himself even more accessible than the Pope does today. One difference will be that with Maitreya there is no danger of assassination. He is and will be invulnerable. That is one danger and worry which will not engage the minds of the governments whose work it will probably be to organize His tours. For Him personally it will be a gigantic task.

Will He have specific and differing 'missions' in the various countries? (Oct. '82)

No doubt His functions will differ from country to country, and He will go with that purpose in mind. I think He will try to use His good offices in whatever capacity they can best be used. He is here to serve the world, and I think it is in that light that He will present Himself to the world. He will not present Himself as knowing everything and come to do everything for us, but if people and governments ask His advice or ask for His judgement—His sometimes 'Solomon's' judgement—in decisions, for instance, in the Middle East or Northern Ireland, He will certainly give His guidance and help. Despite the fact that these situations seem insoluble, it may be that people will accept from Maitreya advice and suggestions that they would never accept from lesser beings.

Will Maitreya teach each nation about its soul purpose and its part in the Plan? (July/Aug. '86)

Yes. Not only Maitreya but the Masters, too, will elucidate the inner destiny of the various nations. Each nation has some unique contribution to make to a civilization, while some nations, because of their rays (each nation has a soul ray and a personality ray), their size, whether male or female, have often a decisive role to play. Each nation has an occult purpose and 'motto' or role in the unfolding evolution of the race.

Do you think the governments of the world will accept the Christ at first? (Jan. '86)

Some undoubtedly will, while some may be slower to accept His counsel. I am thinking of countries like the Soviet Union and China, which have no religious means by which to approach Him. The peoples of these countries, however—like the people elsewhere in the world—will force their leaders to implement the principle of sharing. In a very real sense, despite their lack of personal freedom, these countries are already nearer to the implementation of sharing and justice than are the Western democracies.

Will London remain His 'headquarters?' (Oct. '82)

No. In a sense, He will not have any 'headquarters.' His residence in London now is, I believe, a temporary measure. His journey around the world should take several years—two or three years, at least. Then He will go, from time to time, to any other particular country or countries where the need for Him is the greatest, where He can be of most use, can best serve at that time.

Will Maitreya continue the spontaneous and miraculous cures and healings of Declaration Day? (Oct. '82)

As I understand it, He will not. The spontaneous healings of Declaration Day will be a phenomenon restricted to that day, as further proof, if more proof were needed, that He is indeed the Christ. No doubt, as He has always done, He will continue to heal and cure, but this will be on a private basis, not done in a big, public, spectacular way.

So private individuals will have access to Him to ask for healing? (Oct. '82)

No, I do not mean it in that way. Simply that only the patient will know of it, it will not be 'advertised' healing. He will not be the World Healer. But of course, the Masters (some of Them) are in the world and more will emerge later. This will result in a tremendous stimulus to spiritual or esoteric healing.

This will be accompanied by a growth in understanding of the process of disease and of healing. So we, ourselves, will perform healings, as many do now, which at one time would have been considered miracles. But I do not think that Maitreya will be publicly engaged in healing activities.

Would it not be impossible for Maitreya to operate because people would be asking for healing all the time? (Nov. '85)

You will find that this is not so. The presence of the Masters and the stimulus They will give to many healing processes will answer people's needs. They will quickly understand that Maitreya has other work to do besides individual healing.

The Agent of Divine Intervention

Let's suppose that Declaration Day is delayed for awhile and that the world finds itself in crisis, on the brink of a nuclear war—would Sanat Kumara, the Lord of the World, and Hierarchy allow the planet to be destroyed? (Nov. '82)

I believe that Hierarchy, or rather Sanat Kumara behind Hierarchy, would not allow the planet to be destroyed and would not allow humanity itself to be annihilated. I also believe that the Christ's presence is the guarantee that the inner decision necessary for peace—that is, sharing—has already been taken by humanity, whether it knows it or not. The Christ has said this so many times that we simply have to believe it.

Is it true that Sanat Kumara is directly involved in the nuclear issue? (Nov. '82)

Yes. Since the secret for the creation of the atomic bomb was released by Hierarchy to the allied scientists during the war from 1939 to 1945, Sanat Kumara is now directly involved in any use of nuclear weapons and, I believe, would not allow such a catastrophe.

War by accident is another possibility and, of course, on the surface it would appear that this could take place at any time. The safeguards for the control of such an eventuality are still in the hands of fallible human beings. If there were such an accidental release of nuclear weapons they, too, can be neutralized, even in flight, by Hierarchy. We would not be allowed to devastate the planet.

Will Maitreya wipe the slate clean, the karmic debt of mankind? (Apr. '84)

No. The Christian Church's concept of a vicarious atonement is a misunderstanding of the Christ's function. He came in Palestine, and has come again now, to show the way, to lead, guide and inspire, but not to go against the Law of Karma. We must save ourselves through response to His teachings.

You say that since the Christ returned in July 1977 fewer people have died in earthquakes. Please explain. (Nov. '84)

One of the main reasons for the Christ's presence in the world now, actually ahead of the planned date, is to act as the Agent of Divine Intervention to mitigate the effects of the earthquake activity which has been mounting for 150 years. In the several years before 1977, there was hardly a month without a major earthquake and great loss of life. In 1976, over 600,000 people died in earthquakes. In 1977, 2,800 died, and each year since there has been a dramatic fall in the long-term average toll of earthquake deaths, despite the fact that earthquake activity has continued unabated. This shows the success of His intervention.

You say that Maitreya acts as "the Agent of Divine Intervention to mitigate the disasters in the form of earthquakes which are taking place." How then do you explain the recent Mexican earthquake? (Nov. '85)

Maitreya acts as the Agent of Divine Intervention precisely to mitigate the effects of, but not to prevent, earthquake activity, which is the result of the magnetic pull on our planet of a great cosmic body in space. But for His intervention, even more tremendous suffering would have occurred in the many major and minor earthquakes since 1977.

In Mexico, Maitreya and His workers shifted the epicentre of the earthquake from a few miles west of Mexico City to 250 miles south-west, well away, it was calculated, from the capital.

Mexico City has around 18 million inhabitants. Some 5,000 (the official figure) died, all of them in the 'downtown' area of the centre of the city, in the high-rise flats, hotels, etc. Eminent Mexican architects have since come forward, accusing the town councils of corruption in building such high edifices without the proper reinforcement necessary in an earthquake zone. These deaths could have been prevented by correct building methods. It is interesting—and instructive—to note that it is only these buildings, shoddily built, which collapsed; the roads and streets did not open or cave in as they might have done under earth movement, while the rest of the city was untouched.

Why did Maitreya only begin to mitigate the effects of earthquakes when in the mayavirupa body and not during

the last 2,000 years in his 'body of light' in the Himalayas? (May '84)

One of the main reasons for Maitreya's entry into the everyday world in 1977 was precisely to act as the Agent of Divine Intervention. This is only possible because He is physically present among us—as an Avatar.

You said that Maitreya has reduced the number of deaths from earthquakes. Yet we learn that thousands are dying from droughts and floods. Why doesn't He lessen the effects from these also? (July '84)

Earthquakes and their effects are something over which we have no control, nor are we responsible for their cause, which is cosmic. For this reason the Christ can intervene. The effects of droughts and even the causes of floods, on the other hand, we can deal with, had we the international will to do so. Humanity must learn interdependence and co-operation. Were the Christ to intervene (even if the Law allowed), we would do even less ourselves for the victims of drought and floods.

Since the earth is teeming with creatures both evolving and involving, it is apparent that there never is a time when all forms reach fruition simultaneously. Yet we know that at intervals the earth changes the tilt of its axis, resulting in a total termination of life-forms. The Tibetan, in the Bailey books, and the 'space people' hint broadly about a time of impending crisis. We, in our generation, have seen so many of the New Testament prophesies fulfilled that we must assume the prediction of Matthew Ch.24 must surely also have to take place. My question is: Maitreya and His Disciples would not presume to perform a 'quick fix,' making all humans eligible for a next estate, so how do you see all life coping with a so-called cleansing of the earth by fire? Do souls enter their rightful places in the astral or

etheric planes awaiting a re-balancing of the earth—or don't you envision that kind of event in any foreseeable future? (July '85)

This question comes under the heading of the 'catastrophe complex.' First of all, with respect, we do not know that "at intervals the earth changes the tilt of its axis resulting in the total termination of life forms." I do not know which books the questioner reads, but to my understanding this is nonsense. The earth is indeed currently pulled slightly off its true axis. This is the result of the magnetic pull of a great body in space, and is the cause behind the increased incidence of earthquakes over the last 150 years. Certain widespread earth changes are destined to occur, but not for another 700-900 years from now. This will not necessitate the large-scale destruction of life-forms which the question suggests.

Does Maitreya confirm predictions (from Ruth Montgomery's book, *Strangers Among Us*) about the tilt of the earth's axis in the 1990's and the need to prepare for it? (Nov. '85)

I cannot speak for Maitreya, but the Masters are one on this—as on every question—and for my own Master I can say quite definitely that there is no truth in this prediction. It is one that is widespread, is a powerful thought-form on the astral planes (its source), and is the result of the fear engendered in people's minds at the end of an age. Those who spread these false predictions of fearful catastrophe play, knowingly or not, into the hands of the forces of darkness, whose intention always is to foment fear and chaos.

CHAPTER III

THE EXTERNALISATION OF THE MASTERS OF WISDOM

[For further information on the Hierarchy, readers are referred to *The Reappearance of the Christ and the Masters of Wisdom*, by Benjamin Creme.]

The Hierarchy

Can you say something of the notion of "Hierarchy?" It seems to be derived mostly from diverse esoteric teachings, while most traditional Eastern teachings express the individual's ability to achieve the highest possible state by turning within. Is the Hierarchy an internal structure? (July/Aug. '83)

The Spiritual Hierarchy of this planet has been in existence for about 17 million years. However, since the ending of the Atlantean civilization and the break-up of the Atlantean land mass (of which America is a remnant), the personnel—Masters and high initiates—of the Hierarchy have worked esoterically, behind the scenes of our everyday life. From Their retreats in the mountain and desert areas of the world, They have been the guiding inspiration of our successive cultures and civilizations.

Through the activity of the three great departments in the Hierarchy—under the Manu, the Christ and the Lord of Civilization—the evolutionary stimulus and guidance of all the manifold areas of planetary life takes place.

The trans-Himalayan Lodge is responsible for the training of disciples in Europe and America, but the "traditional Eastern teachings" are likewise part of Hierarchical endeavour.

The Indian tradition has been largely oriented to the devotee, but that is just a stage through which all aspirants pass. With the growing mental focus of humanity, Hierarchy can look for a more conscious co-operation in his own evolution on the part of the disciple.

Why do the Masters live in mountains and deserts? (Jan. '86)

During Atlantean times the Masters of those days worked openly. They were the priest-kings, the God-like Beings who created the various scientifically advanced civilizations whose knowledge has been lost. At the destruction of Atlantis the Masters retreated to the mountains and deserts, leaving humanity to regenerate itself while They acted as the stimulus behind the scenes. For the first time since those days the Hierarchy of Masters and initiates is returning now to work in the world.

What is the White Lodge or White Brotherhood? (June '83)

The Spiritual Hierarchy, made up of the Masters and initiates of the Wisdom, the fifth or Spiritual Kingdom. It is a reflection of the Great White Brotherhood on Sirius.

Are the Masters a group of people? (May '83)

The Masters form a group, They have only group consciousness. They have no personality consciousness at all; They think and work and live in terms of group consciousness. That is not to say that They are not all quite different in quality and character, depending on the particular ray under which They are formed and which They express.

They have their differences of opinion on how to proceed in dealing with a particular point of the plan, different ideas of whether humanity is ready for this stimulus or that, whether it is too soon, or whatever. But They work habitually from what is called the Buddhic level of consciousness, as a group. They are in continuous telepathic rapport with each other.

When we say "May Christ return to Earth" in the Great Invocation, do we mean the Christ Consciousness now that the Christ, and twelve Masters, are here? (May '85)

No. The Christ Consciousness is an energy embodied by the Christ for this period of human crisis. Since His decision to reappear, announced in June 1945, this has flowed into the world in enormous renewed potency. "May Christ return to Earth" should now be said in relation to the Spiritual Hierarchy as a whole. Only twelve Masters (besides Maitreya) are in the world now, but there are sixty-three Masters connected with the human evolution. Of these, some two thirds will eventually take Their places among us, slowly, over some twenty years. The Invocation forms a telepathic conduit which draws Them, under law, into the world.

You have said that from the Spiritual Centre in the Himalayas emerge great Avatars, a fact which will become obvious shortly. How will this become obvious? (Feb. '84)

From the Spiritual Centre we call Hierarchy emerge great Avatars, but this is not confined to the Himalayas. These mountains happen to be the base of Maitreya's retreat. When Maitreya reveals Himself to the world He will, of course, explain where He 'comes from.'

In the book *Esoteric Psychology* Vol. 1 (by Alice Bailey) I read that the rays 2, 3, 5 and 7 will have their focus in the modern world through (or in) four human beings. Does

this refer to the Externalisation of the Hierarchy? Or is one of these four beings Sai Baba? (Oct. '83)

Sai Baba is on everyone's lips but He is not meant in this case! These ray energies will be focused in the everyday world by the Chohans of these rays—Masters of the sixth degree, heads of the major ashrams on these rays. It is therefore part of the process of the externalisation of the work of the esoteric Hierarchy. Three of Them are already in position in the modern world. (*Oct. 1986*: All four Masters are now in the world.)

Why is the Master K.H. (Koot Hoomi) to be the next Christ and not the Master Jesus? (Nov. '85)

The Hierarchy's organization is divided into three departments, each under one of the three Rays of Aspect (rays 1, 2 and 3). The Christ is the head (the Great Lord) of the 2nd ray department. This post is always held by a 2nd ray Master, which the Master K.H. is. The Master Jesus is on the 6th ray, and is the head (the Chohan) of the major 6th ray ashram.

Esotericism is very much based on the study of the seven rays. Of which ray is esotericism itself an expression? (June/July '83)

It is not possible to say that esotericism is the expression of this or that particular ray. All the departments in the Hierarchy are involved in esoteric work since the Hierarchy has worked esoterically for so many ages. The teachings are given out through the Teaching Department under the Christ which is on the 2nd ray, but the Master Morya, head of the major 1st ray ashram, is responsible for the stimulus of all the esoteric and occult groups and societies.

Where would the Masters of the Hierarchy have gone if They had not chosen to stay on this planet? (Sept. '85)

It depends on Their destiny. Some choose the path of Earth Service; others go to higher planets in the system while still others leave this system and go to Sirius. There are seven paths of the Higher Evolution which determine a Master's future: 1) the Path of Earth Service; 2) the Path of Magnetic Work; 3) the Path of Training for Planetary Logoi; 4) the Path to Sirius; 5) the Ray Path; 6) the Path the Logos Himself is on; 7) the Path of Absolute Sonship.

Who is the Guru of Maitreya? (Nov. '85)

He does not have a guru in the sense which I assume the questioner means. He looks for advice and enlightenment to Sanat Kumara, the Lord of the World.

Disciple Jesus and Maitreya

[For further information, readers are referred to an essay, "Initiation and the Gospel Story," in Chapter V.]

We read in *The Reappearance of the Christ and the Masters of Wisdom* that the body of Jesus was used by the Christ for the last three years of Jesus' life. After the Crucifixion, the consciousness of the Christ re-entered the body of Jesus and resurrected the body, thereby becoming a Master. Have I understood this correctly? (June '85)

I am afraid you are under a misapprehension at this point. The Christ was already a Resurrected Master when He overshadowed and worked through Jesus for these three years. After the Crucifixion He (His consciousness, that is) did indeed re-enter the body of Jesus in the tomb, resurrected it (in the occult sense of the word), and manifested Himself for some forty days afterwards when He was seen many times by the Disciples and others. This was the Crucifixion Initiation for Jesus, and at the same time the Ascension (not the Resurrection) Initiation for the Christ.

You continue, in your book, to explain that Jesus did not become a Master at this point: Jesus became a Master during the next incarnation as Apollonius of Tyana, and for the past 600 years has had a Syrian body. I would like to know what happened to the body of Jesus of Nazareth? Apparently Jesus (or Apollonius?) does not have this body because He inhabits a Syrian body. I know that Christ presently dwells in a *mayavirupa*, a body that the Christ created for His consciousness. When the Christ's consciousness entered the *mayavirupa*, what happened to His former body (the body used until the creation of the *mayavirupa*)? Could this have been the resurrected body of Jesus of Nazareth? Even so, wouldn't the Christ have had to abandon the resurrected body of Jesus, the very body which should be identical to the image which appeared on the Shroud of Turin? (June '85)

As a fourth degree initiate (not yet a Master), Jesus had not the entitlement of a resurrected body. The Christ had already (based in the Himalayas) such a resurrected body and did not require that of Jesus. He destroyed the resurrected body of Jesus after forty days and returned the light particles (of which it now consisted) to the sun. With regard to the *mayavirupa*, in which the Christ now lives in London, this was created over a period of five to six years, prior to July 1977. His 'body of light,' as He terms it (i.e. His resurrected and ascended body in which He has lived for the last 2,000 years), is now 'at rest' in His valley in the Himalayas. This body is not destroyed but is simply in a state of preserved 'abeyance,' or suspended animation. The consciousness of Maitreya works fully through the *mayavirupa* which He uses today.

Did Maitreya reincarnate in Jesus as a baby or manifest through Him only during Jesus' three-year mission? (May '84)

The process of gradual overshadowing of Jesus by Maitreya began when Jesus was twelve and was more or less complete by the time Jesus was 24. Maitreya later worked through the body of Jesus for the three years from the Baptism, when Jesus was 30, to the Crucifixion.

Was the Christ's true relationship to Jesus known to any of His early disciples? (June '86)

Yes, several of the closest disciples understood the overshadowing process which was used.

You say Jesus never claimed to be God. What about John 10:30: "I and the Father are one." (Nov. '84)

This statement by the Christ (in Jesus) is not a claim to be 'God' but rather a statement that His consciousness was at-one with the Divine consciousness. This is the state of consciousness of the Self-realised and liberated Master.

When Christ Jesus said "I go to the Father," did He in fact refer to Sai Baba? (Mar. '86)

No. He referred to Sanat Kumara, the Lord of the World, in Shamballa (The Ancient of Days in the Old Testament). Shamballa is the centre where the Will of God is known. In "going to the Father" He meant the necessity for Him to embody the Will aspect (and not only the Light and Love aspects) in order to do His work in Aquarius. In the last 2,000 years He has done this and now embodies all three aspects.

When the Christ said through Jesus, "I have other folds," was He referring to the disciples in the Hierarchy who were not in incarnation in Palestine? (July/Aug. '83)

I believe He was referring to the fact that He was the teacher (the shepherd) for many who knew Him by other names—not only as the Messiah, but as the coming Maitreya Buddha, as Krishna, and as the Head of the esoteric Hierarchy.

We are told by the Christian churches that Jesus died for love of humanity and took on the sins of the world at that time. However, we are also told in the esoteric teaching that He was a third-degree initiate who, at the crucifixion, took and demonstrated the fourth initiation. We are told that people who take this initiation are actually clearing a backlog of their own karma. Was Jesus different in this respect, or could it be that in some past life He had treated others as He was now being treated? I understand that at the fourth initiation people react with total love and so help raise the Earth's vibrations. Could that be what the Church means? (May '86)

To be honest, I do not think the Church rightly knows what it means. Theologians have concentrated almost exclusively on the crucifixion, whereas the true import of Christianity is resurrection. Jesus did not "take on the sins of the world" (no one can). That concept is straight out of the old, crystallized Jewish tradition—a blood sacrifice—which the Christ came to end. We are each responsible, through the Law of Cause and Effect, for our every thought and action.

Because He did love humanity, and the Plan probably even more, Jesus underwent physical crucifixion not for personal, karmic reasons, but because He was *asked* to do so, to symbolize outwardly the experience of initiation at that level. The gospel story as a whole is really a symbolic account of the esoteric process of initiation.

Which of the teachings of Jesus are not relevant to mankind today? (Oct. '84)

To my mind, the teachings of Jesus (which are, of course, the teachings of the Christ) are as relevant today as they ever were. The trouble is that we do not live the teachings. In particular, Jesus said "Love one another," and "Feed my sheep." That is precisely what the Christ is saying today.

What of Jesus' words, "The poor you have with you always." Is that not their free will on the path of evolution? (Oct. '84)

Of course everyone—even the rich—has the right to be poor, but how many people elect to be poor of their own free will? Jesus did not mean that the poor *had* to be with us always. On the contrary, much of the meagre funds of His group were spent on helping the poor. His words referred rather to the fact that He would not be with the Disciples much longer, and that it was no waste to spend precious money—that might have fed the poor—on expensive ointment with which to anoint Him.

Will it be necessary for the Christ to include in His teaching, after Declaration Day, an elucidation for the public of the gospel story, or will the introduction by Him of the Master Jesus suffice? (Feb. '83)

It is probable that at a press conference before the Day of Declaration, in answer to the many questions which must arise about His incarnation in Palestine, He will reveal the true facts of the happenings of that time. And, of course, He may refer back, from time to time, to His teachings given then. I believe, however, that the introduction by Him of the Master Jesus (and the other Masters) will, after the initial explanation of the continuity of revelation, suffice.

I wonder if, in this new age, our Christian Bible will be used or will there be something to replace it? (Nov. '83)

Within the Christian churches, the Bible will continue to be used for some time. It is obvious, however, that the presence in the world of the Christ and the Masters—including the Master Jesus—will necessitate a profound reinterpretation of the meanings of that symbolical work. Much will be discarded, but much will be found to be relevant when correctly interpreted. It will be the task of the Master Jesus to guide the Christian churches into the light of the new dispensation. Eventually, Maitreya will inaugurate a new world religion based on the esoteric science of initiation.

The Bible mentions that Jesus was one of the "Order of Melchizedek": one who is without beginning or end. Can you explain who Melchizedek is and what his order is about? (Feb. '84)

To my understanding, Melchizedek is another name for the Christ, and the Order of Melchizedek, I believe, stems from Babylonian times. It was an esoteric order of disciples training for the first two initiations.

Was Jesus an Essene as some think? (Nov. '85)

Yes, both Jesus and John the Baptist received their early training in the Essene Community.

Please explain the immaculate conception and the virgin birth of Jesus. (Mar. '86)

My understanding is that the disciple Jesus was conceived in the normal human way—that is, there was no 'immaculate conception,' nor would one be required for a third-degree initiate, which Jesus was at birth. The idea of the immaculate conception is an invention of the Church Fathers to emphasize the divinity of Jesus as the 'Son' of God. The same idea of immaculate conception is found in other religions to support the 'divinity' claimed for the founder or inspirer.

There are many paintings of Jesus—are any of these a good likeness of either Jesus or Maitreya? (Dec. '82)

When you see the Master Jesus you will see that He is not so different from some paintings of Him, particularly those which depict Him as being thin-faced, dark-eyed and pale. El Greco comes to mind. These resemble Jesus quite closely. And many people have had inner visions of Jesus as He is. He is now in a Syrian body some six hundred and thirty-eight years old, not the body in which He appeared in Palestine. But of course that is not Maitreya, nor is Maitreya's body built in the likeness of Jesus. The Christ is in a *mayavirupa*, a self-created manifestation. It is built to resemble exactly His 'body of light,' a resurrected and ascended body which is now 'at rest' in the Himalayas.

What religion is the closest to practicing the beliefs put forward by the Christ 2,000 years ago? (Oct. '85)

There are individuals in every religion who practice the precepts of the Christ—even if that is not true of the religion as a whole. Today, I suppose, the Bahai are the closest, with Buddhism, where it is not too crystallized, second.

Which of the world's major scriptures is the least distorted or discoloured?

The teachings of Esoteric Buddhism.

Recently I came across a book by Levi Dowling entitled *The Aquarian Gospel of Jesus the Christ.* Is this a 'true'

book? Was it actually taken from the Akashic Records, as it claims? (Apr. '85)

This is the kind of question I do not like to deal with in public. It is better that people make up their own minds on such things, and I have no wish to set up as an authority. But having answered the question on the Seth material in the previous issue of *Share International*—in for a penny...!

My information is that the Aquarian Gospel is indeed taken from the Akashic Records (which exist on the overlapping area of the highest (7th) astral and the lowest mental planes). It is about 80 per cent accurate—and, therefore, 20 percent inaccurate.

(1) Are any of the newly-discovered gospels, such as *The Gospel of Thomas, The Secret Gospel of Mark,* or *The Gospel of Mary,* genuine accounts of the acts and words of Jesus? (2) Are there others not yet discovered?

(1) *The Gospel of Thomas* is, more or less, a genuine account of the acts (less so of the words) of Jesus. (2) Yes.

In *The Holy Book and the Holy Grail,* by Michael Baignet, Richard Leigh and Kenzie Lincoln, it is supposed that Jesus' descendants form an occult brotherhood which is now at work to put a priest-king in power at the head of a united Europe. Does this suggestion bear any resemblance or connection to the plans of Hierarchy (e.g. in relation to Jesus' role as the future Pope)? (Apr. '84)

There is no resemblance or connection whatsoever between the plans of Hierarchy for its externalisation and the fancies and fantasies of this book, one of the many in this time of 'false teachings' as foretold by the Christ.

Jesus did not have any descendants nor have Hierarchy plans to put anyone, priest-king or otherwise, 'in power' in Europe or anywhere else.

It is also incorrect to see the Master Jesus' role as the future Pope. Rather, by His taking over direct control of the churches, the true apostolic succession will begin.

The Masters in the World

What role and what tasks will the Masters take on? (Sept. '82)

Like the Christ, the Masters, too, will act as advisors on matters of all kinds, relating to all aspects of our lives. As I have said, there will be a Master in what one might call a presidential post in certain countries and in these countries you will find, therefore, some aspects of Hierarchical government, perhaps forming a two-tier system with a democratic form of government. One does not preclude the other. Many young people are very suspicious of the term "master." They see it as conferring some authority over us. This is not the case; a Master is simply a master over Himself and the forces of nature. By token of Their experience and Their spiritual achievement, a degree of Hierarchical supervision will be seen to be totally acceptable within a democratic framework.

How many Masters are now in the world? Will more come? (Aug. '82)

There are eleven Masters now in the everyday world, and one more will take His place soon. Eventually there will be forty Masters, but that is over a long period of time. At first, the initial group of twelve will be introduced to the world by the Christ, as His disciples. Some of them are the disciples who were with Jesus in Palestine: the one who was John the Beloved, now the Master Koot Hoomi, will be among them; St Paul, now the Master Hilarion; and St Peter, now the Master Morya; also the Master Jesus.

How many Masters are in America now? (Mar. '84)

Connected with the human evolution there are six Masters now in America, North and South. Three of Them are in dense physical bodies. Of Those in charge of the sub-human and deva evolutions there are forty-five in the Americas. Only two of this group are in dense physical bodies.

You say that there are now twelve Masters in the (modern) world. Is one of Them in Paris or in France? (Apr. '86)

No, not at this time, but shortly a Master will take up His position near Paris.

Do the twelve Masters already in the world have twelve different functions? (Oct. '85)

Certainly the Masters have different functions, depending on Their ray and particular line of work. Some will teach, while others will be concerned more with world problems of a political and economic nature. Still others will inspire the new architecture, painting and music, while the attention of some will be directed to science and the inspiration of the new 'holistic' science, integrating science and religion. The Masters are, all of Them, engaged in many different areas and tend to specialize along Their ray-line, while working together, of course, in the fulfillment of the Plan.

Will all the Masters externalise their ashrams? (Oct. '82)

No. It depends on the particular Master and the response in the various countries to the Masters' work—some will be more responsive than others. Some Masters are even now experimenting along these lines with various groups in different parts of the world. This is a long-term project.

Are the Masters going to stay in the world as long as Maitreya? If so, do They too have *mayavirupa* bodies? (Mar. '83)

The majority of the Masters will go on to higher work, but some Masters, especially the highest initiates, the sixth degree 'Chohans,' will remain, and one, the Master Koot Hoomi, will become the Christ in the Capricorn age. The Master Morya will become the Manu of the sixth race.

Many of the Masters now use the *mayavirupa* vehicle, but in Their case the construction principle is different. That used by Maitreya has no parallel in the history of the world and is absolutely permanent. The *mayavirupas* used by the Masters are not permanent and need constant refashioning.

It is said that individuals who have taken the Christ or Buddha initiation have the free will to decide to return in a physical body to help the people. In the book *Jewish Traditions in the Kabbala,* by Van Leeuwen, it is said that, according to the Kabbala, this is not possible; they can help from their own plane but not on the physical. Which of these views is correct? (Apr. '86)

I find this rather a strange question to address to me, when I have been saying for years that the Christ is in the world *in a physical body*. There is no law which states that a Christ or a Buddha cannot return in a physical body. This is determined by circumstances and Hierarchical Plan. The classic mode of return is to take over the body of a disciple, specially prepared for this task. The mode used by the Christ today is the creation of the *mayavirupa*, in which He has lived in London, fully physically, since July 1977.

Why does Maitreya have to have a manufactured body when the Masters are able to keep Theirs for thousands of years? (June/July '85)

Some Masters do retain a body for several thousands of years (Maitreya is one such), but the more usual practice is to create (and recreate) the *mayavirupa* (body of illusion). This was done by Maitreya in the five to six years before July 1977. The Masters do not normally live 'in the world,' i.e. the everyday world, surrounded by millions of people, toxic fumes, etc. Maitreya has created a body which is basic or resistant enough to allow Him to do that—for the whole of the Aquarian Age—and yet which is sensitive enough to the higher spiritual vibration to enable Him to do His work as the World Teacher and to convince us of His stature. The majority of the Masters Who are returning with Him do now and will in the future use self-created *mayavirupas*. However, these are created by a different method than that used by Maitreya, which is unique.

Do Masters change Their bodies of manifestation? Do They change rays? (Feb. '84)

Masters do (infrequently) change Their bodies of manifestation in one of two ways, depending on Their degree: by rebirth or by the creation of a *mayavirupa*, a self-created body. Usually They do not change Their ray structure, but can do so for specific purposes if necessary.

Master Jesus

Will we see the Master Jesus after the Declaration of Maitreya or before? (Mar. '84)

After. None of the Masters will declare Themselves until the Christ has declared Himself.

What purpose is served by the appearance of Maitreya that would not be served by the return of Jesus Christ? (Sept. '84)

The question implies a misunderstanding of the relationship between Jesus and the Christ. The Christ, Maitreya, worked through Jesus (for three years). This time the Christ Himself has come as the World Teacher for all humanity. The Master Jesus has a special relationship to the Christian churches wherever they are found.

Does the Catholic Church have a specific post-Day-of-Declaration role? (May '86)

Yes, as a unifier of the Christian approach—provided that, in the light of the new reality which the Christ's presence presents (and that of the Master Jesus, Who is in charge of the Christian churches), it is flexible and resilient enough to renounce its manmade dogmas and doctrines, political and economic power, and social control.

Is Jesus in charge of both the Christian and Jewish churches, or is Maitreya, and not Jesus, now the Messiah of the Jews? (Apr. '85)

Jesus is in charge (has under His care the stimulation and guidance) of the Christian Churches, East and West. The Jewish people still have to recognize Jesus as their Messiah and also Maitreya as the World Teacher, not only in the religious field but in all departments.

Why does the Master Jesus retain the name of a previous incarnation when He was not yet a Master at that time? Is there any energetic reason for it, or does He have other

names or titles, adopting the 'Master Jesus' merely for convenience to esotericists? (Feb. '83)

He does indeed have other names and titles within the Hierarchy, known to some of His close disciples, but Jesus is His name in His best-known incarnation, known today throughout the world. There are obviously symbolic and psychological reasons, therefore, why He should continue to use it.

Do you know of any connection between the recent invitation by the Lutheran Church in Rome to the Pope to come and speak there (a unique event) and the presence in that city of the Master Jesus? (Feb. '84)

There is no direct connection between that invitation and the presence of the Master Jesus in Rome. Rather, this event, unique as you say, is a further example of the growing momentum of the ecumenical movement which indeed has the energy of the Master Jesus behind it.

Who was the Master who was the source for *A Course in Miracles*? (May '81)

The Master Jesus, through a disciple (discarnate), through a disciple.

In the list of the Rays of Initiates we find that Jesus of Nazareth was a fourth degree initiate, while Apollonius of Tyana was a fifth degree. Essentially, this would harmonize with what has already been stated in your "Reappearance" book on this matter. However, when we speak of the Master Jesus are we referring to the Jesus of Nazareth or Apollonius of Tyana? They appear to be listed as two different individuals (as they exist today), but are

they? Or can we refer to the 'Master Jesus' as either Jesus or Apollonius? Please clarify this. (June '85)

The Master Jesus quickly came into incarnation again as Apollonius of Tyana (as stated in my book), became a Master in that life, and lived and worked in Northern India, where He was buried. From this fact has come the legend (and several books based on that legend) that Jesus did not die on the cross, but went to Northern India and was later buried there.

The Master Jesus, as He now calls Himself, has had two more physical bodies since that of Apollonius, and is now in a Syrian body of some 640 years of age. He calls Himself the Master Jesus rather than Apollonius or any other title because it has a special significance for the Christian churches. Historically, of course, the Master Jesus and Apollonius of Tyana were two separate manifestations of the same individuality, but He continues to be known within the Hierarchy as the Master Jesus and it is by this name that He will be known in the coming time.

Other Masters

Are the Masters Morya and K.H. (Koot Hoomi) presently in physical bodies? (Nov. '84)

According to my information, yes. They will be among the first group of Masters to be introduced to the world after Declaration Day.

Why do some Avatars grow old? (June/July '85)

Some do and some do not. Certain 'hidden' Avatars, such as Babaji and Sanat Kumara Himself, do not grow old, and the body in which Maitreya now presents Himself will not grow 'old' throughout the Aquarian Age. Avatars such as Ramakrishna, Ramana Maharishi, Sai Baba and others who take a human body inevitably undergo human dissolution. But this happens only when Their purpose in incarnating is fulfilled.

Would you please discuss the lesser-known Masters, such as Mozart, Blavatsky, Abraham Lincoln, Beethoven, Serapis, the English Master, etc., as to Their ray, whether They are in incarnation now, and who and how They influence or inspire on the physical plane? (Apr. '83)

H. P. Blavatsky and the Masters Who were Mozart and Beethoven are not in incarnation at the present time. Blavatsky is on the 1st ray and is a fourth to fifth degree initiate; Mozart and Beethoven are on the 4th ray of harmony and have taken the fifth initiation.

H. P. Blavatsky works to help the Master Morya in His manifold endeavours along the 1st ray line. This includes the stimulus of the various esoteric and occult societies, in an attempt to bring their thinking along more correct lines.

Abraham Lincoln is on the 1st ray and is a fourth degree disciple of Shamballa rather than Hierarchy. The Master Serapis is a Chohan (sixth degree Master) of the 4th ray, while the English Master is on the 3rd ray and has taken five initiations.

These three individuals are in incarnation, Abraham Lincoln living not far from His monument in Washington, which He frequently uses as a focus for His energy. The Master Serapis works mainly with the Deva or angelic evolution and is aided in His work by the Master who was Mozart. The English Master works mainly with the political and economic groups world-wide, seeking to guide them into a synthesis.

Which Masters worked through H. P. Blavatsky for the writings of her books? (July/Aug. '86)

The Masters Morya, Koot Hoomi, and Djwhal Khul.

Why would Ascended Masters need to live on the planet? Could they not do the same things without reincarnating? (Nov. '84)

In the first place, only a very small number of the Masters are ascended, i.e. have taken the sixth initiation. Secondly, if They are ascended, or at the least resurrected, and yet take incarnation, it is because They are able to do (or need to do) in incarnation what They cannot do out of incarnation. Who are we to judge or limit the activity of Ascended or Resurrected Masters? They are returning to physical plane activity as preparation for entering the Way of the Higher Evolution—Their next step in evolution as a group.

Is it possible that an Avatar will incarnate as a group—for example, to show us how to act as a group or to emphasize group consciousness? (Nov. '84)

This is a popular idea among some groups and individuals, especially in connection with the reappearance of the Christ. It stems from a belief in the Christ Principle or Consciousness manifesting through humanity, the idea being that as that Principle demonstrates on a wide-enough scale, the reappearance of the Christ takes place. This outflow of the Christ Principle (which He embodies) is only *one* of the three modes of manifestation of Maitreya, the others being the overshadowing of the minds of certain disciples and His physical presence in the world. My information is that no Avatar today, or in the future, will incarnate as a group.

Contacting Masters

The Master D.K. has said that to meet a Master on the physical plane would be, for the average person, very disorganizing to their vehicles. Does this still hold true in your

view of the externalisation of the Hierarchy? (July/Aug. '83)

It is perfectly true that for the average person, the close encounter (if one might so express it) with the tremendously heightened vibration, or livingness, of a Master would be very upsetting for his various bodies, unprepared as they would be for this higher stimulus. Therefore, it is probable that even after the externalisation of the Hierarchy is an acknowledged fact, the contact of the average person with Masters will be somewhat remote—by radio and television. It is for this reason (among others, of course) that the externalisation will take place only slowly, over many years.

Nevertheless, some Masters have been undergoing special training which will allow Them to live more closely with humanity, and Maitreya Himself, because of the special characteristics of His body of manifestation (*mayavirupa*) which is created in a unique way, can live in the closest proximity to average humanity.

Must the Master contact the student when the time is right, or can the student contact the Master? (June '85)

The law is that the Master *may* contact the student when the student is ready, but this will only happen when he or she can be of service to the Master's plan.

I have been trying to get in touch with a Master or Teacher on the inner planes for years and had no success. Is there a reason for this? (Oct. '84)

Mere desire to contact a Master is not sufficient to bring about that contact. The aspirant or disciple must show by his capacity, objectivity and desire to serve that he can be useful to the Master's work. There is an ancient adage: "When the pupil is ready, the Master comes." Contact with 'guides' or 'teachers' on the astral planes, of course, needs no special capacity except a certain mediumistic faculty which I personally believe should be avoided.

Why is the Master so stern and unapproachable at times? What lesson is to be learned from a sternness without an answer? Or a reproach without an apparent cause? (July/Aug. '86)

I wonder which Master the writer means. To my knowledge she is not in touch with a Master and the question therefore is a result of glamour.

I know I have never found my Master to be stern or reproachful and unapproachable only on rare occasions when higher work engaged His total attention.

Given the number of initiates in incarnation above, say, the second degree who have ongoing contact with an externalized Master, why are not some, at least, making known in some way the fact of the Reappearance?

This question shows a basic misunderstanding of the relationship between Masters and second-degree disciples, and also about the role of disciples in general in the externalization process.

There are around 240,000 disciples of the second degree in incarnation at present. They are to be found in all fields. Of these, only a tiny minority have "ongoing contact with a Master," externalized or not. The vast majority do their work in politics, industry, science, or wherever, without necessarily knowing anything about Hierarchy or Masters, far less the facts of the Reappearance. And if they heard of these facts (as some of them must have), they would not necessarily believe them. Almost all disciples of the second degree and many of the third work under subjective (soul) stimulus and inspiration.

Also, where disciples do work consciously in contact with a Master, they would know their particular role and be inclined to stick to that. Each to his task.

Why has your Master's name not been revealed? (Sept. '84)

He has requested me not to reveal it for the present. I know of two reasons, the major one being this: if I were to reveal His name generally, I would have to reveal it to the group or groups with which I work. They would focus their attention on Him continuously in such a way as—by telepathy—to distract His attention. Whether He 'blocked' this or responded to it would involve a waste of His energy and time—and the Masters guard both with care.

Can we communicate through prayer with your Master, or can it only be through you? (June/July '85)

Since no one but myself knows the name of my Master, I really do not see how you can (knowingly) communicate with Him, by prayer or otherwise.

The Tibetan (Master D.K.) talks of esotericists responding to the astral reflection of the Hierarchy rather than the reality. How do you yourself know which you are communicating with? What advice would you give to aspirants regarding discriminating between the two? (July/Aug. '85)

It is true that on the astral planes there are powerful thoughtforms of the known Masters, the astral constructions of devoted aspirants and disciples over the years. Many astrally sensitive people contact these illusory 'Masters' and receive back the 'teachings,' astrally embodied, which at least to some extent have come originally from real Masters through mentally polarized and soul-focused disciples. There are many such instances today, some of them very well known and respected. (There are several groups and probably many individuals who consider that I come into this category of deluded disciples. I leave it to time to prove conclusively that this is not the case.)

To come to the question of how I *know* with whom I am communicating, the real or illusory Master, it is obviously possible to contact an astral reflection and think it a Master, but it is impossible, I would say, to be contacted by a Master (because the disciple is contacted by the Master, and not the other way around) without knowing with certainty that one is so contacted. Obviously, if a Master wishes, for His purposes, to contact a disciple, He will find a way to do so—and leave the disciple in no doubt. This can be either a physical or a telepathic contact. In my case, since I am engaged in this public work of preparation for Maitreya, my Master was at pains to establish His reality—and I insisted that He do so. No astral thought-form can heal. My Master and His Colleagues perform acts of healing which amaze those who know of them. No astral thought-form can make solid objects disappear and reappear (see the preface to my book, *The Reappearance of the Christ and the Masters of Wisdom*). No astral thought-form can or does put the disciple through the intense de-glamourization and disillusioning process which my Master put me through in preparation for public service. No astral thought-form sends a photograph of itself to the disciple in contact. I could go on and on. In a thousand ways my Master has proved His reality to me (and countless others).

The touchstone is *objectivity* and *lack of glamour*. It is true to say that my Master has never made one statement which could feed the glamour or ambition of any individual, myself or others. On the contrary, many disciples have been enormously enriched by His wise advice, objectively but lovingly given.

My advice to aspirants is this: discrimination is the key. Look for objectivity. Beware of those who offer initiations from Masters—with or without a certificate! Beware of those who tell you that the Masters need your very special help (usually financial!) in Their plans. Beware of those of low degree who claim an impossible contact with the Chohans (sixth degree initiates), and beware of any communication, through others or direct, which feeds your ego and glamours and gives you the sense of importance which all long for and few deserve.

Do you think that there was any significance in the fact that your Master's first contribution to *Share International* was on the subject of time? (Aug. '82)

Yes, I must say that I have thought of that too, lately. I thought at the time that it was a curious choice of subject to begin a series of articles for *Share International.* However, I am absolutely certain that everything He does is done with some purpose behind it. It may have been done deliberately to place in our minds the idea that our sense of time, for instance, in relation to Maitreya's emergence was not necessarily the same as that of the Masters. Perhaps He was suggesting that They have an altogether different, broader, more flexible sense of time. It may have some relevance and that may be why he chose that theme to begin His articles. On the other hand, it may have some other significance, for example, to show us how different is Reality from our time-dominated concept and how important it is to consider the problem of time. More than likely both these reasons were behind this choice.

Do dream experiences about any of the Masters have any significance for the individual recipient? (June '84)

It depends on the dream and the dreamer. Most such dreams have no significance, but occasionally the Masters manifest Themselves to disciples in this way. The trick is to distinguish the true from the purely wish-fulfilling.

Does each spirit-soul have only one Master? (June '85)

Each soul normally and eventually is drawn into the ashram of one Master of the same soul ray, although in certain cases, especially in more advanced disciples and initiates, more than one Master may be involved in the development, etc., of the disciple. Apart from that, disciples are frequently 'lent' to other Masters for specific work.

Does each person have a guide? (Mar. '86)

No. Each person has a guardian angel, but 'guides,' usually working on the astral planes, normally work in relation to groups. The Masters of Wisdom, the Guides of the race, Who work only on the higher mental planes, normally work with and through groups of disciples.

Is the Christ the Master of most 2nd ray souls? (Oct. '85)

No, by no means. The Christ, Maitreya, is the Master only of ìMasters and a few fourth degree initiates.

White Eagle writes in his booklet, *The Path of The Soul*, that in difficult times one should concentrate on one's Master. In His qualities one could find courage. Has every Master the spiritual leadership of a group of souls? (Sept. '84)

No, not all the Masters, even among those connected with the human evolution, take pupils or form an Ashram or Group. Some of Them are engaged in work of such a broad and lofty nature in connection with the race as a whole that such work with groups would be impossible.

The Hierarchy and Forces of Materiality

In the chapter on the process of Maitreya's emergence we read that the opposing forces to the light upset the hoped-for and long-awaited rendezvous between the press and Maitreya in July 1985. As the spiritual presence of the Hierarchy increases on the earth, do these opposing forces of the black lodge increase their influence in the world also, and would this account for humanity, stuck between these two forces, seemingly being lost, confused and frustrated with its lot? (Nov. '85)

It is true to say that as the spiritual influence of the Hierarchy increases in the world, the efforts of the black lodge will increase also. However, that is not to say that their *influence* will also increase—they are fighting a losing battle. As Maitreya Himself has said, "The end is known from the beginning," and He foresees total victory for the forces of Light.

While working only from the soul level, the Hierarchy of Masters have been at a disadvantage in relation to the black lodge, which works on the physical and astral planes. With the return of Maitreya and His group of Masters, however, this situation is changed. The lords of materiality will be 'sealed off' to their own domain—the upholding of the matter aspect of the planet.

As a Spiritual Regent, does Sai Baba's role include confronting and sealing away the 'forces of evil' on this planet? (Nov. '83)

Yes. He works closely with the Lord of the World and the Hierarchy in Their continuous supervision of the work of the lords of materiality, negating, so far as possible, their destructive influence. His presence makes possible 'divine intervention' which would not otherwise be the case. That is one of the functions of an Avatar.

The month of August last year (1985) had so many 'accidents' and in each 'accident' date the number 2 was noted. Can the meaning of this be given out? (Mar. '86)

There is no meaning to give out. However, August 1985 saw an unprecedented number of terrorist attacks and meaningless, motiveless killings. People seemed to have gone berserk. My Master predicted this as a result of the attack by the cosmic and planetary 'dark forces' on 31 July 1985 to prevent the contact between Maitreya and media. The attack was contained, but the release of negativity into the astral planes resulted in the crazy behaviour which followed.

Does the recent rash of airplane crashes have anything to do with the energy opposing Maitreya's public appearance on the planet? There was that huge one on 31 July and so many since. Also, does the big earthquake in Mexico have anything to do with it? (Dec. '85)

No, nothing whatsoever. It is simply that the planes, as a generation, are getting on the elderly side, and competition is so fierce among international airlines that I believe corners are being cut in supervision, maintenance, etc. The Mexican earthquake, too, has a totally different cause.

Do the so-called 'forces of darkness' ever impersonate or disguise themselves as the forces of good in order to deceive the well-intentioned, to subvert their intentions? If so, how can we avoid being thus deceived? (Dec. '84)

Yes, this is a common ploy by the forces of materiality. They often imitate the methods used by the Hierarchy of Light to snare the unwary. The best defence against deception is to examine carefully one's motives and to keep them pure and altruistic. The forces of darkness cannot work or influence where the light and love of the soul dominates the actions. Objectivity and selflessness are the keynotes of soul-inspired actions and ideas. When this is the case one is automatically protected.

Is my very fear of this a result of 'dark force' activities? (Dec. '84)

No, it is a common fear. The best thing, to my mind, is to forget entirely the 'dark forces'—to proceed as if they did not exist—and thus give them no energy.

Why does the Hierarchy allow religions to divide humanity and hate each other? (May '84)

It is not Hierarchy's task to allow or disallow any particular action by humanity. We have free will which They do not infringe. They are our elder brothers, but They cannot live our lives for us any more than parents can live their children's lives for them. Gradually, by the suffering which results from our hate and divisions, we learn harmlessness and therefore right relationship.

Why does Hierarchy believe that mankind is worth saving? (Apr. '84)

Because They know that man is potentially divine and in incarnation according to divine purpose.

What is a Yeti? (June '84)

The Yeti—or 'abominable snowman'—has nothing to do with man at all. It is a Himalayan bear adapted to living at great heights. Very shy and not very numerous, its mysterious presence is usually known from its large footprints in the snow. The fact that it frequently walks on its hind legs—thus leaving only two prints—has led to the speculation that these prints are of some animal-man of the ancient past.

The Yeti should not be confused with the rare 'sky-clad ones' who also inhabit the Himalayas. These are men, Yogis, able to live at these heights completely naked (hence the term sky-clad). They are not Masters of Wisdom in the technical sense, but have developed certain yogic practices to a remarkable degree. They would not need to eat or sleep, for example, and feel no cold.

Signs

Could you say something about visions—for example, visions of the Virgin Mary? (Nov. '82)

Visions of the Virgin Mary are mainly of two kinds: those which are put into the minds of the devout by certain of the Masters, or by disciples of those Masters working from the inner planes; and those which are astral imaginings or emanations. In other words, some are simply astral, emotional longings, fulfilled astrally—people long to see the Virgin Mary, they long for help, and it is eventually fulfilled through these astral visions. In the other case, it is not unknown that certain Masters see it as Their work to maintain the talismans, to keep them fulfilled. A vision of Mary is like a talisman, and so is, for example, the Turin Shroud, which was left for the support of the faithful. It helps to maintain their faith in God and a true connection between God and man; it fulfills their yearning for a sign from God. And people do see not only visions of Mary, but many other things—weeping statues, weeping paintings. I have seen a photograph which when taken was simply a view of a landscape, yet when it was developed had the figure of the Master Jesus in the middle of the photograph. And more recently there have been several photographs of clouds, taken by different people in aeroplanes at different times, on which the standing figure of the Christ is clearly superimposed ('coming in the clouds'). There are many such manifestations.

They are real. However, some of the "visions" are not real, they are simply astral emanations or projections.

What is the significance of the many reports of weeping statues of the Mother Mary and even of statues which move? (Sept. '85)

They are signs, given for the faithful (in a religious sense) to assure them of the continuing love and concern for them of God and His representatives. Many of the Masters (the Mother Mary is now a Master but not in incarnation) activate statues or paintings of Themselves in this way. The proliferation of these signs today is an indication of the end of the age and the assurance of divine succour in times of crisis. They can also be seen as the signs of His presence to which Maitreya refers in Message No. 10.

Why is the image of Mary apparently used so often when the Masters project 'visions' for people?

There would be little point in projecting a vision of an unknown Master. The well-known and much-loved symbols of Jesus and Mary (in India, Krishna or the Mother) are used precisely because they are recognizable. Mary, especially, is adored as the ever-loving and protective Mother.

UFO

How would we recognize a hostile as against a friendly UFO? (May '84)

There are no hostile UFOs. The various tales of allegedly hostile UFOs notwithstanding, the UFO manifestation is the result of interplanetary co-operation and is totally peaceful and beneficent in intention. This co-operation, of course, takes place between our Esoteric Hierarchy and the other planets. Stories of hostile action on the part of UFO occupants, I believe, are the morbid imaginings of frightened humans. Science fiction writings and the cinema have been largely instrumental in creating this kind of fear reaction. They have done a disservice to the understanding of the UFO phenomenon by projecting this negative thought-form.

Do UFOs pick certain people by ray or otherwise to make themselves visible to? (June '85)

As I understand it, no. Sometimes it is done for some major purpose, but as often as not it is relatively haphazard, providing they think the person will be open and not too scared. It is never their intention to scare people. If you have read my book, *The Reappearance of the Christ and the Masters of Wisdom*, you will know that I believe the UFOs (and their occupants) to be of etheric physical and not dense physical matter and their solid appearance to us to be a temporary phenomenon.

Does a UFO become invisible by bending the light-rays? (May '84)

No. The UFO is normally invisible, being made of matter of the four etheric planes—mainly (80 per cent) of matter of the two highest and 20 per cent from planes three and four. They are made visible to our sight by lowering the vibrational rate of these atoms and are rendered invisible again by returning to their normal frequency.

Would the Space People intercede for us if there was an atomic war by using their technology to stop the missiles? (May '86)

I believe they would. Having given permission for the atomic secrets to be released to the Allied scientists during 1942, Sanat Kumara (Lord of the World) would be involved in any nuclear conflict.

CHAPTER IV

SPIRITUALITY AND LIFE IN THE NEW AGE

Spirituality

"The word 'spiritual' does not refer to religious matters so-called. All activity which drives the human being forward towards some form of development—physical, emotional, mental, intuitional, social—if it is in advance of his present state is essentially spiritual in nature..."

In this statement from *Education in the New Age* by Alice A. Bailey, the Master D.K., I believe, focuses the shift in emphasis which must be made in our relationship to the world, and reflects a completely new approach to activities other than the strictly religious. He also said that the monopolization by the religious groups of the term "spiritual" has been the greatest triumph of the forces of evil on this planet. The general view is that whatever is "religious" is "spiritual," whereas all other activities are profane or mundane. So long as we go to church on Sunday, we can spend the rest of the week creating the most corrupt, dishonest and irrational political, economic and social structures and conditions. We have separated the spiritual from every aspect of our being except the religious life and have relegated it to a limited role as "the inner life." This has allowed us in our outer lives to live corruptly and dishonestly and has resulted in the difficulties which now confront the world, where we now face the possibility of total destruction at the touch of a button.

We have prostituted science, just as we prostitute every aspect of divine knowledge, to the mammon at the pole opposite to our divine nature, a divinity which we have recognized only in religious terms and in the religious field.

We do not see man as a spiritual being except when he enters a church or adheres to some particular religion. Therefore all political, economic, or social structures which deny a religious connotation to life (for instance, the present-day systems in the communist world) are considered deeply evil. Indeed, aspects of their social organization may be evil—the totalitarianism, the denial of individual freedom are definitely evil—but to a large extent they are based on profoundly spiritual principles: Liberty, Justice, Equality, and Fraternity, which are at the root of not only the French Revolution, but of every revolution since that time. The problem is, of course, that the spiritual ideals remain largely ideals only.

In this coming time we shall have to make a shift in consciousness to include every aspect of our being in our definition of "spiritual." All our structures must be based on the inner Oneness of humanity and reflect that reality. As souls we are One; there is no such thing as a separate individual soul. We have to create political, economic and social systems which allow that inner divinity to express itself.

We have built systems which are based on the wrong principles: competition, division, separatism and inequality, all in direct opposition to the inner reality. The inner reality is man's Oneness, a shared divine nature which is potential in every single human being, and which needs the correct outer forms to allow the inner radiance to be expressed. Much of the violence of today is the result of the tension between man's knowledge of himself, inwardly perceived as divine, and his inability to manifest that recognition on the outer plane. He feels he has no control over the political and economic structures which put him into sharply- divided categories—a virtual caste system. He reacts against the outer circumstances, which bear no relation to his sense of himself as a divine being. He is at war with himself and, as an extension of himself, with the society of which he is a part. This is at the root of a great deal of the present social tension and violence in the world. Only by a re-education of humanity about the true nature of man as a threefold reality—spirit, soul and personality—and of the Law of Cause and Effect in its relation to the Law of Rebirth, can a true expression of man as a soul take place.

This will condition our new systems. Until we grasp that all people are divine, we shall not be able to create institutions sufficiently responsive to the inner divinity without corrupting that divinity. The churches today, to a large extent, have corrupted the divinity of which they speak because they have become so dogmatic, so doctrinal, and so separative in that dogma and doctrine that they have lost the tolerance, the sense of goodwill, of brotherhood, which should be the basis of the religious notion of God: a common Fatherhood and therefore the fraternity of all men. When this is applied to the political field our systems will reflect that reality.

Likewise in the economic sphere, we must institute the principle whereby all peoples everywhere can share together the goods of the earth. The greatest division in the world today is the economic disparity between North and South, the industrialized nations and the Third World. One third of the world usurps and wastes three quarters of the world's food and at least eighty per cent of the world's resources and energy, while the Third World makes do with the rest. The tensions inherent in this imbalance are driving us inexorably to chaos. These are the central findings of the *Brandt Commission*, among others. Their report, *North-South: A Programme For Survival*, recognizes the dangers inherent in this imbalance. Until all people everywhere can eat and live freely as fully accepted members of the human family, there will be no justice in the world. While there is no justice there will be no true peace; if there is no true peace in the world today, there is no future for the world.

We are now facing a crisis which is essentially spiritual, but which is working out in the political and economic fields. Hence the Christ's decision to work within the sphere of politics and economics, and hence His emphasis on the principle of sharing, which, He has said, is the key to all future progress for man: "When you share you recognize God in your brother." "Man must share or die." Sharing is a divine principle, and until we recognize that all structures must reflect that inner divinity we shall not make one further step in our evolutionary journey. As soon as we do realize it, we shall open the door into an entirely new situation.

There is a wonderful statement by the great Spanish poet, Federico Garcia Lorca, about the ending of hunger:

"The day that hunger is eradicated from the earth there will be the greatest spiritual explosion the world has ever known. Humanity cannot imagine the joy that will burst into the world on the day of that great revolution."

That may seem a very ambitious statement, but it is a recognition, I believe, that the eradication of hunger in a world of plenty is humanity's first step into its divinity because it is the first step into right relationship of man to man. As soon as we recognize that we are One and begin to share the resources of the world among all peoples, we take the first step into becoming gods. Therein lies the essential spirituality of the new economic structures, which must be based on sharing because they must be based on man's divinity. Sharing is a divine activity and goes further than the distribution of the world's resources: we all share our divinity. We are really One on every level—physical, emotional, mental, intuitional and social. On all these levels sharing can take place.

There is an enormous division, even in the 'new age' groups today, between those who see political and economic action not only as essential but as a great spiritual movement for rebirth, and those who feel that politics is a dirty word, that economics is something only the poor deal with. I am often appalled at the callousness of so-called 'spiritual' people as they view the starving millions of the world. So often the plight of the dispossessed is explained away as their 'karma' through which they are learning a lesson. Simple, straightforward, ordinary human compassion, one might think, would lead to a concern for their well-being.

Politics, economics, science, culture, and education will soon be fundamental spiritual endeavours of humanity, embodying every aspect of the spiritual life. The religious groups, the so-called 'spiritual' and 'new-age' groups, do not have a monopoly of spirituality. In fact, the Master D.K. has said that the so-called esoteric and occult groups are the most glamoured of all the groups. I have also found them to be the least effective. The real changes in the world, the real shifts in consciousness, are being made on the political and economic front. It is through political and economic change that the structures will be rebuilt which will allow the spirituality inherent in all peoples to be reflected. The Christ will show that the path of the spiritual life is broad and varied enough to accommodate all people. In every endeavour, in every department of human life, the awareness and knowledge of God can be sensed and expressed. All can contribute their awareness of this moment-to-moment experience to the many-coloured pattern which will grow as a result of that shared experience. (Jan. '82)

Aims and Possibilities

The goal for humanity in this coming age is the creation of group consciousness, the sense of being integral parts of a Whole. The new energies entering this planet from the constellation Aquarius work in this direction; their intrinsic quality is synthesis, universality.

We are about to witness profound changes in all our institutions and structures—political and economic, religious and social, scientific, educational and cultural. These changes will take place as humanity grasps, stage by stage, its essential Oneness, and adopts the measures necessary to implement that Oneness.

The first human priority is the saving of the millions now starving to death in the Third World. A crash programme of aid on a world scale will be needed to alleviate their plight. No effort should be spared to ease the distress now being suffered in some of the poorest areas. There is nothing more urgent or important to do in the world today. All else must follow this primary human necessity.

The Christ will call for the acceptance of the principle of sharing through the redistribution of the world's resources—the food, raw materials, energy and technological expertise, largely usurped (and wasted) today by the developed nations.

When we have accepted the principle of sharing (which principle will be forced on the governments by world public opinion), each country will be asked to make over, in trust for the world, that which it has *in excess of its needs*. Every country will be invited to make an inventory of its assets and needs. Fed into computers, these statistics will provide a United Nations Agency, set up for the purpose, with the information on which a rational redistribution of the world's resources can take place. In this way a better balance between the developed and underdeveloped world can be achieved. It has been estimated that the redistribution programme will take two to three years to implement. The plans and blueprints for the scheme, drawn up by high initiates—economists, financiers and industrialists of great achievement—have long been in existence, awaiting only the demand of humanity for their implementation. A sophisticated form of barter will replace the present economic systems.

There is no doubt that there will be opposition from those more-privileged members of society who will see in the changes which must take place a loss of their traditional status and power; but the need for change will become so overwhelmingly obvious that they will find themselves increasingly powerless to halt the momentum.

For several years, in five major centres (New York, London, Geneva, Darjeeling and Tokyo) groups have been trained by a Master in the precise legislation which will change our present chaotic political, economic and social structures along more rational (and more spiritual) lines. With the minimum of cleavage, the minimum disruption of the existing social fabric, far-reaching changes can be expected over the coming years. The democratic system will still hold, and will be seen to be right and effective when it is, for the first time, truly directed to the common good. The participation of all sections of society in the construction of the new social order will ensure the speedy adoption of the measures necessary for its implementation.

The key to a more harmonious political climate is the acceptance of the principle of sharing. Both the democratic and the communistic systems are in process of transition, and as they evolve they will become less mutually exclusive than they now appear to be. Greater world harmony will result.

The United Nations Assembly will come into its own as the international legislative body. The work of the Assembly is inhibited today by the lack of support given it by the major powers, in particular the USA and Russia, and by the existence of the Security Council with its power of veto. The Security Council has outlived its usefulness and now must make way for the more broadly-based voice of the Assembly to be heard. The United Nations is the blueprint for a future World Government of federated independent states. It is not part of the Divine Plan that the nations should live under one political system. Democracy and Communism are each the expression, more or less distorted, of a divine idea. In their eventual perfect expression each will give to the world a model of social organization suited to different peoples in different circumstances. "Unity in diversity" may be said to be the keynote of future political groupings.

Profound changes are already taking place in the industrialized world with the advent of micro-technology. Machines, ever more sophisticated, will increasingly take over the means of production. Today's problems of unemployment will become the problems of leisure. Education for the right and fullest use of leisure will be of paramount importance. Eventually, all the artifacts of our civilization will be made by machines, thus freeing man for the exploration of his own true nature and purpose. In time, these machines will be made by an act of man's creative will; we have, as yet, scarcely touched the surface of the potential of the human mind.

The immediate need is to transform work processes to free from mechanical drudgery the countless millions who now know no other meaning in their daily work: "Let me take you into a world where no man lacks; where no two days are alike; where the joy of Brotherhood manifests through all men." (Maitreya's Message No. 3.)

The Advent of the Christ and the emergence of the Masters of Wisdom will bring an enormous sense of relief and reduction of tension to the world. The gain in physical and emotional well-being will be considerable. Much of the physical disease in the world today has a psychic cause: the strains, the tensions and fears inherent in our divided society and world. Given true hope for the future, the general health of humanity will improve.

Quite apart from this, new approaches to discovering the causes of disease will be made. The existence of the etheric planes of matter, i.e. matter finer in substance than gas and normally invisible, has long been postulated, and accepted by esotericists as axiomatic. This is the next area of matter due for investigation by our exoteric scientists. Kirlian photography and the work of Wilhelm Reich have already pointed the way. It will be realized that the health of the physical body depends entirely on the etheric "double" or "counterpart-body." The force centres (or "chakras," as they are called in the East), which focus the etheric flow, have their counterparts on the dense physical plane in the major and minor glands of the endocrine system. We are just beginning to understand how important to our well-being is the correct, interrelated functioning of the endocrine system. This in turn is dependent on the proper functioning of the vital etheric body which substands it.

The alternative, so-called 'fringe' or complementary medicines of today (they are really very old indeed) will take their place beside the more orthodox methods. Teams of doctors and healers of various disciplines will work together, each bringing their particular insights and gifts for the greater benefit of the patient. The Masters are, without exception, adept in the esoteric healing arts, exemplified so dramatically by the Christ in Palestine. Their inspiration and guidance will quicken the pace of experiment and discovery and lead to results undreamt of today.

There is, parallel to the human, another great evolution, the Angelic (or Deva, as it is known in the Orient), which has much to give and to teach humanity in connection with disease and its cure. In the not too distant future, very real contacts will be made between the two evolutions which will result in a great expansion of man's awareness of his true nature and of his place in the scheme of things. This whole subject is so deeply esoteric and abstruse that only the briefest mention of it can be made here.

Certain diseases such as syphilis, tuberculosis and cancer are endemic in humanity and unbelievably old. It will take a long time to rid the world entirely of these scourges, but eventually it will be done. And in the meantime, enormous strides will be made in their control and in the amelioration of their effects, as is already the case with tuberculosis. The universal adoption of cremation as the only hygienic method of restoration to the earth of the body after death will speed this process. For countless ages, through burial, diseases of the physical body have been absorbed into the earth to be reabsorbed in vegetable and animal tissue. This has occurred for so long that the Earth itself is contaminated.

The coming age will see certain profound changes in human perception which will give to humanity an altogether deeper and richer experience of the Reality in which we live: telepathy and etheric vision will become part of normal human equipment rather than being, as now, relatively rare. We are all telepathic (we share this faculty with the animal kingdom), but with most of us it occurs unconsciously, spasmodically, without any control or intention. Gradually, in this new age now dawning, telepathy will become the normal mode of communication between people at the same stage of evolution. The Christ's overshadowing of all humanity on the Day of Declaration foreshadows the future ability of humanity to communicate mentally, telepathically, at will, over any distance. Lying will automatically become impossible and speech will gradually die out.

We know, today, three states of physical matter: solid, liquid and gaseous. Esotericism postulates the existence of four further states of matter above gas, the etheric planes. We live in an etheric ocean, our etheric bodies being more complex concentrations of that ocean. The Master Djwhal Khul has prophesied that a change in the physical eye will occur to confer the "double focus," etheric vision, which allows the perception of these subtle planes. A whole new world will open for humanity; the beauties of the subtler planes will be revealed. Many of the world's great cities are built on etheric power points; the quality and tone of these energetic concentrations will become a major source of discovery and study.

One of the most profound changes which will take place will be in our approach to death. Man will lose his fear of death. Humanity will come to accept and understand the Law of Rebirth; that the death of the body is but the transition to a new and freer state; that the soul in its long journey in incarnation takes vehicle after vehicle through which to reflect itself on the physical plane. Death will lose its terror. When the body is old and depleted in strength, death will be cheerfully sought as the doorway to renewal and further experience.

The Christ will affirm the slow, gradual evolution of man through the process of reincarnation (the Law of Rebirth), and through our understanding of this Law and its relation to the Law of Cause and Effect (the Law of Karma) will come the sure basis for the establishment of right human relations. We will come to understand that our thoughts and actions from moment to moment set in motion causes whose effects make our lives what they are, for good or ill. So we will see the need for harmlessness in relation to others, a harmlessness based on the 'will to good,' expressing itself as goodwill.

The Christ will proclaim the truth that the Kingdom of God exists on earth, and has always existed, in the fact of the Spiritual Hierarchy of Masters and Initiates, and that one day, through His Agency, all His people will be members of that Kingdom. The Ancient Mysteries will be restored, and man will know himself as the divine Being that he is.

All people, eventually, even those not engaged in the religious field, will share the sense of a spiritual basis to life. All will endeavour, in whatever field of human activity they may be engaged, whether political, scientific, educational or artistic, to give expression to this sensed inner truth and will build a culture and a civilization directly reflecting their experience that God, Nature and Man are One. Then revelation will follow revelation, until we will find ourselves in possession of that knowledge which will open for us the secrets of life itself and will allow us to become conscious creators and co-workers with God. This will be possible when humanity's will and God's will are one and the same. A creative interplay between God and man can then take place, and the true nature and purpose behind the human evolution will become apparent.

This will lead to the creation of the Divine Science known only to the Masters of Wisdom. One day, through man himself, this science will become the instrument whereby the forces of the universe can be harnessed and utilized in the service of the Divine Plan to further the evolution of all kingdoms in nature. Under the guidance of the Hierarchy of Masters, man will find himself able to control forces and energies of which he is today totally unaware, and of which today he is totally at the mercy. He will be able to transcend time and distance by the power of his thought and to create modes of travel so silent and apparently motionless that fatigue will disappear. Through the power of sound he will build his artifacts and control his environment.

Naturally, all of this depends on our ability to surrender our little separate wills and bring them into line with the Divine Will and Purpose. It is to this end that the Christ and the Masters will work. Theirs is the task so to lead and guide that we willingly, gladly, make this surrender ourselves, in the light of our own soul's vision of the scope and majesty of the Plan.

A new era of peace and goodwill is dawning in the world. Nothing can now prevent the inauguration of this era of tranquility and equilibrium. The cosmic forces released into the world by the Christ are definitely making themselves manifest on the physical plane and will continue to do so in ever-mounting potency. These forces will lead to results which at the moment seem to be impossible of achievement. More and more, these energies will condition the ways of our thinking and feeling, and will lead eventually to that desired state of fusion and synthesis which will be the keynote of the Aquarian age. Then we will recognize the fact for so long hidden and unmanifested: that Humanity is One, part of One Life. (June '82)

[This article is largely extracted from the "Introduction" to *The Reappearance of the Christ and the Masters of Wisdom* by Benjamin Creme.]

Political and Economic Change

Religious programmes for elevating human consciousness and improving human character have, on the whole, worked on a few devoted souls, but left the masses yet unreformed and unenlightened. What makes you believe that this current programme (of Maitreya) will have any different effect? (Nov. '85)

It is true that the changes in human consciousness have been slow, but one only has to compare the general awareness of the masses of humanity today to that of the Middle Ages or of Palestine in Jesus' day to realize how far we have advanced. World-wide education and communications have transformed humanity over the last two centuries and prepared it for the changes which must now come. Also, it is not simply a 'religious' programme for improving human character which Maitreya brings. It is a spiritual inspiration which addresses all aspects of our lives—political, economic, religious and social. Above all, in this coming age the Great Exemplars, the Christ and the Masters, will be living openly among us, inspiring, guiding and stimulating all to reach their highest aspiration and potential.

Throughout the ages there have always been men and women of good and evil. Will not the evil that persists make world-wide bliss impossible? (May '86)

I am not actually talking about world-wide 'bliss.' It is obvious that until *everyone* is perfect—which is an evolutionary process—there will be imperfection (what the Churches call sin). I think you have to see 'bliss' in relative terms. The Masters know continuous bliss and it will be a very long time until *everyone* experiences that. But for those who are now starving to death, just to have guaranteed regular meals would be 'bliss'.

Why, in your opinion, is there a rise in religious fundamentalism in the world today? (Jan. '86)

Inevitably, at the end of an age and civilization there is a breakdown of existing religious, political, economic and social structures. Due to their age, these structures are crystallized and weakened by the withdrawal of the energies which brought them into being. Sections of society begin to respond to the new energies which a new age brings and, as they search for and demand new forms, a polarization is set up.

Under the threat of the new, those in love with the old forms take up an increasingly fundamentalist position, seeking against the tide of history and evolution to preserve the past, the status quo. This can be seen throughout the world today in every sphere, not alone in the religious field.

In what light will the Christ be seen by the world? In what capacity will He act? Will He and the Masters form some new institution? (Sept. '82)

After Declaration Day He will be seen as the spearhead of all forward-looking, progressive movements for change. Eventually, this will mean total change of all our institutions. Some time after Declaration Day He will introduce twelve Masters to the world and some of Them will take certain very high posts. One or two will take their places, I do not know how soon, at the head of certain governments in key nations in the world. Another Master will be in charge of a new agency to be set up within the United Nations to oversee the redistribution programme. They will act in the most international way, not forming, as I see it, any new named team or separate agency, but They will be leaders of world thought and opinion and, of course, the stimulus behind all ideas in the rebuilding of the world.

Will the Christ and the Masters form a world government? (Sept. '82)

As I understand it, They will not form a world government. World government will come inevitably as a logical result of the acceptance by humanity that it is One, and that realization will grow from the acceptance of the principle of sharing. Sharing is the basis of all change and progress in this coming time.

The United Nations today forms the nucleus of a future world government. At present it does not have the power which a world government might need, but only because these powers are not given to it by the major nations, America, Russia and China, for instance. The Security Council stands in the way of a true functioning of the UN Assembly, the real basis of a future world government. It should be stressed that world government does not signify a dictatorial, supra-national regime, imposing laws on nations which, willy-nilly, they must obey. It will be the result of a federation of independent states, something like the British Commonwealth or the United States of America. Before the Union, none of the states of America could conceive of giving up autonomy and sovereignty, a condition which is found quite natural now. By the same token, many of the nations today see no possibility of giving up a degree of sovereignty which one day they will accept as perfectly natural to do in the interests of world groupings and world government.

Each country will retain its own language, culture, political system, and so on. It is not the intention of Hierarchy to attempt to create a one-governmental system throughout the world.

So the political and legal systems will be maintained in all countries? (Sept. '82)

Political forms will be retained according to the customs, tradition, history and ray structure of each nation, only in more perfected forms than now. The world's legal matters which concern global issues, for instance the exploration of the seabed or space, or mineral deposits in the world, and so on, will be governed by international law.

Will the Christ play a part in this world government? (Sept. '82)

No, but certain of the Masters will. The Christ will not be the head of the world government. Naturally, He (and the Masters) will be available to give advice if necessary. He is the World Teacher, not its political head.

Very likely, the world government will have some sort of office like that of Secretary General of the United Nations which could be held alternately, by agreement, by representatives from the various countries, high initiates, or perhaps even Masters.

Does the Christ have any particular political bias? (Oct. '82)

No. You will find that the Christ does not align Himself with any particular political ideology or stance. He is not a member of any political party. You will see that He speaks for all people, especially the poor, for East and West. The world's problems are not simply party-political problems; sharing the resources of the world is a global issue, one for the UN as a ìwhole to deal with. He will appeal to the goodwill and compassion in all people everywhere, of whatever party, political persuasion, or none.

Did Maitreya establish both capitalism and communism, which will be united by Him (the "eye" of the Triangle)? (Nov. '83)

No. Both capitalism and communism are man-made, but in response to ideas sent into the mind-belt by Hierarchy. There are no plans to 'unite' these two systems.

Do you consider communism as a world threat? (Oct. '84)

No. The threat to the world resides in the rivalry, in the paranoid fear and hatred of each other between so-called communist Russia (and, to a lesser extent, her allies) and so-called democratic America (and, to a lesser extent, her allies). There is no such thing as true communism or true democracy. Both are divine ideas (but as yet woefully inadequate expressions of the ideal), and each is in a state of transition towards that ideal. In time, both systems will be seen to be less mutually exclusive than they now appear to be. The key to this harmony is the acceptance by both of the principle of sharing.

How can we (the West) disarm without allowing ourselves to become dangerously vulnerable? (Oct. '84)

I think it is foolish to expect the West or the Eastern Bloc countries to disarm unilaterally. Disarmament will only come when a condition of trust is established. Only the principle of sharing (advocated by the Christ) will create that trust—and hence disarmament and peace. That is not to say that we should not use every effort to *reduce* armaments of all kinds, East and West.

Political tendencies at this time are directed in a way contrary to sharing and disarmament. Is this a case of polarization of conservative and progressive forces? And, if so,

can this polarization be overcome by peaceful means or will a 'revolution' be needed? (July/Aug. '84)

What we are witnessing is certainly a polarization of the progressive and reactionary forces in the world. Through this polarization humanity can see clearly the dangers of continuing in the ways of the past. The Love energy of the Christ is the "Sword of Cleavage" which brings about this polarization. The plans of Hierarchy are for a gradual transformation of our political, economic and social institutions with the minimum of cleavage and trauma; certainly not revolution in the usual disruptive sense.

If we, humanity, have accepted the principle of sharing, why is there so much support for the Reagans and Thatchers of the world? (Nov. '85)

Because of the polarization which now exists. The Reagans and Thatchers represent the old order and are the expression of humanity's fear of change (despite inner awareness of its inevitability)—hence their reactionary form of conservatism. They each see themselves as bulwarks against communism. I do not know about Mr. Reagan, but Mrs. Thatcher (because of our electoral system) is in power with a minority vote of the British people and is very unpopular with many sections of society.

What is the relation between the strong conservative preferences in, for example, Holland, Germany, England and America, and Hierarchy's plans? Are these the death throes of the egocentric capitalist order? (Oct. '83)

The natural tendency of any institution under threat is to return to first principles, to 'dig-in.' This is obvious in the religious field where, feeling deeply threatened by science and a more enlightened view of evolution and religions other than Christianity, the active Christian groups, especially in the USA, have become more and more fundamentalist. The whole world is caught up in a ferment of change and desire for radical change such as it has never before experienced. Inevitably, the rich nations—the ones mentioned in the question—resist the changes which they know will weaken their privilege and power. These changes must come if the world is to survive, and what we are witnessing is a last-ditch stand of the old order to delay, as long as possible, the inevitable. Conservatism, of course, has its useful function, too, in slowing down the speed of change. Hierarchy has to perform a delicate balancing act in stimulating necessary changes but at such a pace as will not create too much chaos, cleavage and trauma.

Does a nation such as the United States or Great Britain have the moral obligation to intervene in another nation's internal affairs when these affairs have led to murder, evil and a total disregard for human rights? (June '84)

No, I do not believe any nation has that right (let alone obligation). Much of the present world tension would be relaxed if the major powers (I am thinking in particular of the United States and Russia) would stop interfering in other nations' internal affairs. Both are fanatically committed to their own ideal, their own (very partial) view of reality, and tend to see the manifestation of evil in every action or process in the opposing 'camp.' No nation has the monopoly of wisdom or right. The proper forum for the examination and, if necessary, condemnation of a nation's actions is the United Nations. Let the US and Russia give the necessary power (and money and support) to the United Nations by ceasing to use it for propaganda purposes, and by renouncing the use of the veto in the Security Council. Were they to do this the world would be transformed very quickly.

Would you please comment on the Palestinian problem? (Nov. '83)

I suppose this means: has this great significance for the world; does it influence the Christ's emergence? I think I have made it clear elsewhere that it does not influence the Christ's planned emergence.

The Palestinian situation is tragic, to say the least. There is no doubt that the Israelis have gone too far this time (November 23 saw the Israeli invasion of Lebanon), even from their own point of view. There has been an immediate karmic result for them. There is a coming together of the Arab states with the USA which there has not been before. This will force the Israelis into accepting a kind of compromise in that area which they have fought against accepting for 30 years—a homeland for the Palestinians. The Middle-East problem will never be resolved until this is done.

Many people believe that the Palestinian situation—the invasion of Lebanon, the massacre of Palestinians in Lebanon—has increased world tension. I believe this is only on the surface. Despite these abrupt tense situations like the Falklands crisis, the Middle-East fighting, and so on, there is an underlying move towards greater peace and harmony among the great powers than there has been for a long time. Russia and China, for the first time in many years, are beginning a dialogue, a series of talks specifically aimed at reducing tension. This is new. The action of groups marching in Europe and America demanding the reduction or the abolition of nuclear weapons has changed the thinking of governments about detente in Europe. Despite the outer flare-ups, therefore, I do personally experience a decreasing of tension on a world scale. These outer upheavals are only to be expected and, of course, they are given the greatest publicity, whereas there is a steady coming together of the nations which gets no publicity at all.

Biblical scholars consider the number '40' in the bible to represent testing and probation. The 40th anniversary of the foundation of the state of Israel will occur in 1988. Do you think something extraordinary will happen in the Middle East in the next several years? (Jan. '86)

Yes. Since the inception of the Israeli state in 1948 the Middle East has been the 'powder-keg' of the world, endangering world peace through the tensions thus created. There cannot be true peace in the world until 'the Middle East question' is settled. This settlement will not take place until the Palestinian people have their rightful homeland there. The Israelis, of course, claim an even older right to Palestine, based on ancient heritage. Were all the world's peoples, however, to return to the lands of their forefathers of 2-5,000 years ago, no people would be living where they now live. So great have been the migrations of humanity during that time that such a claim to ancient rights is a mockery of justice.

So deep are the feelings aroused in both sides, so entrenched are the positions which each adopt, that I believe that Maitreya alone has the spiritual authority to point to the solution and achieve its implementation. Whether a separate Israeli state continues to exist or not, whether some form of power-sharing will be evolved, a solution to the Middle East problem must be found—for the sake of world peace. The situation, of course, is bedevilled by the actions of the Powers, in particular the US and the Soviet Union. They are responsible for the support and arming of their respective 'champions' to maintain their 'sphere of influence' in the area, vital today as one of the major oil- producing areas in the world. The answer, as always, rests in the acceptance of the principle of sharing, which will lead eventually to the abolition of frontiers and rabid nationalism. Further, the discovery of the fusion process for using nuclear energy safely will diminish dramatically the importance of the Middle East.

Are the people ready for all that this means? Will they really want sharing? (Oct. '82)

The Hierarchy, through the Master D.K., has said that the hearts of men are sound, especially the ordinary people. They are ready for peace, justice and sharing. They long for peace. Already the peoples of the world march and demonstrate for peace. Soon they will march calling for justice and sharing. Maitreya Himself said, in Message No. 135: "Forming themselves into groups, men of goodwill will brandish aloft their hopes and dreams of justice and peace. This clamour will light the torch of truth among the nations and at its centre shall I be found."That is exactly what is happening now, in the USA and in Europe, with the Peace Marches. This, to me, shows that the people are ready for sharing and for the Christ. It shows that they are ready for His words. In this way, as He speaks, He will focus and evoke that demand and aspiration. There is no government on earth that can withstand the focused, determined will of educated world public opinion.

Has man really free will when he has to choose between sharing and the annihilation of the world? (July/Aug. '84)

It is precisely in making that choice that man exercises his free will. There is implied in the question the suggestion that the threat of annihilation is being held over mankind if we do not share. That threat is there, of course, but it comes from man himself—our own actions—and not from any outside agency.

The rich sharing their wealth with the poor—isn't that communism? (Oct. '84)

No, it is true Christianity! (It would also be true communism, if such a thing existed.)

Considering what happened 2,000 years ago in Palestine, won't the powers that be again resist the principle of sharing and therefore Maitreya's teachings? (Oct. '85)

No doubt 'the powers that be'—that is, those in positions of privilege and power—will indeed do their best to halt or slow down the changes that Maitreya will call for. The international banking and financial community will probably be among the last to accept the need for sharing, but they will find themselves less and less able to halt the momentum of change; the cry for help and justice from the Third World will be increasingly loud and difficult to ignore.

The world today is a very different one from that of 2,000 years ago. Then, the Christ spoke to ignorant and superstitious peasants, totally under the domination of the priests. Today, world-wide education and communications have prepared the people to make their own decisions and insist on their implementation.

You stated: "Those who remain adamant will eventually find themselves in the minority and will have to live with it or withdraw from this life." What does the phrase, "withdraw from this life" mean? How will this be accomplished if "there will be no force applied"? (Apr. '84)

Obviously, there are many for whom the proposals of Maitreya will be unattractive—those who do not believe in the principles of sharing and justice if it means an end to their privilege and power. They will find it impossible, however, to halt the momentum of change, and eventually will have to adapt to the new conditions or withdraw from the mainstream of life into some remote area. Change will come, not because Maitreya or anyone else will enforce it, but because it must; the alternative is annihilation.

You say that fundamentalists and those in the banking industry will be the last to accept Maitreya. Why is this; will He alter the currency or medium of exchange? How will this be done? Will this be done worldwide? (Feb. '84)

I have said that probably the (Christian) Church leaders and the fundamentalists will be among the last to accept Maitreya as the Christ; this, of course, because they will tend to see Him as the anti-christ, who, they believe, will precede the Christ into the world at the end of the world—Armageddon. Their ideas are already fixed about the mode of His return. I have said that "the international banking and financial groups will be among the last to accept the need for a new economic and financial order."

This is plainly evident today in the resistance of these groups to the ideas of redistribution put forward by the Brandt Commission and others. How much more so will they resist the more radical ideas of Maitreya. It is important to remember, however, that He will not alter anything. All decisions for change, and the speed of their implementation, are in our hands. Maitreya will only counsel and advise, but eventually He will advise the withdrawal of money until man loses the lure of it. A sophisticated process of barter will replace the present chaotic economic systems.

How can the ordinary individual help to redress the imbalance of the world's resources? To whom should we be giving our support? The Ecology Party seems to be saying the right things, but who would have the power to bring about the drastic economic changes required? (June '84)

No political party today, based as they are in the power structures of the past, has the answers to the world's needs. This is a global problem and can only be tackled on an international level. This will take place due to pressure on the world's governments from the peoples themselves—the countless millions of dispossessed (and also aspiring possessed) under the inspiration of the Christ.

There are, however, a great many non-governmental agencies who do invaluable work. They would value your support. Their names are so well known as not to need repeating here. Give your support to every individual, agency or organization which advocates sharing of resources as the key to ending world problems.

Do you agree that we have to be discriminating about the principle of sharing? After all, it says in the Buddhist scriptures that "to share in the life of the foolish will lead to the states of woe." (Sept. '85)

No, I do not agree. The use of the word 'sharing' in the Buddhist scripture quoted means to *adopt* the life of the foolish, which of course is fraught with danger. This is to do with the principle of sharing in the sense of the redistribution of the world's resources.

In response to your message many groups have been set up in various countries to tackle the problem of hunger; there are, among others, 'Share' in America and 'Peace through Sharing' in the UK. What is their main function? (Dec. '82)

As is probably known, I have stood on a very broad platform in relation to the reappearance of the Christ. This has enabled people to respond to the ideas according to their own lines of interest and potential. Many people find my information interesting but not necessarily believable. However, they can and do respond to the idea of sharing and many have focused on action to end world hunger. To me, this is a perfectly satisfactory response to my message.

In London, 'Peace through Sharing' was launched by the group with which I work. We initiated the movement but play no part in its organization or direction. It was started precisely to provide an opportunity for those who believe that peace is only possible through sharing.

The function of groups like this is educational. Their work is to educate people to see that peace is dependent on the correct distribution of the world's resources, which is what the Christ says, what the Brandt Commission says, and more and more people are beginning to realize the truth of this.

In a previous issue of *Share International* you gave the actual recipe for the home solution of *Oral Rehydration Therapy* (ORT), which can save the lives of thousands of Third World children suffering from diarrhea. Please could you reproduce it? (June '84)

The formula appeared in the February 1983 issue of *Share International.* It is: eight teaspoonfuls of sugar added to one of salt in a litre (approx. two pints) of boiled and cooled water. It is based on the discovery that glucose accelerates the body's absorption of salt and water.

Is it possible that humanity can pick up thoughts of peace if a large section of people transmit peace thought at one time (like the 'Peace Bomb' organizers claim)? Can it work like the '100th monkey' syndrome where if 100 monkeys learn a trick by imitation, all other monkeys everywhere can do the same trick without learning it? (May '84)

I have no doubt that the focused thoughts of large numbers of people can and do influence the thoughts and actions of others, whether for peace or otherwise. Telepathy is a fact in nature and is behind the efficacy of prayer and invocation. Hence the need for the control and right use of thought because the lords of materiality, the dark forces, use the same procedure to foment hatred and fear of war, of catastrophe, of different races or ideologies. The '100th monkey' syndrome does not work in man's case because of his ability to think. The monkey builds in an instinct which becomes generalized while man makes individual choices through thought.

What do you think of the meeting of the Pope with the Dalai Lama and of his visits to Muslim countries? What is his message? (Apr. '86)

I would say his purpose is to achieve a unity of response to world problems from all the religious groups. He is very much concerned about the problems and dangers which exist today and seeks to use his position and prestige as Pope to inspire the governments of the world to find a remedy.

Do you believe there should be women priests? Would women make as good priests as men? (July/Aug. '86)

There is no reason why women should not be priests, and I have no doubt, assuming equal individual calibre, they would make as good priests as men.

Environment and Education

Does the implementation of the Lord Maitreya's Teachings also give a solution to the problems of environmental pollution? (Apr. '85)

Yes, most certainly. You will find that the basis of Maitreya's teaching is right relationship: between man and man (and woman); man and God; and between man and his environment, the planet. We will come to understand that man, nature, and God are One, and that proper care of the planet (and all the kingdoms in it) is essential to the well-being of the whole.

In practical terms, we can look forward to a much simpler style of living (the developed West, that is) without the gross over-production (through competition) and waste of resources that we have today. The built-in obsolescence which is so much a part of modern industrial policy will have to be replaced by regard for conservation of materials and the environment. Noise pollution, one of the most harmful to health through its effect on the etheric body and the nervous system, although seldom emphasized, is relatively easy to deal with.

There is talk here of irradiating our fruits and vegetables before they go to market. It sounds very dangerous to me, and I wrote my assemblyman about it. But I thought, before I write more letters, I would see if I could find out if it really is harmful. Could you ask your Master? (Dec. '85)

You are quite right in opposing the irradiation of fruits and vegetables before they go to market. There is enough radiation in our environment, natural and unnatural, without eating more. Even more dangerous is the ability of unscrupulous businesses to pass off produce as 'fresh' when it is already decaying and unsuitable for consumption. This is already happening in Europe with shellfish.

What is the significance of the Chernobyl incident in terms of the viability of nuclear power as a safe means of energy? (June '86)

It is obvious that this unfortunate accident demonstrates, once again, how volatile and potentially dangerous is our present (fission) method of using nuclear energy. Significantly, the Russian scientists involved have said that the explosion and subsequent overheating of the fission rod occurred in a way which could not have been predicted from current scientific knowledge. If this is true, therefore, the same dangerous situation may well exist in every nuclear plant in the world. That being so, there is only one answer to the problem: *the closing down of all nuclear plants and the abandonment of the current fission method of extracting energy from the atom.* This would release the resources for full-scale research into the fusion process—already theoretically possible. Using a simple isotope from water, available everywhere, the fusion process of the future will give us unlimited energy for all our needs, safely.

Incidentally, my Master, commenting on the Chernobyl accident, said it was serious but that the radiation threat was not nearly so widespread or as dangerous as Western media had made out, nor were the numbers of people killed anywhere near the Western speculation. This has since been admitted by the American head of the International Atomic Energy Agency. My Master also said that within about a week after the accident the Space Brothers (our brothers from other planets) would begin neutralizing the worst concentration of nuclear radiation, up to the limits of karmic law. They had sought and received permission from the Lords of Karma to act on our behalf in this way.

One of the saddest aspects of this disaster, to my mind, was the reaction of the Western, chiefly US, media and governments. Instead of an expression of sympathy and supportive desire to help in such an emergency (the US did eventually offer to send experts to help), there was immediately a squalid attempt to make the utmost political and propaganda capital out of the Russians' discomfiture. Now it is clear that the Russians all along had told the truth about the incident. That they were not believed is, of course, a direct result of their policy of secrecy in the past. Perhaps they will learn that openness and honesty in international relations pays.

How dangerous has been the result of the Chernobyl accident? Is it still dangerous, and is it especially so for pregnant women? (June '86)

As stated above, it seems that the accident was serious but not nearly so dangerous as was thought, especially in the West. It would appear that no special precautions can or need be taken now. It is not particularly hazardous for pregnant women except for those in the immediate vicinity of the plant.

This is not to say that this being so we can safely continue with this form of energy. On the contrary, Chernobyl was almost an even greater tragedy and should act as a timely warning to look elsewhere for energy.

Do you think education will take a new direction in the future? (Nov. '83)

It is obvious that with the growth of unemployment through the technological advance in manufacturing which is taking place even now, there will be more and more need for education for leisure. People will have infinitely more leisure and can avail themselves of the possibilities for exploring the wealth of culture and knowledge which we have available now. People have to become more creative, in the sense that everyone is basically creative, yet only a relatively small number of people have the possibility of expressing and developing their creativity. Leisure is essential for this. Most people are so devitalized by repetitive work processes, by poor conditions, by the sheer deadness and sameness of their activities day by day, that creativity is almost the last thing you could expect. Education for leisure will release in people the possibility for the development of their inner skills, talents and potential in a way which could hardly be envisaged at present.

Quite apart from that, the focus of education in the future will be towards the fulfillment of soul intention and purpose. The knowledge of individual ray structure, and the potential and limitations which that structure gives, will become of major concern. The child will be seen as a soul in incarnation with certain purposes. Education will be the means to enable these purposes to be carried out.

What do you think are the most significant things we can teach children to prepare them for the Aquarian Age and world sharing? (Mar. '86)

Obviously, much emphasis should be given to the Oneness of humanity and the need for justice and sharing. I would say a global, international view of the world and the idea of service to the world should be inculcated plus the need for demonstrated love and an inclusive spirit to engender right relationships. The most important factor, of course, is parental example.

We all agree that capital punishment is wrong, but what is the sane alternative? (June '85)

With respect, we do not all agree that capital punishment is wrong—otherwise hangings and executions would no longer take place. For example, here in 'enlightened' Britain there is a powerful lobby to bring back hanging for certain offenses, and I believe it true to say that if we had a referendum on the issue, a majority would vote for its retention.

I do not believe that long years of incarceration in prison is a humane alternative either. People who commit crimes serious enough to invoke capital punishment are manifestly 'sick' and need treatment of one kind or another. I think a combination of psychological treatment, social re-education, and a long period of socially useful community work might produce better results than long prison sentences. Above all, a change in society itself to reduce the tensions, frustrations, envy, sense of inadequacy, and so on, which are behind a great deal of our present crime, is essential.

The Arts

Will we see a flowering of the arts in the future? (Jan. '83)

Yes, but I think it is true to say that the art of today must reflect the disintegrative processes of society in general and must share some of the plight of our present collapsing civilization.

The conditions for a tremendous flowering of the arts are not with us yet, although just as great composers and artists are born and work today as at most other times. The Master D.K. has prophesied that the 4th Ray of Harmony (as it is called) will be coming into incarnation early in the next century and will lead to a massive development of the creative life, in combination with the 7th Ray of Organization. That combination produces the very highest type of artists and will lead to a regeneration not simply in what are called the "creative arts," but in our lives. Everyone will become creative in their living in an altogether new way. The Master D.K. has likened the art of today, in relation to that of the future, to children's building bricks in comparison with great cathedrals like Durham or Milan. There is no doubt that there will be a great flowering of creativity in the future.

Is it correct that Master K.H. will be responsible for the inauguration of the new kind of music in the new age? (Feb. '83)

That is not my information. As I understand it, this stimulus will come in the main from the activities of the Ashram of the Master Rakoczi and the various departments within His sphere as the acting Mahachohan for the coming age. This would undoubtedly involve the 4th ray ashrams of which the Master Serapis is the Chohan.

What is the esoteric function of music? (Feb. '83)

Music is ordered sound, and before the end of this century, according to the Master D.K., we shall build with the scientific use of sound, whether this is by means of 'music' (Joshua fought the Battle of Jericho and the walls came tumbling down) or by precise use of sounded mantras remains to be seen. Certainly music at its highest is an expression of soul experience and must therefore reflect some aspect of reality. So the esoteric role of music must be to reflect the musician's experience of the inner reality. That is a totally different thing from the music which simply excites, pleases, quietens or otherwise affects the emotions, which is more usual.

Many people think that we no longer have any great artists and composers. What is your opinion? (Sept. '83)

Society is very fragmented today. Would we necessarily recognize the great artists? Did we recognize many of the great artists of the past like Rembrandt, Vermeer of Delft, and others, or artists of the more recent past like Cezanne, Van Gogh, Gauguin, early Matisse, Picasso and so on? I think people always lament that there are no great artists 'today' because their eyes and ears are only open to the past, and therefore easily assimilable, art. Many people would not agree that there are no great creative artists now. For instance, Stockhausen is thought by many to be a great composer. However, the average man has not heard of him. The point is that the arts do not relate directly to society as they did in the past. Society was much more homogeneous than it is now, so you currently have a small minority of people aware of the arts, responding to the new, recognizing the value of the exponents of the new, while the vast mass of people have no connection with these avant-garde composers or artists. They are totally distanced from them.

That is not to say that there are not composers and artists today who are just as creative and inventive as at any other time. It is certainly more difficult today. Every composer, every artist, has the feeling that he has to make everything from the beginning, that he can no longer rely on any kind of tradition or accepted style which would be valid for any length of time, that he has to remake art in his own image over and over again. This places an enormous strain on the creative process. Artists burn out quickly or their art is rapidly superseded by fashion. The emphasis, therefore, is on originality at all costs.

What does pop music do to the structure of the human being both physically, emotionally and mentally? Is it of any value? (Feb. '83)

Pop music, simply because it is usually over-amplified, does seem to have a bad effect on people's hearing. But of course this would be true of any music which is over-amplified; it has nothing to do with the kind of music. The main impact of pop is on the physical body through the insistent rhythms and beat and through the excitation of the emotional body. It is for this reason that young people find it excites them, physically and sexually. The effect of pop concerts is obvious, creating a mass 'high' of energy on the physical and astral planes. It is specifically for, and comes out of, the masses.

Almost all well-known composers have been male. Is this due to the fact that Earth is female and there is a negative/positive reaction? (Mar. '86)

No. Most well-known composers have been men because, until now, women have not been taken seriously as creative equals with men and have largely been denied the training and stimulus which makes for major achievement.

Health and Healing

Will our physical bodies undergo a slower rate of destruction in the new age? (Sept. '85)

Yes, most certainly. With the gradual eradication of disease from the planet, man's physical body will take much longer to "wear out." The removal of social tension, too, will do much to prolong the usefulness of our physical vehicles.

Alice Bailey gives us information in *Esoteric Healing* about the chakras or centres becoming active during the evolution of humanity. For example, in Lemurian times man responded to energies on the physical plane, and in Atlantean times to astral energy also. Now we are working more on the mental plane. How do these energies relate to the chakras or centres and levels of healing? (Apr. '83)

In Lemurian times, humanity responded to energies of the physical plane flowing through the centre at the base of the spine and the sex centre at the sacrum. Atlantean man utilized both these centres but responded, too, to astral energy flowing through the solar plexus. As Lemurian man's goal was the perfecting of the physical body, that of Atlantean man was the perfection of the astral-emotional vehicle. Our race (the Aryan) has the goal of perfecting the mental vehicle. This occurs as a result of a gradual shift upwards of the energies below the diaphragm to the centres above the diaphragm until all are synthesized in the centre between the eyebrows, the ajna chakra. This is the directing centre from which all mental type of work should be done.

When the crown chakra at the top of the head is sufficiently active and receiving the spiritual energies of the soul, a magnetic radiance is set up between the ajna and the crown centres and their physical plane correspondences, the pituitary body and pineal gland respectively. From that magnetic interaction the 'third eye' is created (it is not the centre between the eyebrows).

All true esoteric healing takes place from the soul level, using the higher centres as the manipulative agents of the energy. There is, of course, a lesser type of healing, much in evidence today, which uses the solar plexus of the healer.

Is the healing process known as 'laying on of hands' related to alignment of the chakras. (Mar. '86)

Yes. All energy entering the body comes into the etheric vehicle through the chakras. In laying on of hands, the energy moves through the chakras in the palms of the healer into the patient. The source of energy depends on the evolution of the healer. Most commonly it comes from the solar plexus centre of the healer, his or her own life force. It often involves energy which the healer has invoked from his or her own soul and sometimes from the soul of the patient, which will augment the energy of the physical body. There are also many healers who work under guidance, consciously or unconsciously, from some higher source. Some disciples on the inner planes, and even Masters, work through certain individuals without the individuals necessarily being aware of it. Most often, the aim is the removal of stasis and correct balance of the chakras.

Concerning the chakras in the hands: (1) Must there be an actual laying on of hands for effectiveness in healing? (2)Would the right hand be considered the 'hand of power?' (July/Aug. '85)

(1) No, it is not always essential for the hands to actually touch the patient—different healers have different methods—but touching does seem to add a dimension of actuality to the healing process. The patient will usually feel the warmth and the flow of energy from the hands, which is a psychological 'plus.' (2) Yes.

Scientists say that no heat or change in temperature is measurable on their instruments when a healer's hand is held over (or touches) a patient. Yet often the patient experiences a sensation of heat. Is the heat imaginary or is the energy unmeasurable on present-day instruments?

I wonder which 'scientists' the questioner means. There have been a large number of experiments in which heat (experienced as such by the patient) has been registered on heat-sensitive instruments during healing. The heat occurs on the etheric plane and is due to the friction between the patient's etheric 'envelope' and the healing energies conveyed by the healer.

Does the removal of a spleen have any effect on a person's spiritual development? (June '86)

If a spleen is removed then the etheric counterpart of the spleen continues to do the work of the physical organ (the real activity is on the etheric in any case), while the solar plexus takes over some of the spleen's role as distributor of energy, if necessary. This would have no effect on the spiritual development.

How does one obtain healing powers? (May '85)

I believe all people have the potential to transmit healing energies from some source or other, usually their solar plexus or their own soul. Meditation and service are the key methods of strengthening and fulfilling that potential.

In healing, can one do harm if there is not total knowledge of the patient's karmic situation? Are there ways to avoid doing harm?

Crucial to this is motive. It is the love of the soul which creates in its reflection—the man or woman—the desire to heal.

Not everybody is attracted to healing, but everyone can heal. Everyone can be a channel for the healing energy of love. That love energy may demonstrate itself in different ways, through different individuals, and along different ray paths, but it is the primary motive which drives the individual to heal.

Everybody is a 'born' healer, but not everyone is drawn to heal. People are drawn to other things, to write, to talk, to inspire, to guide, to educate, whatever. For example, Beethoven would not have been as useful laying his hands on a few people as writing the music which is deeply, spiritually, nourishing, and in that sense, healing. Likewise with Mozart. Of course, if either had wanted to, they could have been healers. They were healers, and they are healers. Music, at that level of soul inspiration, is healing, in the highest sense of the word. I do not mean it necessarily cures diseases of the physical body but it calms and attunes the spirit through the nervous system, attunes you to your own spiritual nature. In that way it is healing.

Should you, then, lay hands on everyone who asks that you do? You must use your intuition, this is the only guide you have. Many years ago I used to give healings and was getting wonderful results. Then I read Esoteric Healing by Alice A. Bailey, and realized that I knew absolutely nothing about healing. I knew even less about the Law of Karma, and how that might govern someone's illness or cure. So I stopped giving healings for many years. Later, my Master told me: "You could have gone on, I was behind you. I was doing the healing." But I did not know that then. When a Master heals, He knows exactly how much energy in which particular chakra, is necessary, possible, right, to use. That is something we do not know. We work blindly.

But if the motive is loving, and the healing is left to the healing powers of the Love of God or the Masters, or whatever you call it, what is right will be done. Keep yourself, the personal healer, out of it. Each one of us is a healing channel if we want to be, and when asked, we have the human duty to try to help.

Is the heart chakra affected when someone suffers a 'broken heart?' (Feb. '84)

Yes, but indirectly. A 'broken heart' has nothing to do with the heart chakra but with the emotional body. The chakra affected therefore would be the solar plexus. But any major disturbance in its function would affect the transmutation of energy from the solar to the heart chakra and thereby affect the heart chakra.

I was wondering whether it is possible to employ the recorded messages from Maitreya for healing purposes over the radio or otherwise (without the rapport with a Master)—perhaps in hospitals and mental institutions where there would be hospital radio/broadcast services? (July/Aug. '83)

Yes, certainly, that should be possible. I have no doubt that the energies released from these recordings would be beneficial to many types of patients.

I have a young friend undergoing hypno-therapy to overcome her shyness and sensitivity. What are Hierarchy's views on hypnotism? (July/Aug. '83)

I cannot speak for Hierarchy, but my view is this: hypnosis as a therapeutic process is immeasurably old, at least in the East. This science of suggestion has been debased in the West by stage hypnotists, but in fact it is a very useful tool in reprogramming our subconscious computer. All of us have been conditioned since childhood by restrictive, negative suggestions which, in many cases, cause great limitation of expression and much suffering in later life. Hypnosis, skillfully done, can help to reverse this process with positive suggestions. The problem is that the beneficial results may be only temporary. The very best hypnosis, giving suggestions which last, is self-hypnosis. Any good hypnotist will proceed with the intention of bringing the patient to self-hypnosis. Regressions into past lives by hypnosis is another matter.

Will Djwhal Khul be making available the *true* teachings on healing that earnest students like myself await? (May '86)

As I understand it, yes. Not only D.K. but a group of Masters will be releasing more information which will open the doors to the new healing methods.

Is one particular Master in charge of each major branch of esoteric healing, or is one Master in charge of all spiritual healing, or do They all work generally in this realm? (May '85)

Not all the Masters are engaged in healing work but the majority of Them are, in one way or another. Each ray has its own specific approach to healing and so They work along Their own ray line. They also work in groups and very often through groups on the inner or the physical planes. My Master, for instance, works with a group of three other Masters, either directly or through disciples (individuals or groups), on both the inner and outer planes and, of course, with different branches of the Deva evolution.

Are devas used by Masters in healing? (Nov. '85)

Very much so, especially, but not exclusively, the green and violet devas, the "devas of the shadows."

In 1937, Edmond Szekely was given permission by the Vatican to translate some Nestorian Christian gospels held in their library. The first of these to be translated formed a very beautiful little book which Szekely titled *The Gospel of the Essene*. It gives teaching on the cure of disease by eating a raw vegetarian diet, by fasting and by sun and water, i.e. by naturopathic means. Did Jesus actually give these teachings? (Nov. '85)

Yes, more or less. By that I mean that, trained by the Essenes, He subscribed generally to these teachings but that is not to say that He prescribed them. His teaching was about relationship—of man to man and man to God. He was not a fanatical raw vegetable faddist. In fact, by all accounts He ate fish, drank wine, and, I believe, ate goat chesse. Being a high initiate (4th degree), His method of approaching disease was one of response to individual need, (a) out of compassion, and (b) to demonstrate a philosophical or psychological truth. I think it would be untrue, therefore, to call Him a naturopath concerned with physical disease.

Is the pendulum an authentic and reliable tool for receiving guidance and information? (May '85)

In certain fields the pendulum is indeed a useful tool. The important thing is to know the limitations of its use. It is often used as an 'oracle' to prescribe actions and decisions which rightly should be taken by the person him/herself. It reflects whatever is desired from a subconscious level and therefore, to my understanding, is quite useless as 'guidance.' The pendulum absorbs and responds to vibrations emanating from people or objects and (on the basis of like attracting like) can relate that vibration to the same (or similar) vibration. Hence its value in homoeopathic prescribing, where the vibration of the patient can be related to the vibration of one or more remedies for the condition. It is extremely sensitive to mental

The Mystery Schools, both preparatory and advanced, will be set up in various parts of the world to supply the necessary discipline and training for the initiatory experience. The Christ will go from country to country visiting the temples which will be built in those particular countries and there bring millions, in group formation, through the experience which we call initiation.

How soon will this take place? (Oct. '82)

Even over the next fifty years—so many are now standing on the threshold, ready for that extraordinary event—hundreds of thousands will go through the portals of initiation.

Why don't the Mystery Schools give out the same information as you? (Aug. '82)

Which Mystery Schools? There are no Mystery Schools as yet. They will be opened in the future, but not until we have set the world to rights, implemented the principle of sharing, and the Christ is inaugurating the new world religion. There will be two in the UK, two in the USA, for instance. These are on ancient sites where Mystery Schools existed in Atlantean days. There are some deluded groups who call themselves Mystery Schools, but true Mystery Schools do not exist yet.

As humanity today has the opportunity to tread the path of initiation in the thick of everyday life, does this mean that specific exoteric training will become available to aspirants? Could we expect an externalization of the Halls of Learning and of Wisdom? (June '83)

It is precisely in the thick of everyday life that the renunciations and expansions of consciousness which lead to (and constitute) initiation take place. Nevertheless, according to the Master D.K., the plan is that the esoteric ashrams of the Masters, which constitute the Halls of Learning, will become externalized on the physical plane. But it is important to remember that all initiatory work is self-initiated and self-regulated. The Master works by hints and stimulus and presented fields of service rather than by direct training as we might understand that word.

What are the good and bad points of Freemasonry? (May '84)

The Society of Freemasons is the oldest on earth, dating back to Atlantean times. Locked up in its rituals and symbols are some of the secrets of initiation. When the necessary purification has taken place freemasonry will constitute one of the paths of initiation. This purification is necessary because of the accretions over the last eight thousand years which have discoloured the teaching. For many members today, of course, it is little more than a social and businessmen's club.

Will Freemasonry still be a masculine order? At least in the Netherlands there exists a mixed Freemasonry, as well as a female association, but these are not recognized by 'regular' Freemasonry. (Sept. '84)

Once again the Netherlands, which in so many ways is in the vanguard, has got it right. (There are, of course, co-masons in Britain and other countries.) Freemasonry, as one of the Paths to Initiation, will be open to all those men and women who fit themselves for entry to the Mysteries, and for whom, according to ray, Freemasonry is the natural path.

CHAPTER V

EVOLUTION AND INITIATION

The Process of Evolution

The process of evolution takes place alike on individual, planetary and on cosmic levels. As we progress in this, the human kingdom, we shall recognize that it is a very important kingdom in the scheme of this planet but is nevertheless a transitional phase between the animal and the spiritual kingdoms, and that the evolutionary journey which each of us is making takes place under laws which govern throughout cosmos. There is nothing in the whole of cosmos which, under the law of correspondences, is not proceeding under these same laws of evolution.

We are, essentially, Monads, sparks of God, demonstrating divinity at our tiny individual level. We have within us the potentiality of all divinity, and the process presented to us to demonstrate that divinity is rebirth. Rebirth is a process which allows God, through an agent (ourselves), to bring Itself down to Its polar opposite—matter—in order to bring that matter back into Itself, totally imbued with Its nature. It is an extraordinarily interesting and beautiful thing that is taking place in creation. It is amazing in its beauty, its intricacy, its logic, in the opportunity also for creative change, because it is not a fixed mechanical thing but an extraordinarily beautiful living process.

We are Monads either of Will, of Love, or of Intelligence. The Monads reflect themselves as souls, differentiating themselves into seven distinctive energies or ray types. The soul, the true Self, the inner man, demonstrates itself again on the physical plane, taking a personality of one or other of these energies, which may well change from life to life; a mental body, an astral body and a physical body, the rays of which may also change, running the gamut of these various types until it has built into its vehicle all the qualities of all the rays, synthesized in this solar system by the 2nd ray of love-wisdom. In this way, the soul can demonstrate itself as love through its succeeding personality expressions more and more—until it is doing so totally.

The aim of the evolutionary journey (in the first place) is to bring the vibrations of the physical, astral and mental vehicles into frequencies so similar that the person is an integrated whole. There has to be this synchronicity of vibration to make possible the great crises of the evolutionary journey called initiation.

When the individual is ready for training for the last few laps of the evolutionary marathon, the soul brings its vehicle, the man or woman, into meditation of some kind. That very first time it might be a very fleeting experience, but sooner or later meditation becomes an important activity in the life.

The soul does this in order eventually to grip its vehicle in such a way as to form a link, a channel, through which it can send its energy and its nature into the vehicle and so work out its purposes. The soul, when it takes incarnation, does so with certain plans and purposes, and the incarnation is the opportunity for the vehicle to carry out the soul purpose. This occurs over and over again, and of course the nearer you get to the final straight, the end of the marathon, the more correctly, the more fully will you be demonstrating the plans and the purposes, the will, of the soul. All that we know of purpose and meaning in life comes from the soul level.

The nature of the soul is to love and to serve, and to sacrifice itself for the Plan of the Logos. The soul has no other purpose than to serve through love and sacrifice and it is indeed the self-sacrificial will of the soul which brings it into incarnation. Groups of souls come into incarnation together (however unaware the individual personality might be that it is one of a vast group of souls), each group expressing a particular type of energy and brought into incarnation specifically to handle that energy.

The ray energies come into manifestation cyclically. For the last 2,000 years, life on this planet has been dominated by the 6th ray of Idealism or Devotion. With its advent, enormous numbers of 6th ray souls were brought into incarnation because they have the ability to express the qualities of that particular ray. We are now in a period when the 7th ray of Organization or Order is coming into manifestation. There are always several rays (never more than four) in manifestation at any given time, but the 7th ray will bring in very large numbers of 7th ray souls and people with 7th ray personalities who will be able to handle the new incoming energy. In the article written by my Master for *Share International* (Vol.5, No.7/8), He talks specifically about the coming into incarnation of groups under a particular ray quality giving the possibility of the correct handling of problems. He begins with the esoteric truism that every period brings into incarnation those souls equipped with the ability to meet with and handle the problems of the particular time.

Every cycle obeys this law. Whatever problems we are faced with in the world we can be sure that in incarnation, or coming into incarnation in the immediate future, will be groups of souls equipped to deal with them. As the Master says, this is the guarantee of progress for humanity; it gives us hope and provides an insight into the working out of the Plan. We are faced today with extraordinary problems because we are at a transitional phase between one age and another. But as this age proceeds, in another, say, 300 years or so, groups of souls will come in who will meet a completely different situation. An altogether more stable one will pertain. These groups will be equipped with the knowledge, the insights, qualities and abilities to demonstrate more of our divine potential, above all the sense of Oneness, of fusion, which is the basic evolutionary aim of this coming cycle.

We are entering the "crisis of love." This is the experience which the human race faces as it enters that period in its evolutionary journey when it will, as a whole, demonstrate the quality of Love and take its place in the Kingdom of Souls, the Esoteric Hierarchy. During the Aquarian age, the aim of the Christ, Maitreya, the Hierophant at the first two initiations, will be to initiate millions of people, in group formation, into the Hierarchy. Eventually, by the end of the age, the vast majority of humanity will have taken their places in the Spiritual Kingdom, the Esoteric Hierarchy, at some stage or other. Vast numbers will take the first and some will take the second initiation. This is an extraordinary event to be happening on a mass scale. It shows the success of the evolutionary Plan as it is envisaged by the Lord of the World, Sanat Kumara, on Shamballa, and carried out by His agents, the planetary Hierarchy.

As does everything in Cosmos, evolution proceeds according to definite laws. The result of evolutionary experience and progress is to come into deeper awareness of these laws and of the mechanism by which they govern the energies at the basis of all creation. God, it might be said, is the sum total of all the energies in the whole of the manifested and unmanifested universe and at the same time the laws governing these energies, and their interrelationship. God, as it says in the Bible, is a consuming fire. God is energy, fire; not one fire but many fires. Their interrelation and interaction creates the visible and the invisible universe. As we understand their working, we become manipulators of these laws. The Logoi of the various planets and great Beings like the Christ and the Buddha have evolved into awareness of these laws, have understood their workings and know how to manipulate them correctly, scientifically, in accordance with the Plan of the Solar Logos.

Evolution of the Soul

How did the human race come into existence? (Dec. '85)

According to the esoteric teachings, the human race began eighteen and a half million years ago. At that time, early animal-man had reached a relatively high state of development. He had a powerful, co-ordinated physical body, a sentient feeling or astral body, and the germ of mind which could later form the nucleus of a mental body. The energy of mind, the fifth principle, was brought to this planet from Venus by the 'Lords of the Flame,' and an enormous stimulus to evolution resulted. The human egos (souls), waiting on their own soul plane for just such an opportunity, then took incarnation in animal-man for the first time. The individualization of animal-man became a fact and the human story began. The Biblical story of Adam and Eve is a symbolic presentation of this historical event.

Why do some writers say that we are fallen angels? What happened? (Sept. '84)

This relates to the biblical 'fall' of man from 'paradise.' Essentially, each of us is a soul in incarnation, a solar angel. On the soul plane, each soul is an individualized part of one Oversoul; the separation we experience on the personality level is an illusion—the great heresy. The 'fall' refers to the decision of the human souls to come into incarnation for the first time, eighteen and a half million years ago, to leave 'paradise'—the soul's natural state of perfection—for the experience of 'the fruit of the tree of knowledge.' This is a great sacrifice for the human soul, for it involves severe limitation of its sphere of expression. The sacrifice is willingly undertaken, however, to carry further the Plan of Evolution of the Logos of the planet. Thus the 'fall' is really symbolic.

If this is so, is there a relationship between 'the fall' and suffering? Without such a fall, could we have grown towards God without suffering? (Sept. '84)

Without such a 'fall' there would be no evolution. The soul knows no suffering. Suffering is the result of the inability of the personality to correctly or fully express the nature of the soul, which is entirely self-less, knowing no sense of separation. Evolution (as it pertains to man) is the process whereby the personality, functioning under the principle of desire, is gradually brought through suffering to renounce the blocks or impediments to the soul's expression on the physical plane. The way to end all suffering, the Buddha taught, is to end desire. This is the path of renunciation, which takes one to liberation from desire—the pull of matter—and to total at- onement with the divine source.

Although humanity is One, we are also individual because of different experiences in our various incarnations. But, putting karma aside, is there something innately individual about each of us? (Apr. '83)

Humanity is ensouled by a great Deva or Angel and each human soul is part of that Oversoul. Nevertheless, each one of us is uniquely individual and contributes that individuality to the Whole.

If the Bible teaches that we are created in the image of God, why do you believe in evolution? (Oct. '84)

They are not, to my mind, mutually exclusive concepts. Surely it is possible to see man as created "in the image of God," that is, having the potential of all Divinity inherent within him but needing the evolutionary process to manifest that potential in its completeness. The Christ and the Masters of Wisdom have completed that process (as far as this planet is concerned).

They are perfect—Gods—but have *evolved* to that perfection and so can demonstrate the Divinity potential in us all.

Is evolution a force that cannot be stopped? If we did blow ourselves up, where would our souls go? Would they evolve later on another planet? What would they do in the meantime? (Apr. '84)

Evolution is indeed a process which nothing can halt—only delay. If we were so misguided as to blow ourselves up, we would continue on our journey on some less evolved planet, losing the benefit of millions of years of evolution. This would be a descent into a primitive existence, "a descent into hell itself, the climb upwards from which would be endless and fraught with unutterable pain and suffering."

What is meant by the "Cosmic Magnet" referred to in the Agni Yoga teachings?

The Cosmic Magnet is the sum total of the forces and energies which spiral through space under the Laws of our Universe. It is their cyclic manifestation which is responsible for the evolution of systems, planets, and kingdoms.

If you consider the cyclic movement of our solar system and the influence of the constellations, you would almost think that spiritual evolution is something automatic. Can we resist the Aquarian energies or is our free will a fake? What influence do we have ourselves on the institutions and ways of thinking in the world? (Nov. '85)

Our free will is not a 'fake' but is limited. We can withstand the force or movement of evolution for a time—and suffer thereby—but eventually the power of the cosmic magnet sweeps us up in its irresistible pull to advance. It is useful to realize how important our influence is, and can be, in the inauguration of the new institutions and ways of thinking.

Why is it necessary for a new Avatar to come after the Aquarian Age, which will be such a good era? (Nov. '84)

Evolution proceeds in spirals. Compared to the past, the Aquarian Age will see humanity make enormous advances on its spiritual path; it will be a golden age. But compared to the achievements of the future, humanity as a whole will have taken only the first steps. Until all is perfected, the need for Avatars will remain, each greater than the ones before, each showing us the way ahead to even greater achievements.

What is the ultimate aim, in esoteric terms, for the journey of each individual along the evolutionary path? (Oct. '85)

Many answers could be given to this question. One might be: complete at-one-ment and identification with the Purpose of the Logos.

Once the survival of the species has been guaranteed and fusion has taken place, what then will be the purpose of man? And what is his purpose—is this known, or is it yet to be created as man evolves? (Nov. '84)

The ultimate purpose of man is known only to the creating Logos and those few, like the Christ and the Buddha, who have Logoic consciousness. There are several 'blueprints' of that perfection, all of which are possible. Man himself, as he evolves and creates co-operatively with the Logos, will determine which of these possibilities actually precipitates.

If the soul is perfect, why does it have to evolve? (Apr. '84)

It is the soul *in incarnation* which evolves. The soul, perfect on its own plane, incarnates in order to evolve or spiritualize matter. This is its service to the Plan of the Logos.

'Man's soul is perfect.' Was Hitler's soul perfect? (Oct. '84)

Yes, of course. Like every other soul, Hitler's is divine. The evil personality of Hitler was completely cut off from his soul's influence and so could be used (actually obsessed) by the exponents of evil. He is thus a 'lost soul.'

We keep hearing that many 'old souls' are incarnating at this time. To what does the term 'old soul' refer? (July/Aug. '86)

There are said to be 60 billion souls in and out of incarnation, and they vary enormously in their life experience. An 'old soul' is one which through long and frequent incarnational experience has travelled further along the path to final perfection than the many 'young souls' who started on the evolutionary journey much later (in time). 'Old souls,' therefore, represent the most advanced units of the human kingdom.

Are today's children more evolved than previous generations? (Jan. '83)

Many children now coming into incarnation are more evolved than the previous generations. They are more sensitive to the spiritual energies—and they are more intuitive. This is part of the process of evolution. Each period brings into incarnation the people who are equipped to deal with the problems of their era. They are able to provide solutions to problems peculiar to their time. We have reached a point now when more children are being born who are equipped for the new time; they will transform our life. In the next twenty-five to thirty years the world will be radically changed. Many of those being born now will have an awakened intuition. (There is, in fact, a new sub-race being formed, the sixth sub-race of our fifth root race. See the article by my Master, "Reason and Intuition," in *Share International*, Vol. 1, No. 9.) Just as we have begun to perfect the ability of the lower rational mind, of which our science and technology are expressions, so the incoming souls who will form the beginnings of the sixth sub-race will evidence more intuition. Intuition is a function of the higher mind. You can see it in some children now; it brings with it certain faculties—direct knowledge and telepathy, for instance. Telepathy is potential in all people. When, through meditation and service, the aura becomes magnetic, telepathy follows as a direct result. Naturally, it can be developed by training and practice, but it is an inborn faculty as yet underdeveloped in most people. Gradually, more and more relatively advanced people will come into incarnation; they will have this and other skills well developed. In fact, eventually speech will die out; telepathy will take the place of speech, which will only be used in relation to those who have not yet developed the telepathic ability.

In the Master D.K.'s works, He refers to the awakening of 'slumbering entities' as an actual fulfillment of prophecy for the future time; can you shed any more light on this curious mystery, as this obviously refers to other than the reappearance of Maitreya? (Apr. '84)

These 'slumbering entities' exist as Avatars awaiting the point in the evolution of humanity when They can usefully be invoked. This requires the presence in the world of certain other entities and certain groups of relatively advanced men.

Evil—has it always existed on planet Earth, or did it invade it? (Sept. '85)

What we call evil exists in that aspect of God that we know as matter. It is inherent in substance itself and is the outcome of the activity of divinity in the previous solar system. In that first system, God was intelligent activity working through the form or matter aspect. In the present (second) solar system, God is love but that love is imperfectly expressed through matter, hence the evil.

Do you advance if you don't exercise free will? (Oct. '85)

No. In reality we only have the potential for free will. Free will can only function when we make decisions based on choices. This presupposes the ability to think, and so free will only manifests when people think—as humanity as a whole is now beginning to do.

While asleep are we in communication or at-one with our souls? (July/Aug. '84)

It depends on the level of sleep. For most people, there are points of very deep sleep in which soul-contact is established and the spiritual batteries are re-charged. These are followed by phases of relatively light sleep during which dreaming takes place—an activity of the lower mind.

I have been told by a psychic that my health problems are due to wrong diet which is causing obsessive thinking which is preventing soul contact. Could this be true? I am hesitant to believe this without a higher authority. (Mar. '86)

Don't accept me as a 'higher authority,' but, oh dear, what nonsense! If soul contact were dependent on what you eat, anyone at whatever point in evolution would have access to his or her soul by a simple change of diet. If only it were so easy! I cannot understand how people can take these so-called 'psychics' seriously.

Gurdjieff speaks in one of his books about the organ 'kundabuffer' which is said to have been implanted in man by Hierarchy in the earliest times. This was necessary after a disaster: the earth was said to have been hit by a comet and at the same moment the moon came into existence. The moon threatened to fall back on earth. When everything was in balance again the organ 'kundabuffer' was taken away. Down the ages the name of this organ was corrupted to kundalini. It seems to be a fairy- tale, but Gurdjieff isn't just anybody who can easily be dismissed. Can you comment? (Dec. '84)

Of course it is not true—but not entirely untrue either. It is an allegory. It refers to the time of the destruction of Atlantis. For millions of years a long spiritual tradition had been maintained and many great spiritually-based civilizations had flourished under the guidance of the Hierarchy of the time. Men knew their spiritual descent and heritage and were directly aware of their inner reality as souls.

After the destruction of Atlantis (no comet fell on Earth), all this changed. The Hierarchy of Light retreated to the mountains and deserts, working from then only on the consciousness plane (the plane of the soul). A 'kundabuffer'—a 'kind of buffer'—arose between man and his perception of reality. He forgot his divine origin and slipped back into primitive ignorance and darkness, from which he is gradually evolving back to the light through the agency of the unseen Hierarchy of Masters. Kundalini, of course, is the serpent power, the energy of the earth itself, the Mother aspect, coiled at the base of the spine. The reference to it by Gurdjieff is not simply a flight of fancy but contains a truth. It is when the kundalini is awakened and rises through the chakras (prepared for it in advance) that the inner spiritual perception and powers make themselves apparent.

Is it possible that we incarnate on other planets during our evolution? (June '86)

For most people the earth is the area of activity from the beginning to perfection. In some cases, however, towards the end of the incarnational cycle, a period or sojourn on the higher planets may become possible. This is governed by intricate laws governed by karma and spiritual opportunity.

Is our evolution hindered by having a variable star (the sun)? There is a theory that the sun's irregular emissions create violence and tensions in humanity. (May '84)

No. The energetic emissions of our sun obey cosmic laws. They create tension—without which there would be no evolution—but not tensions and violence. These are the result of humanity's wrong handling of these impersonal energies.

Evolution of Life-Forms

How can man with 'animal origins' have spiritual needs? (Oct. '84)

Behind this question, of course, is the century-old controversy between the Fundamentalist Christian groups and Darwin's theory of the evolution of the species: if man is created by God and in God's image how can he have evolved from animal beginnings? The controversy arises from a complete misunderstanding—by the Christian groups—about the nature of the evolution proposed by Darwin. His theory, of course, describes the evolution of the physical body of man, which indeed evolved, over millions of years, from early animal-man.

The divine aspect in man, the soul, incarnates in that animal body to bring its divine nature into manifestation on the physical plane. Man is the unique condition in evolution where spirit and matter meet. In this way matter is gradually spiritualized—the true purpose of man is to spiritualize matter. Thus, until perfected, man as a personality with physical, astral and mental bodies—all of which are matter—needs the spiritualizing influence of his true reality as a soul and, beyond that, as a Spark of God.

You have stated that in terms of the form aspect, each kingdom evolves from the one below it. In *The Secret Doctrine*, however, H. P. Blavatsky states rather emphatically that in this fourth round the human kingdom, including its forms, evolved as a separate species. Would you please clarify this?

There is no contradiction between these two statements. It is true that the human body has evolved from the animal kingdom, but the individualization of early animal-man in Lemurian times (eighteen and a half million years ago), when the human souls first took incarnation, and the introduction of the energy of mind which made this possible, have created an entirely new species. From the *form* aspect, no animals evolve to be men; they can only do so from the stimulus of the consciousness aspect. And, of course, men do not incarnate as animals. The species are quite separate now.

Who or what created all the marvelous life forms on Earth? Did they at one time 'materialize' from another dimension, such as the astral plane? (Jan. '86)

All the forms through which the One Life manifests itself were originally thought-forms in the mind of the creating Logos, the Heavenly Man ensouling this planet. They are brought into being by the work of the 'active builders,' the deva or angelic evolution, both sub-human and super-human. They work with primordial substance, precipitating the forms we see in all their variety from the 'etheric' to the 'dense' physical. (The physical plane has seven sub-planes, of which our physics recognizes only the lower three: dense, liquid and gaseous.) The forms 'materialize,' therefore, not from the astral but from the etheric physical planes.

Have all of us gone through the stages of minerals, plants and animals into that of humanity? If so, is it correct to say that the elements (minerals) of the present will be the people of the future? (Sept. '84)

The question posed in this fashion shows a confusion of life and form. As life, that energy has certainly gone through all the forms which we call mineral, vegetable, animal and human. We are the expression of a life at our level. That is not the same as saying that we have been minerals or that the minerals of today are the men of the future.

Will all life forms pass through a human stage of evolution? (Mar. '84)

Yes. Every life form in the universe is in the process of becoming human or, having been human, of becoming superhuman. This is as true for every tiny devic elemental (constituting the matter of our physical, astral and mental bodies) as it is for the Heavenly Man, the Logos of this planet, in whose body of expression we ourselves are tiny centres of force.

Animal Kingdom

You state that the animal kingdom evolves through us, and that we in turn have grown out of the animal kingdom.

How did the lower kingdoms evolve before man appeared on the evolutionary scene? (June '84)

One must distinguish between evolution of the form aspect and evolution of the consciousness. From the form aspect, each kingdom has grown out of the kingdom below—the vegetable from the mineral; the animal from the vegetable; the human from the animal; and the spiritual (the esoteric Hierarchy) from the human. From the angle of *consciousness* each kingdom evolves through the activity of the kingdom above it.

Does the animal kingdom, in its own curious way, already sense the coming of the Christ and the benefits to its own kingdom, as perhaps witnessed in the intensive increase in various species moving physically closer to the centres of civilization, e.g., foxes, badgers, squirrel, birds, etc.? (Nov. '83)

In the sense that the animal kingdom could be responding to the 'idea' of the Christ's return, no. It can make no such mental response or be aware of benefits accruing to itself from His presence. However, on the astral level, the animal kingdom does and will respond to the Christ's energy. Its emotional life will be stimulated thereby.

I believe the reasons for the increase in animals (normally found only in the wild) near large towns, etc., will be found in changes in their natural habitat rather than in their response to the Christ's presence.

What are the Masters who are in charge of the animal kingdom doing, precisely? (May '84)

One of Their tasks is selecting those animals who, from their close association with man, already demonstrate a measure of individuality which makes them fit for entering the human kingdom when the door into that kingdom is reopened. These animals include not only cats and dogs but horses, elephants, oxen, camels, who have associated themselves occultly with man. They are even now being set apart from the group but will not go through individualization for some millions of years.

Birds provide the bridge from the animal to the deva evolution, entering into that rather than into the human kingdom.

Mineral Kingdom

Where did the mineral kingdom come from? (Sept. '84)

The mineral kingdom is a precipitation on the dense physical plane of the energies of the etheric physical planes. The 'blueprint' of the mineral forms already exist on the etheric planes.

Planetary Evolution

You have said that Venus and other planets are far more evolved than the Earth. Can you give the planets in order of their evolution? (July/Aug. '86)

The seven sacred planets are of course the most evolved. A sacred planet is one in which the Heavenly Man, the Logos of the planet, has taken the cosmic correspondence to the third (or higher) initiation in man. In order of evolution these are: 1) Uranus; 2) Mercury; 3) Vulcan; 4) Venus; 5) Jupiter and Neptune; 6) Saturn. The non-sacred planets in order of evolution are: 1) Mars; 2) Earth; 3) Pluto and a hidden Planet; 4) a hidden Planet.

Does Halley's Comet have anything to do with the cosmic aspect of the reappearance of the Christ? (Jan. '86)

No. Halley's, like all comets, is "spinning a cosmic web," as my Master puts it. Comets carry matter and energies of differing frequencies from one part of the Galaxy to another, creating thereby complex networks of energy throughout galactic space. They sow the seeds of future development wherever they appear, thus carrying out the purpose of "the One about Whom naught may be said," the unimaginable Entity Who ensouls the Galaxy.

You say that comets exchange 'frequencies' between solar systems. Do they also exchange groups of souls between planets? If so, did the comets Halley and Kahoutek perform such functions? (June '86)

No. The exchange of souls between planets takes place on an altogether more 'local' level. The activity of comets is galactic.

In *A Treatise on Cosmic Fire*, Master D.K. speaks about our "Cosmic Centre." Can you give more information as to where and what this is? (June '86)

This refers to our galactic Logos, "the One about Whom naught may be said."

Devic Evolution

What is the significance of the greater contact with the devic line of evolution for mankind? (Dec. '82)

These are two great parallel lines of evolution which will eventually come together in the very distant future to form what is termed the 'divine hermaphrodite.' Each complements the other, as a kingdom, the human representing the masculine and the devic the feminine aspects of the one reality. Devas are the 'daughters of feeling.' They work through feeling and through the perfection of feeling, whereas we work through mind and the perfection of mind. So we have, each of us, a great divine quality to give to the other.

The devas are referred to as the 'active builders,' and the Hierarchy is called the centre for the energy of the builder aspect (*Telepathy and the Etheric Vehicle* by Alice Bailey). What is the correlation here? Are not the devas involved in a separate, although similar, evolution to ours? (Jan. '86)

Hierarchy is the centre where the Love of God is expressed. Love is the building aspect, the magnetic, cohesive force binding the particles of matter together; it is also the relating aspect, relating spirit to matter. The devas are indeed the 'active builders,' working intelligently with substance to create the forms of all that we see, under the control of Hierarchy. Working with the Christ aspect—the building forces—Hierarchy sets in motion and oversees the implementation of the Plan through the agency of the devas. The deva evolution is a separate, parallel evolution to the human.

Is it possible for humans to merge into the Devic evolution? (July/Aug. '84)

The Deva evolution is very complex, being both sub-human and super-human. There are many very evolved Devic entities, now super-human, who once were human. All life-forms are in the process of becoming human, being human, or going beyond the human stage.

You said Maitreya has brought into the world certain great devas who will work closely with humanity. Do you mean that some people will consciously work with the devas? (Dec. '82)

Not everyone, but, more and more, sensitive members of the race will learn how to invoke them and to perceive, contact and receive teaching and training from them. This is a specialized activity. I know many groups claim such contact today but I believe that to be more or less fantasy, glamour.

You mentioned in your articles about elementals which make up our bodies. Would you explain the nature of these elementals? (July/Aug. '84)

Our bodies (physical, astral and mental) are made up of the life-forms of tiny devas on each of these three planes. Our bodies are literally made up of theirs, and in this way the devas gain the life-experience which eventually will equip them for human consciousness. They are infinitesimally small, myriads being required to create the substance of our vehicles.

Some people say they have experienced the sighting of fairies; is it possible these are the same entities as elementals? (July/Aug. '84)

No. Correctly, fairies, gnomes, etc., are 'the lower builders,' using the elemental substance of etheric or astral levels to create the vegetation of the earth.

The Gospel Story and the Path of Initiation

The evolutionary journey on which we are engaged is marked off by five major points of crisis, major expansions of consciousness, the five steps to Liberation and Mastery. These are the five planetary initiations which free us from further incarnational experience on this Earth. All of the Masters have taken these five initiations (some have taken further, higher initiations), and Their presence in this world is the result of a conscious decision to serve the Plan of Evolution and not from any need, through personal karma, to incarnate.

The esoteric process we call initiation is an artificial forcing process introduced into our planet in mid-Atlantean times to speed up the evolutionary process. Without it we would inevitably arrive at the same point of development as we evidence today, but it would take millions of years longer to do so.

In those far-off days, a crisis occurred in another part of this solar system which required the presence of some of the most advanced members of the Hierarchy of our own planet, Who at that time were from Venus. The process of initiation was introduced, therefore, to enable the most advanced members of Earth's evolution to undergo this forcing process, and so equip them to take over the lower posts in the Hierarchy, thus releasing the Senior Masters for other work.

The highest initiation possible for an Earth man at that time was the third initiation, and among the first group to reach that achievement were the Christ and the Buddha, Who have remained at the forefront of our evolution to this day.

Seen from the esoteric standpoint, the gospel story is really the story of initiation, a story presented to humanity again and again, in different ways, long before Christianity. The account of the life of Jesus is the symbolic presentation, dramatically re-enacted for us, of the initiate's journey to Perfection.

The first initiation is called the Birth of the Christ and is symbolized by the birth of the Disciple Jesus at Bethlehem.

When the evolutionary energy which we call the Christ Principle or Consciousness is awakened in the human heart (the spiritual heart centre at the right side of the chest), the man or woman becomes ready for preparation to take the first initiation.

It is important to realize that the person is already an initiate before he or she stands before the Initiator. The human soul, the first master, brings its vehicle to the point of initiation through its life experience and meditation. Then the Master (of the Hierarchy) steps in, and by a combination of stimulus, testing and presented service opportunity, prepares the candidate to come before the Hierophant to receive the impact of the energy from the rod of initiation which He wields. The Christ, Maitreya, is the Hierophant at the first and second initiations, the third and higher initiations being taken before the Lord of the World, Sanat Kumara, at Shamballa. "I am the Way." "No man can know the Father except through me." These sayings of the Christ are esoterically true, but they have been interpreted by the churches, quite wrongly, to mean that Christianity (or, more correctly, Churchianity) is the only religious path, that only if a man accepts the (man-made) dogmas and doctrines of the Christian Church can he know God. The Christ embodies the Christ Principle on this planet. That is an energy which flows from Him to us. It is through the manifestation of this Principle that we re-orient ourselves and enter the Initiatory Path. In this sense, He is indeed "the Way." Likewise, only when one has stood before the Christ at the first two initiations can one open up contact with the Monad, the Spirit, the "Father in Heaven," which leads to the third initiation before Sanat Kumara, the Lord of the World.

The "born-again" Christian groups have an inkling of the truth, in that the first initiation is the "second birth" of the Bible; but, of course, this is an experience shared by millions today throughout the world, and not exclusive to the "born-again" Christians.

The first initiation demonstrates control over the physical body, in particular over the tiny devic (or elemental) lives which make up the physical body of man. The second initiation demonstrates control over the astral emotional body or elemental lives which make up that vehicle. This is called the Baptism Initiation and is symbolized for us by the Baptism of Jesus at Jordan.

The third—the first true, soul, initiation—is called the Transfiguration and is symbolized by the Transfiguration of Jesus on the Mount. It demonstrates control over the mental elemental and body and brings in Monadic or spirit contact and energy for the first time: "The Jewel in the heart of the Lotus."

Jesus entered the world at Bethlehem as a third degree initiate and so simply symbolized these three stages of growth for us. He had to undergo the fourth initiation and did so in full physical fact to dramatize, symbolically, for our sake, the experience of Renunciation. In the West this initiation is known as the Crucifixion; in the East it is called the Great Renunciation, when all is renounced—position, family, even life itself if necessary—for the higher spiritual life.

Then follows (and this is the core of the Christian gospel story) the fifth initiation, the Resurrection, symbolized by the resurrection of the body of Jesus after the Crucifixion. Each initiation attracts to the bodies of the initiate matter of subatomic particles—literally, light. By the fourth initiation the bodies of the initiate are three-quarters sub-atomic or light. This process is completed at the fifth or Resurrection Initiation, when the initiate stands free from the pull of matter forever, a perfected Master. The evolutionary goal has been achieved and the Master has finished his life experience on this planet. His choice of whether to remain on this Earth and so serve the Plan of our Planetary Logos is His alone.

There are higher initiations which call the Master to further effort. The Ascension, symbolized by the ascension of the Christ after His appearance before the disciples in the resurrected body of Jesus, marks the sixth initiatory experience and confers Cosmic Consciousness and total immortality of the body to the Ascended Master.

Seen in this way, the gospel story holds before humanity the promise of Divinity, a Divinity realized not alone by one extraordinary man, the "Son of God" but a Divinity attainable by all who make the necessary effort to expand their consciousness to include the spiritual levels; a Divinity achieved, too, by a scientific process, of which the Christ and the Masters are the custodians, the process of initiation. (Apr. '82)

The Requirements for Initiation

I have shown the gospel story as the presentation to humanity, in symbolic form, of the esoteric path of initiation. Many people today stand on, or at the threshold of, that path, yet very little is known about the actual requirements for these great expansions of consciousness which constitute initiation. It would seem appropriate, therefore, to devote some time to touch on these requirements, remembering always that an article of this kind can do no more than cover, rather superficially, the basic essentials. Initiation is a complex, profoundly esoteric and mysterious subject, and those readers who wish to read more deeply about it are referred to the writings of the Master D.K. through Alice A. Bailey, in particular to *Initiation, Human and Solar*.

It is important to remember that initiation is a process, not a ceremony (although it does involve ceremony), nor the successful passing of an examination. It is the result of a gradual expansion of consciousness. It is a growing awareness and demonstration of the spiritual realities which lie back of our outer physical plane expression—our Higher Self or soul, and that of which the soul itself is a reflection, the Divine Monad or Spark of God. It is a process whereby successive and graded stages of unification and at-one-ment take place between the man or woman in incarnation and these higher aspects of our three-fold constitution.

There are a great many minor but five major planetary initiations. Each one represents a definite stage of integration and at-one-ment reached by the initiate. The goal is achieved when, at the fifth initiation, the liberated Master stands in full at-one-ment with the Monad, His "Father in Heaven." He has expanded His consciousness to include the spiritual planes and needs no further incarnational experience on this planet. For the Master there are higher at-one-ments—with the planetary and systemic Logoi—with which we need not concern ourselves.

Initiation indicates a point achieved, but does not bring about that achievement. Life itself is the field of development of the process; it is the experiences, the trials and failures of everyday life, and the gradual mastering of oneself that brings about the control over matter and the consciousness on all planes that characterizes the Initiated Master.

Technically, initiation is an artificial, scientific process which speeds up the evolutionary process; historically it is very old. It is not obligatory—individual men can take as long as they like to achieve perfection—but it provides the means whereby those who are ready and willing to make the effort, to undergo the trials and tests, and above all to make the sacrifices and renunciations which initiation demands, can speed the journey of evolution immeasurably, and thus serve more fully the Plan of the Logos.

The requirements for each initiation have necessarily changed as mankind has evolved; each new stage reached by humanity as a whole pushes upwards these requirements. Today, from the Masters' point of view, the third is the first true (soul) initiation, the first and second being really preparatory, demonstrating the control of the vehicles—physical and astral respectively—of the personality. Through these purified and integrated bodies the divine inner man, the soul, makes its presence felt, gripping the vehicles and shining through the personality. When that integration includes the controlled mental body, the third initiation can be experienced. Synchronicity of vibration is the key to this process. The soul can only manifest itself to any great extent through vehicles of analogous vibration. It is for this reason that so much emphasis has been laid, in all teachings, on purity—of physical body, of feelings, of mind and of motive.

The process of purification rightly starts on the Probationary Path; by the time the Initiatory Path is being trodden, the *habits* of purity are expected to be already established and automatic.

The physical body is the first to undergo purification, and for those in preparation for the first initiation a vegetarian diet becomes essential. Meat eating has a lowering effect on the vibration of the physical body of man and must be eliminated from the diet. It is interesting to note how many people today, especially the young, are turning to vegetarianism. There is no doubt that this relates to the fact that several millions now stand on the threshold of the first initiation; consciously or unconsciously, they are responding to the inner precepts of the soul.

Consciousness on a plane is a very different thing from control on that plane, and initiation is the result, not only of consciousness, but also of control. At the first initiation the control of the soul (or Ego) over the physical body must be well advanced. The desires of the body for eating, drinking, sex, sleep, rest, must no longer dominate. That is not to say that the aspirant must no longer eat, drink, sleep or have sex, but all of these should be in moderation, regulated, and under the control of the soul. This control is really over the physical elemental. All our bodies, material and spiritual, are made up of the bodies of tiny devic (angelic) lives or elementals, the so-called lunar and solar pitris. The lunar pitris form the physical, astral and mental bodies of the lower man, while the solar pitris constitute the body of the soul—the causal body.

The first initiation is called the Birth Initiation. It is the result of the birth of the Christ consciousness in the cave of the heart, and aspirants who have undergone this experience will have oriented themselves towards the spiritual life—which does not necessarily mean the religious life. A general rightness of conduct and thinking and an attitude of goodwill will be demonstrated. The character will still have many faults (the ideal is seldom attained), but a new and more comprehensive and inclusive attitude to all beings will be shown, and the desire to serve will be strong. As a result of the control of the physical elemental a greater creativeness will manifest itself. This is due to the shift of the energy flow from the lower chakras to the throat centre. It is not by accident, therefore, that the culture of any civilization is created by the initiates.

The second initiation demonstrates emotional control, control of the astral elemental, just as the first demonstrated control of the physical elemental. This initiation is said to be the most difficult. The initiate, enmeshed in the fogs of desire, of the astral mists, has to clarify his responses to reality and free himself from emotional bondage. So powerful is the astral nature of man that this is an enormously difficult task and can take many lives to achieve. The soul, through the agency of the mind, has to control the emotional body and make it limpid and clear for its true purpose: a fitting vehicle for the buddhic or intuitional level of consciousness.

The fifth principle of mind, working through the mental body, acts as the director and organizer of astral reaction and thus as the dispeller of glamour. The Master D.K. has written: "The second initiation is a profoundly difficult one to take. For those upon the first or second rays of aspect it is probably the most difficult of them all." However, with the advent of the Christ, acting as the dispeller of glamour on a world scale, the way forward for the large number of aspirants now approaching this experience will be facilitated, and many, having long ago taken the first initiation, will pass through the portals for a second time during this life.

The second initiation behind him, the initiate has to learn control of his mental vehicle. Just as the fogs of glamour on the astral plane have had to be dissipated, so now the illusions of the mental plane must be dissolved in the light flooding in more and more brightly from the soul. The third initiation, the Transfiguration, demonstrates the completely integrated personality, soul infused and responding now to the energy of the Monad. Love, wisdom and dynamic will, the attributes of the soul, now shine clearly through the personality, and a creative life of world service and effectiveness ensues.

These first three major planetary initiations must always be taken in incarnation, on the physical plane. In this way the initiate's consciousness is demonstrated through both mind and brain.

To conclude this brief and necessarily incomplete account of the requirements for each initiation, I quote again from the writings of the Master D.K.: "When a man takes the fourth initiation he functions in the fourth plane vehicle, the buddhic, and has escaped permanently from the personality ring-pass-not. This great act of renunciation marks the moment when the disciple has nothing in him which relates him to the three worlds (physical, astral and mental) of human evolution. His contacts with those worlds in the future will be purely voluntary, and for the purpose of service." (*Rays and Initiations*, p.696.)

"The life of the man who takes the fourth initiation, or the Crucifixion, is usually one of great sacrifice and suffering. It is the life of the man who makes the Great Renunciation, and even exoterically it is seen to be strenuous, hard and painful. He has laid all, even his perfected personality, upon the altar of sacrifice, and stands bereft of all. All is renounced, friends, money, reputation, character, standing in the world, family, and even life itself." (*Initiation, Human and Solar*, pp.88-9.) (Mar. '84)

Expansion of Consciousness

What is meant by the "wilderness experience?" (Dec. '82)

This relates to the period after Declaration Day. It is an experience for the whole of humanity—humanity will be faced with a choice and make the decision to reject gross materialism. Mankind today is shackled by materialism. It has rejected its relationship to God, to reality, to the whole natural world of which it is a part. Man has despoiled that world and stands in totally wrong relationship with himself—and with his brothers and sisters. In place of correct relationship, he has set up a material existence which is altogether false. I do not mean that one should not have washing machines, or cars, or have a meal in a restaurant, and so on. What I mean is that a large section of humanity—some two-thirds of the world—lives in utter degradation and misery, while at the same time one-third of the world lives in luxury.

This is obscene. If you go to Southern California, West Germany, or Japan, you will see luxury and opulence which are unthinkable in large sections of the world. It is this deeply unspiritual situation, the lack of right relationship, to which I refer as the gross materialism which we will need to reject. For a time, humanity will have to give up its lust for goods, for material living at the expense of the spiritual life. There is nothing wrong with prosperity. What is wrong is that it is partial, unrelated to the inner reality, the divinity of man and to the world as a whole. Then it is grossly unjust.

The wilderness experience, particularly for the West, is the acceptance of a simpler way of life, so that all people everywhere can live. In fact, one of the Christ's main tasks is to release humanity from the glamour of materialism. It is this glamour, this fog of unreality, which prevents man from knowing who he really is and what the meaning of life really is.

You said group consciousness is the aim of the evolutionary purpose in the Aquarian age. Please explain.

Evolutionary progress up to now has been to fashion individuality. That has to be achieved before it can be overcome. The potent, self-serving, highly integrated individual has to give way, eventually, to the world server. The essence of Aquarian consciousness is the concept of the group. The energies of Aquarius, streaming to us in ever-mounting potency with every year that passes, will create, inevitably, the conditions for group consciousness. The Aquarian energies cannot be sensed, apprehended and utilized except in group formation. It is not possible to do so on an individual basis.

The key to this change in consciousness is love, and through love, service. As you serve you become more decentralized, until eventually you are totally identified with that which you serve—humanity, then creation itself. Then you have group consciousness, the consciousness which the Master knows.

The Spiritual Triad has three levels: atmic, buddhic, and manasic. The atmic is the level from which the Will of God, the will and the purpose of the Monad is reflected. The buddhic is the level from which Love-Wisdom is reflected and the manasic level reflects Higher Mind. These three levels are the spiritual planes, and each of them manifests itself in turn. The Higher Mental or manasic level makes itself felt first, because it is closest to the lower mental, our normal focus. What we call intuition is really the action of that manasic level. When we have a feeling that we know something, when we do not even think about it but just know it, we are really working from the manasic level. True intuition is something else.

To the Masters, intuition is really group consciousness, the action of buddhi, Love-Wisdom. It demonstrates itself on the physical plane through the purified astral vehicle as non- separative group consciousness. We do not have this yet, but over the next 2500 years that kind of consciousness will gradually become the norm among the groups in the world.

A great Avatar, the Avatar of Synthesis, has been invoked by Hierarchy. Standing behind and working through the Christ, the energy of this Being works through Hierarchy as a group and humanity as a group. It works through the United Nations Assembly as a group (not through the Security Council whose members have a veto and work against group expression in the United Nations). The energy of the Avatar, a synthesizing, fusing, blending energy, flows through the United Nations Assembly, blending eventually the nations of the world into one serving unity. They will then serve the world as a whole instead of their own separate national interests, as they do now.

The group through whom it most potently works is the New Group of World Servers. They are the link between Hierarchy and humanity because they have a foot in both camps. They are, all of them, disciples. They will have taken the first and perhaps the second, some of them the third and a few the fourth initiation. They are World Servers. They are not necessarily the esotericists of the world but are in every single human department; in every field they are giving expression to their sense of humanity's needs in this time of transition.

They are the hope of the world. Through them the new civilization will be built. They are now seeking to set in place the foundations on which the new structures—political, economic, religious, social, scientific, educational, cultural—will be built; to create the civilization of the Aquarian age, the most important aspect of which will be the creation of group consciousness, the sense of the One humanity, the realization that God, nature and man are One.

The Master Morya in *Leaves of Morya's Garden*, II (by Helena Roerich) talks about "primary energy." What does He mean by that? He also talks about "discipline of the

spirit." Does He mean discipline of the personality? (Oct. '84)

Primary energy is psychic energy, the energy of consciousness itself. By "discipline of the spirit" I believe He means the bringing into the evolutionary path (He is talking to initiates and disciples) the energy of Spiritual Will, which gradually replaces 'aspiration' with its emotional overtones.

Starting with the first small group of men around Jesus who became disciples and apostles, being in the presence of the Christ has transformed character and immeasurably speeded up man's spiritual evolution. On the Day of Declaration will this happen to a great part of humanity? (May '85)

On the Day of Declaration itself, no, we cannot expect such tremendous changes to occur. All evolutionary change proceeds slowly, and people will remain pretty much as they were for a long time (measured in terms of evolutionary advancement). What will happen is that the *best* in people will be evoked by the Christ, and as humanity makes the needed changes in political, economic and social spheres (in which our spiritual crisis is focused today), that best will become more and more the norm. The Day of Declaration will surely evoke an enormous sense of relief from tension and fear, however, and inspire millions into a new life of aspiration and service.

Does the fact that the continent of Atlantis is re-emerging at 2.5 inches a year, and that this process will be completed in 700-800 years' time, have any connection with the raising of humanity's consciousness towards the spiritual realm? (May '85)

Atlantis is slowly rising (at three to four inches a year, not two and a half) in a controlled fashion which will take some 800-

900 years. During that period, humanity will undoubtedly make an enormous expansion of consciousness, but the two events are not linked in any direct way.

[For further information on Atlantis, see the chapter on Ancient Civilization in *The Reappearance of the Christ and the Masters of Wisdom*, by Benjamin Creme.]

In *Discipleship in the New Age*, the Master D.K. states that America is a remnant of old Atlantis. How can this be? Atlantis sank below the sea long ago and was located far out in the Atlantic Ocean—or so I thought. (July/Aug. '86)

America is indeed a remnant of old Atlantis (which gave its name to the ocean), but the emphasis is on the word 'remnant.' A large part of the huge Atlantean continent, which stretched to Western Europe, sank beneath the waters of the ocean. The major catastrophe occurred about 98,000 years ago. One last remnant, the island of Poseidon, where the Azores now remain, sank about 15,000 years ago.

Can wisdom be taught? (May '85)

No. Wisdom is an attribute of the soul and unfolds naturally as the soul manifests through the personality. Knowledge can be taught; wisdom is loving understanding or knowledge illumined by love. It proceeds from the buddhic level of consciousness.

In an interview with you in *Holistic Health Magazine*, you say that having the figure of the Buddha on an ashtray is not blasphemy. What is your definition of blasphemy? (June '84)

In that interview I said (jokingly) that having His figure on an ashtray meant that the Buddha had 'arrived'—after 2,600 years! It is, of course, hardly a mark of respect and would never happen in the East (just as the Christ's figure on an ashtray would be unlikely in the West), but it is not blasphemy. Rather than such ignorant disrespect or irreverence, I would define as blasphemous that which runs counter to the spiritual reality of life. A clear example of blasphemy, therefore, is the existence of millions of starving people in a world of plenty, while the inner spiritual reality is the Oneness of all humanity.

Since the rearing of cattle for meat is an uneconomical way of using grain (as cattle consume more than humans), is it not therefore necessary to encourage the spread of vegetarianism in the world? And does meat-eating not hold back one's spiritual growth? (Oct. '85)

Feeding grain to cattle is certainly an uneconomical way to use it (in absolute terms; in reality, however, it is much more complicated). Despite this fact, there is actually no shortage of grain in the world—it is simply not properly distributed. Vegetarians as a group are very ready to encourage others to give up meat-eating and of course use every possible argument to support their view. However, according to the Master D.K., meat-eating is perfectly correct for the masses of humanity; it is on the path of discipleship and especially on the initiatory path that meat should be eliminated from the diet.

There is no simple answer to the second part of the question—it depends on the point of evolution of the person involved. At a certain point, yes, meat-eating retards spiritual progress, since the atomic structure of meat is not well-absorbed by the human system. After a certain stage, however, meat can safely be eaten—or not, as the initiate chooses.

Stages of Initiation

What is the importance of knowing one's stage of initiation? (Apr. '84)

It is not essential to know the exact point where one is on the Path. There are many active initiates working in the world with no conscious knowledge of being initiate. On the other hand, to know at what stage one is is useful, provided the knowledge does not feed one's glamour—either the glamour of achievement or the glamour of self-depreciation. It helps to put things in perspective to know that one has such-and-such a distance yet to travel on the Path, that there are those more advanced as well as those less advanced, and that we are all going forward together. It helps, too, to give purpose to life to know, not just theoretically but definitely, that one stands at a certain point. This invokes the will. The danger, of course, is that this knowledge can invoke a sense of complacency, of satisfaction with the achievement already made.

Is it possible to work out what one's point of evolution is? (Feb. '84)

Yes, it is possible to work out, with a fair degree of accuracy, one's point of evolution—if one is reasonably objective. Study the requirements for initiation as given in *Initiation, Human and Solar*, by Alice Bailey. Consider as objectively and honestly as possible how far you fulfill these requirements or not. In this way you should be able to assess your probable point in evolution. Of course, objectivity and self-knowledge are of the essence here: I know of someone just on the point of the first initiation who, after studying the above work, concluded happily that he was between the third and fourth initiations! A glance at the ray chart of initiates will further help self-assessment. It puts things in perspective to realize that powerful world figures like Gandhi or Hitler were second degree initiates. Remember that the disciple is known by his control of his environment, while the initiate is recognized by the extent of his world service.

[Please refer to the appendix for the list of Initiates; the Rays and stage of evolution (or initiatory degree) of some of past major figures of the world.]

What can one do consciously to speed the process of mental polarization other than, or in addition to, transmission meditation? (Sept. '85)

Mental polarization is the result of a gradual shift in consciousness from the astral/emotional to the mental plane, and covers the period between the first and second initiations. The astral vehicle is the most powerfully developed body which humanity has; it has taken millions of years to perfect it, and most people are dominated by its action (or rather by the astral elementals of which it is fashioned). The Master D.K. has written that the greatest service you can give to the world is to control the astral vehicle. This is done from the mental plane and takes many or several lives to accomplish.

The astral planes (there are seven in all) are the planes of illusion or glamour. When the fogs of glamour are dispersed by the light of the mental plan, a gradual shift in polarization takes place. Many people confuse the emotional and mental processes. They imagine they are 'thinking,' when in fact they are clothing their emotional reactions in astral thoughtforms which they mistake for thoughts. Anything, therefore, which focuses the mind, which brings it into action in every situation or reaction, speeds the process of polarization. Meditation, of whatever kind (except that state of negative reverie which is so often mistaken for meditation), is a prime mover in this direction; a diligent determination to look as impersonally and honestly as possible at all one's reactions, in every situation, especially the most disturbing; an understanding of one's ray structure—and therefore of one's glamours; a dedication of one's life to serving humanity, leading to greater decentralization. All of these help to shift the consciousness onto the higher plane, thus bringing the light of the soul into each life situation.

In *Letters on Occult Meditation*, D.K. says in reference to the emotional body: "It is a complete unit, unlike the physical and mental bodies." How and why is the astral/emotional body considered more of a complete unit than the mental and physical bodies? (July/Aug. '86)

Because it is more completely developed. More time (twelve million years) was spent over its development—twice that of the physical body, while only a fraction of that time has so far been devoted to the evolution of the mental body. The full development of the physical vehicle has had to wait for a refining process—only now becoming possible on a mass scale—which will give etheric vision to the race by a development of the physical eye. Then there is the subtle change in the atomic structure of the body of the initiate which eventually confers physical immortality on the Adept.

The mental unit of humanity as a whole is far from completion.

How does one receive the first initiation? (May '86)

One's soul brings one to initiation through meditation and service, the Master acting as a kind of midwife for "the birth of the Christ in the cave of the heart." When the candidate is ready—when his or her chakras can stand the impact of the energy from the rod of power—he or she is brought before the Christ, the Initiator at the first and second initiations.

If I had a mystical experience, how could I know if it was the first initiation or not? (May '84)

If you had a mystical experience you could be pretty sure that it was not the first initiation! As the inner man, centres ablaze with fire from the rod of initiation, returns to the physical body, the first reaction is almost always one of physical disequilibrium. Frequently, a sense of impending death—despite every indication of good health—is the strongest sensation. These purely physical reactions may be followed, sooner or later, by vague memories of mystical events or ceremonies, but this is not always the case.

Why do we have to take initiation in physical incarnation? (Apr. '84)

Initiation is really the demonstration of the gradual spiritualization of matter by the soul. Each initiation records and stabilizes a higher vibration and confers a growing proportion of light to the vehicles. This can only happen on the physical plane.

Do people who have taken the first or second initiation in a previous life find that they possess, without effort, the abilities achieved in the previous life (i.e. the control of the physical body, the control of the emotional body in the case of the second degree initiate)? Or do they have to reaffirm these abilities by again taking these initiations before proceeding to higher work (in which case I presume that the process is easier)? (July/Aug. '84)

The degree of control (which may well not be complete despite having taken initiation) achieved in any life is carried over into the next. The vibrational rate of each body is determined by the vibrational rate of the permanent atoms (physical, astral and mental) around which the matter of the new bodies is formed. Each initiation is taken once only and stabilizes that vibratory rate.

In *Initiation Human and Solar* (by Alice A. Bailey), the Master D.K. says that at the first initiation it is usually the heart centre that is vivified, and the throat centre at the second. Then in *Rays and Initiations*, he says that with the first initiation the energy of the sacral centre is moved to the throat, and with the second the energy of the solar plexus is moved in part up to the heart centre. What centres (chakras) are usually involved, and how, for the first and second initiations? (July/Aug. '86)

The centres involved at these two initiations are exactly as quoted from D.K. above. I think the reader's confusion arises out of the fact that the *results* of these energetic transferences take a long time to be established. For example, at the first initiation the heart centre is, indeed, usually the one vivified. This brings about the "Birth of the Christ in the cave of the heart," the awakening of the Christ Principle in the spiritual heart centre (at the right side of the chest). From then on—and this usually takes several (average six to seven) lives—the aim of the disciple is the control of the astral/emotional plane by himself directing its energies through the power of the Christ (Principle) within. This *gradually* shifts the energy of the solar plexus to the heart centre, and the second initiation can then be taken.

Likewise at the first initiation, which demonstrates control of the physical-plane elemental, the sexual energies of the sacral centre *begin* to rise to the throat centre. By the vivification of the throat centre at the second initiation, these energies become available in an altogether more potent fashion for creative work. The culture of an age is always the result of the creativity of the initiates.

When a person takes the first, second or third initiation, is this due to a special activity of Maitreya? (Dec. '84)

Maitreya acts as the Hierophant, the Initiator, at the first two initiations. One of the roles of Maitreya is to act as the "Nourisher of the little ones," "the babes in Christ"—those who have taken the first and second initiations and need His spiritual 'nourishment' to prepare them for the third, the Transfiguration. The third initiation, from the point of view of Hierarchy, is the first true soul initiation.

In this period of quick change and rapid evolution many souls may evolve extra fast. Are there souls now taking more than two initiations in one lifetime? (Sept. '84)

No. There are always several lifetimes between the first and second initiation, but the second and third or third and fourth may take place in the same life. But my information is that, so far, no-one has taken three in one life.

Does a living initiate know of his initiation and his ray pattern? (Mar. '84)

Not necessarily. There are always many initiates, up to and including the third initiation, who know nothing of such matters and who have no interest in esoteric teachings. Indeed, in their particular fields, they may well serve better in this life without such an interest. (I am thinking, for example, of political or industrial 'men of action' who need an outward focus, for whom the introspection which goes with meditation would be a hindrance.) There are many, besides, who have taken the first or even the second initiation in a previous life but have no recollection of the fact—even if familiar with the teachings. Likewise, since esoteric psychology is in its infancy, so to speak, there are relatively very few who know their ray structure. This, of course, will change as the interest in such matters broadens.

How can we account for the apparent disparity between the vast number of people in incarnation effectively accomplishing complex mental work (actuaries, mathematicians, etc.) and the relatively smaller estimated number of those above the level of first degree initiate, or, more particularly, above the degree of 1.5 and therefore mentally polarized?

This is a very interesting question. The answer lies in the fact that the vast amount of intelligent mental activity demonstrated by millions today is still the activity of the lower mind. The truly *creative* mental work of inspired mathematicians, scientists, and so on, is always achieved by initiates of some degree. *That which cannot be taught* is the result of intuition, higher mind, and the outcome of soul unfoldment and influence. Furthermore, 1.5 is only the *beginning* stage of mental polarization, which is not considered complete until around 2.5, when spiritual polarization begins.

Another factor is this: consciousness on a plane (and therefore the ability to use the energies of that plane) is a very different thing from *control* of that plane. The initiate has to demonstrate control on each plane—physical, astral, and mental—as s/he proceeds to perfection.

Would not the ability to think through complex problems with precision indicate initiate status, or could this ability also be due to other factors?

This is basically the same question as the above and, I believe, is answered there. The ability to think through complex problems is the result of training. It demonstrates a high level of ratiocination, but is still a function of the lower mind. If the physical elemental is controlled by the mind, the individual can take the first initiation, and if the astral is controlled, the second initiation. Unfortunately, this is by no means the case in the millions who can think logically and rationally. Around

800,000 only, of those now in incarnation, have taken the first initiation.

How could I recognize a first degree initiate among my friends? (May '84)

The first degree initiate will have established a considerable degree of control over the desires of the physical body. He or she will have a general attitude of inclusiveness and goodwill and a strong desire for altruistic service. Depending on the chosen field of service there may or may not be an interest in esoteric teaching, but a creativeness along some line or other will be demonstrated. Idealism will generally be strong, together with a growing sense of group consciousness. I might add that the initiate becomes increasingly aware of the world of meaning and of a growing need and ability to express that awareness.

Is the person on, say, the third initiation process conscious of the process? If so, how would this be relevant in daily life? (June '86)

It would depend on his field of activity whether he was conscious of initiation as such or not. What he would be aware of—and demonstrate—is a desire, a need, to serve in some capacity. At that stage his service would be potent and on a wide scale of effectiveness.

In your article, the Master D.K. is quoted as saying that the second initiation is probably the most difficult of all for those on the 1st and 2nd rays of aspect. Why so for these rays? (Apr. '84)

Because of the nature and the peculiar intensity of the glamours to be found in people on these rays. Those on the 3rd ray, with the focus more on the form aspect, tend to be more objective. They are more prone to illusion than glamour and therefore find the third initiation the major obstacle.

Gandhi was a second degree initiate and had therefore controlled his emotional body, but he still had difficulty in controlling his sexual desires. Why? (May '84)

There are two points here: the ideal of total soul control of the lower vehicles is not always (perhaps seldom) achieved at this point in our evolution, and many examples of incomplete or unbalanced attainment could be cited. A large measure of control is always reached, however, before initiation can be taken. The other point is this: there is nothing inherently wrong with sexual desires; they are the result of our manifesting through our animal body and are perfectly natural in man. It is simply a question of regulation and control. Gandhi, however, was riddled with sex-guilt. His 6th ray fanatical nature forced him to try to rid himself (and everyone around him) of these, to him, evil impulses—by inhibition rather than transmutation. The inevitable result was that he only increased the desire (through focusing his attention on it), which made him struggle all the harder for control. Had he not been so guilt-laden, and more accepting of the sex function, his soul-control would have demonstrated itself automatically.

Can you tell us how really wicked people such as Hitler and Stalin are second degree initiates and therefore at the same stage on the evolutionary ladder as saintly people like Annie Besant and Mary Baker Eddy, etc.? Did Hitler and Stalin enter the left-hand path in their previous incarnations? Otherwise, it would seem that power rather than goodness is the criterion for progress. (Oct. '83)

It is said that even an Arhat can fall, and an Arhat has taken the fourth initiation and is all but perfected. One has to differentiate between power-hungry people like Stalin, who did some very wicked things but was not on the left-hand path, and Hitler, who very definitely was; indeed, he was totally obsessed, taken over, by the forces of evil, as we term the lords of materiality.

Initiation confers power. The second initiation is a difficult stage in that the initiate has power without the soul-infusing process (which guarantees divine altruism) being as yet complete.

Simple goodness, however, is not necessarily the mark of the initiate. There are countless very good people who have not taken the first initiation. It is really a question of conscious awareness; it is the expansion of such awareness which brings about initiation. This can be along the line of power or intelligence as much as that of love, although one would generally expect the love aspect to be manifest in some way—perhaps in dedicated service to one's country, as Stalin no doubt saw his life's work.

If an initiate back-slides, as in the case of Hitler, does this mean he is then only equivalent to an aspirant, or is he still an initiate—in which case he would presumably have to reaffirm his degree of initiation? (July/Aug. '84)

He would remain initiate of his particular degree, but would have to work off the karma involved in his 'back-sliding' before advancing again.

The Master D.K. criticizes St Paul but often quotes his description of God as the "One in Whom we live and move and have our being," and Paul does seem to be inspired at times. So the question is, was Paul overshadowed by Maitreya? (Oct. '85)

Paul was indeed inspired (by his own soul and by his Master), but he was not overshadowed by Maitreya. He was a third degree initiate. (This event was dramatically chronicled in the

Bible as his 'conversion' on the road to Damascus and his being blinded for three days.) The Master D.K.'s criticism of St Paul (whom He nevertheless calls "that great initiate") refers to Paul's partial distortion of the new teaching to accommodate it to the old Jewish teaching. He overemphasized the divinity of Jesus and made it exclusive. It is St Paul's mysticism which to this day colours the approach of the Christian churches.

Our Western interpretation of the fourth initiation may be a bit distorted. H. P. Blavatsky took the fourth in that life; yet there was no obvious violence. Does this indicate that another form of 'crucifixion,' perhaps psychological, is possible? (Sept. '83)

The fourth initiation is really that of Renunciation, by which name it is known in the East. It does not necessarily mean a life of violent suffering but rather a deliberate renunciation and relinquishment of all that ties us to the three worlds (physical, emotional and mental) of human evolution. As a soul-infused personality, the at-one-ment of the fourth degree initiate is now with his Monad ("Father in Heaven"), and all that he does is done under the Divine Will (the Will-to-Good) for the Hierarchical Plan.

In the West, the crucifixion of Jesus in Palestine symbolized this Great Renunciation for us and has lent its name to this experience.

The life of Madame Blavatsky was by no means an easy one by any reckoning. She carried many crosses, not least the calumnies and betrayals of those nearest to her, besides derision, antagonism and character assassination from a large number of her contemporaries. At least the last twelve years of her life and work were lived in conditions of great physical illness and suffering. Only an indomitable will and the help of her Master kept her in the body.

At what point did Jesus actually take the fourth initiation? (July/Aug. '85)

The outer expression of the fourth initiatory experience for Jesus was the crucifixion—the symbol of the inner renunciation which marks the fourth degree initiate. All initiates, of any degree, however, are already 'initiate' before they go through the final initiatory experience.

If we are souls in incarnation, solar angels, what is left in incarnation after the fourth initiation, when the causal body, soul, disintegrates? (Dec. '84)

At the fourth initiation it is the causal body, not the soul, which is shattered—because it is no longer needed. The causal body is the vehicle of the soul, not the soul itself which is reabsorbed into the Monad or Divine Spark of which it is a reflection. Left in incarnation is the totally soul-infused personality, demonstrating all the qualities and attributes of its soul and relating now to the Monad. The soul is the Divine Intermediary between the Monad and the man or woman in incarnation. The causal body becomes superfluous and is shattered when the fusion of the soul and its reflection, the personality, is complete.

Would you please list the number of initiates at each stage of the path? (Apr. '84)

In incarnation at the present time there are approximately 800,000 who have taken the first initiation; 240,000 who have taken the second; 2-3,000 who have taken the third; and 450 initiates of the fourth degree.

Is there any relationship, direct or indirect, between the progressive states of consciousness described by Maharishi Mahesh Yogi as: (1) Cosmic consciousness; (2) God con-

sciousness; (3) Unity consciousness, and the first, second and third initiations as described in *Initiation Human and Solar* by Alice Bailey? (Apr. '85)

The first, second and third initiations are to do with Unity consciousness, the fourth and fifth confer God consciousness, and the sixth and seventh, cosmic consciousness. I believe that the Maharishi uses the terms Cosmic, God and Unity in a rather different way from the Master D.K., that is, in the reverse order of attainment.

In Vol. III, p.213 and p.551 of *The Secret Doctrine*, H. P. Blavatsky states that Socrates was not an initiate, but in the "List of Initiates" Socrates was a second degree initiate. Why the discrepancy, or what's the difference? (May '86)

From the point of view of the Masters, a person is not truly initiate until the third initiation has been taken; the first two are seen as degrees of integration of the *personality*, while the third is the first true *soul* initiation. So in that sense Blavatsky is correct. However, Socrates (and Plato) was a 2.3 degree initiate, which *for that time* was very advanced indeed.

In the List of Initiates, you state that Leonardo da Vinci was a fourth degree initiate. Where is he now and what is his degree? (June '86)

He is on Sirius. His degree is now the equivalent, on Earth, of an eighth-degree initiate (such as, for instance, the Buddha). He was not in fact from our Earth evolution but was an Avatar from the planet Mercury.

CHAPTER VI

THE SEVEN RAYS

A General View

Modern exoteric science has proved the ancient and fundamental esoteric axiom: there is nothing in the whole of the manifested universe but energies, in some relationship, each vibrating at a particular frequency. The esoteric science postulates seven such streams of energy or rays, whose interaction, at every conceivable frequency, creates the solar systems, galaxies and universes. The movement of these seven rays of energy, in spiralling cycles, draws all Being into and out of manifestation, and colours and saturates it with their own individual qualities and attributes. This is as true for a grain of sand as for a man or a solar system. Each is the expression of a Life.

As far as our own solar system is concerned, these seven energies are the expression of seven great Lives embodied by seven stars in the constellation of the Great Bear. In our system, one of these rays, the 2nd ray, is focused. The other six rays are therefore sub-rays of this basic ray. The manipulation of these subdivisions by our Solar Logos creates every variation of life within His system.

So complex is the subject of the rays, so pervasive and all-embracing is their influence, that it will be possible in this article to skim the surface of their action only, and to show something of their relevance to our lives and relationships. The aim will be to demonstrate the value of knowing the qualities of the rays governing ourselves and our nations and in this way to stimulate the reader to enter into a deeper study of these forces which, on every plane, condition our nature and make us what we are.

The rays are particular types of energy, the emphasis being on the quality which that energy demonstrates rather than on the form which it creates. To say that a man or a nation or a planet is 'on' the 1st or 2nd ray, is to say that they are coloured by, and express the quality of, that ray. Consequently, there are seven ray-types of people, and the idea of the septenate is to be found at many levels and in many branches of our lives: "the seventh son of a seventh son," "the seven sacred Planets." "Seven is a number in magic," as Dylan Thomas put it.

There are three primary rays, or rays of aspect, and four secondary rays of attribute. They have many names describing their many qualities and actions but are usually enumerated as follows:

Rays of Aspect

1st ray of Power, Will or Purpose
2nd ray of Love-Wisdom
3rd ray of Active, Creative Intelligence

Rays of Attribute

4th ray of Harmony through Conflict, or Beauty, or Art
5th ray of Concrete Science or Knowledge
6th ray of Abstract Idealism or Devotion
7th ray of Ceremonial Order or Magic or Ritual or Organization

Cyclically, according to the plan of the Logos, the rays come into manifestation, producing through their influence the succession of civilizations and cultures which mark and measure the evolution of the races. The three major planetary centres, Shamballa, Hierarchy and Humanity, are, respectively, the exponents of the three major rays of aspect: Will, Love-Wisdom and Active Intelligence.

Every human being finds himself on one or other of these seven energies, and all of us are governed basically by five ray forces: the ray of the soul, which remains the same for countless aeons; the personality ray, which varies from life to life until all the qualities are developed; the ray governing the mental body; that governing the astral-emotional equipment; and the ray of the physical body, including the brain. These all vary cyclically. Each ray works primarily through one centre (or chakra), and together they determine the physical structure and appearance, the astral-emotional nature, and the quality of the mental unit. They predispose us to certain attitudes of mind and certain strengths and weaknesses (the virtues and vices of the rays). They give us our particular personality colour and general tone on the physical plane. For the greater part of our evolutionary experience on this earth the rays of the personality govern our expression, but when we are two-thirds of the way along the path, the soul ray begins to dominate and to be expressed.

"Man, know thyself," said the ancient Greeks. "Man, know thy rays," says the esotericist. A knowledge of one's rays provides one with an insight into one's strengths and limitations, one's line of least resistance in this life; and also an understanding of the bridges and the barriers between oneself and others, erected by our individual ray structure. Those on similar rays tend to see things from the same point of view, to have the same approach to life, while those on disparate rays find it difficult to come to an understanding of each other's attitudes and meaning. It will be obvious how this factor conditions the quality of married life. It affects, too, the success or failure of the meetings of leaders of nations, especially when it is realized that each nation is governed by two rays: the higher soul ray, expressing the highest (usually as yet unmanifested) ideals of the nation; and the lower personality ray, governing the people's selfish national desires.

To view history from an understanding of the rays governing the nations and races is to see it in a new light. It becomes obvious why certain nations are allies while others have little in common and are traditionally hostile to each other. It becomes fascinatingly clear why particular ideas, movements and religions flourish at one period and fall into decay at another; why some countries emerge for a time and become dominant influences in the world while others lie fallow, as it were, awaiting their time of awakening through the stimulus of an incoming ray.

A knowledge of the ray structure of some of the great individuals who have created our culture and civilization enables us to see how their rays made them what they were, conditioned their actions and qualities, and shaped their destinies.

The science of psychology is in its infancy. It seeks to understand the workings of the human psyche, and in psychotherapy it works to alleviate the symptoms of stress and disorder. But until an understanding is reached of man as a soul in incarnation, governed by certain ray influences, much will remain obscure. It is the soul which determines the rays (and therefore the influences and limiting factors) of the personality and its vehicles. The new psychology, today esoteric, will begin from that premise. (Jan. '83)

Major Ray Influences

Behind the discord of the present troubled times stand two great energies. The 7th ray of Ceremonial Order or Ritual is (since 1675) coming into manifestation. The 6th ray of Abstract Idealism or Devotion is (since 1625) gradually passing out. Our present problem is the result of the fact that these two highly potent energies are functioning simultaneously, and in roughly equal potency, so that their effects are balanced. Neither dominates.

In consequence, the world is divided politically, economically, religiously and socially into two main groups; and these groups are in confrontation throughout the world. On the one hand, there are the exponents of the 6th ray approach who, from love of the old forms, are holding on to the outworn structures, fighting a last-ditch stand for their preservation. This group forms the conservative and reactionary forces in all fields throughout the world. The other, the progressive forces, are those who are able to respond to the new incoming energies, who sense the need for new, more living forms through which the new age civilization can manifest. The most impatient would sweep everything away, the good as well as the bad, and need the restraining hand of Hierarchy to produce ordered change.

Since long before the Christian era, the 6th ray has waxed in strength (Christianity being the result of its influence), and although it is now on the wane, its qualities saturate and colour all our structures and institutions, all our ways of thinking, feeling and relating.

The characteristic quality of the 6th ray is devotion to the ideal—often a fanatical adherence to the ideal at the expense of all others. This ideal can, of course, be expressed on every level, from the most basically selfish desire to 'make a million,' to an altruistic devotion to a cause or an abstract vision of sacrifice. It is for this reason that the Crucifixion has been the outstanding symbol of Christianity. The sacrifice of Jesus has been seen as a vicarious atonement for our sins. This 6th ray energy has produced, as its culminating type of aspirant, the mystic. In religious terms, the history of the last two thousand years is the history of the growth of mysticism, both in the East and in the West. The great religious figures and saints of Europe have invariably been mystics, while the same (abstract) approach to God has characterized the teachers and adherents of Islam, the Sufis, the Buddhists and the Jains. The fanatical adherence to, and militant advocacy of, their own ideal has, of course, led to the long succession of religious wars which continue to this day.

This same 6th ray influence has been responsible not only for sectarianism, but also for nationalism and patriotism, dogmatic, doctrinal exclusiveness, narrowness of view in science and philosophical schools of thought—in short, it has stimulated the individualistic and separative tendencies in humanity. At the same time, it has presented as abstract ideals the ideas of love and brotherhood, of justice and freedom. These ideals are now firmly fixed in the minds and hearts of aspiring humanity, and need but the influence of the incoming 7th ray of Ceremonial Order to bring them into manifestation on the physical plane.

As the rays move cyclically into manifestation (there are never more than four—and therefore never more than four types of people—powerfully present at one time) they sweep into incarnation those souls along their own line of force. This process is especially marked at the end of one age and the beginning of another. Today is such a time. During the Piscean age now ending, the 6th ray brought in millions of 6th ray souls through whom it could express its purpose and quality. With the waning of its influence, the bulk of 6th ray souls will gradually be withdrawn from manifestation, their places to be taken by souls of the 7th ray which will dominate during the Aquarian cycle.

The major problem for the 6th ray exponent has been that he cannot externalize his ideal. His highest ideals remain abstractions. He cannot bring them down lower than the plane on which he is focused—the astral plane, the plane of the emotions. Under the divine plan, each ray prepares the way for its successor. The 7th ray relates spirit to matter, thus synthesizing these opposites. Through its exponents, it will bring into expression, as a physical plane reality, the ideals and visions of the previous cycles. As the 6th ray fostered separatism and exclusiveness, so will the 7th ray bring about fusion and blended oneness. As the 6th ray stimulated the growth of individuality, so will the 7th promote the group spirit and consciousness. It is an intensely practical ray. Its exponents have their 'feet on the ground' and recognize the need for order, rhythm and ritualistic work. As the 6th ray produced the mystic, the 7th will produce—and is producing—the magician, the worker in white magic. What are the marvels of our contemporary science but magical applications of certain laws? This is the magic of today, at a higher turn of the spiral than that of earlier Atlantean times, when the emphasis was on the 'black' side. The 7th ray was the dominant influence, too, in that far-off time.

These two energies, though dominant, are not the only forces playing on and through humanity, and through all the kingdoms. Rays two, three, five and seven are 'in incarnation,' openly manifesting. Ray four, that of Harmony through Conflict, is always subjectively influential where humanity is concerned—ìthe conflict which it engenders makes for rapid growth—but will not come in until the next century; then, the harmony aspect will be uppermost. Its influence will provide the stimulus for the unfoldment of the intuition and for art of all kinds, including, for the masses everywhere, the art of living.

The 1st ray of Will or Power is not in incarnation, but nevertheless the potency of its destructive aspect has been most powerfully expressed through the leaders of Nazi Germany, the majority of whom were 1st ray exponents, together with others in Italy and Japan. This is the energy of the anti-Christ about which there is so much misunderstanding. It is the destructive aspect of the 1st ray which destroys the old, outworn forms of a dying civilization to prepare the way for the building forces of the Christ aspect. It has done its destructive work which, we shall find, will in due course benefit the Plan.

Since 1975, the creative aspect of this powerful, galvanizing 1st ray energy has been released directly into humanity (that is, without going through, and being 'stepped down' by, Hierarchy). This is the Shamballa Force, the Will-to-good, the force of Life itself. It is released each year by the Buddha at the Wesak Festival in May, and will continue to be released in increasing potency until the year 2000. (Feb. '83)

Virtues and Vices of the Ray Characteristics

The various characteristics and qualities of each of the rays are given by the Master D.K. through Alice A. Bailey in *Esoteric Psychology*, Vol. 1, and others (published by Lucis Trust). They are as follows:

Ray 1: Will or Power.

Virtues: Strength, courage, steadfastness, truthfulness arising from absolute fearlessness, force of will, singleness of purpose, power of ruling, vision, power to good, leadership.

Vices: Pride, ambition, willfulness, hardness, arrogance, desire to control others, obstinacy, anger, solitariness, power for evil.

Virtues to be acquired: Tenderness, humility, sympathy, tolerance, patience.

Ray 2: Love-Wisdom.

Virtues: Calmness, strength, patience and endurance, love of truth, faithfulness, intuition, clear intelligence, serene temper, divine love, wisdom, tact.

Vices: Over-absorption in study, coldness, indifference to others, contempt of mental limitations in others, selfishness, suspicion.

Virtues to be acquired: Love, compassion, unselfishness, energy.

Ray 3: Activity, Adaptability or Intelligence.

Virtues: Wide views on abstract questions, sincerity, clear intellect, capacity for concentration, patience, caution, absence of the tendency to worry himself or others over trifles, mental illumination, philosophic viewpoint.

Vices: Intellectual pride, coldness, isolation, inaccuracy in details, absent-mindedness, obstinacy, selfishness, critical, impractical, unpunctual, idle.

Virtues to be acquired: Sympathy, tolerance, devotion, accuracy, energy, common-sense.

Ray 4: Harmony, Beauty, Art and Unity.

Virtues: Strong affections, sympathy, physical courage, generosity, devotion, quickness of intellect and perception.

Vices: Self-centredness, worrying, inaccuracy, lack of moral courage, strong passions, indolence, extravagance, veiling of intuition.

Virtues to be acquired: Serenity, confidence, self-control, purity, unselfishness, accuracy, mental and moral balance.

Ray 5: Concrete Knowledge or Science.

Virtues: Accuracy, justice (without mercy), perseverance, common-sense, uprightness, independence, keen intellect, truthfulness.

Vices: Harsh criticism, narrowness, arrogance, unforgivingness, lack of sympathy, prejudice, tendency to isolation, mental separation.

Virtues to be acquired: Reverence, devotion, sympathy, love, wide-mindedness.

Ray 6: Abstract Idealism or Devotion.

Virtues: Devotion, single-mindedness, love, tenderness, intuition, loyalty, reverence, Inclusiveness, idealism, sympathy.

Vices: Selfish and jealous love, overbearing, partiality, self-deception, sectarianism, superstition, prejudice, over-rapid conclusion, fiery anger, violence, fanaticism, suspicion.

Virtues to be acquired: Strength, self-sacrifice, purity, truth, tolerance, serenity, balance, common-sense.

Ray 7: Ceremonial Order or Magic or Ritual.

Virtues: Strength, perseverance, courage, courtesy, meticulousness, self-reliance, creativity, thoughtfulness, organization.

Vices: Formalism, bigotry, pride, narrowness, poor judgement, arrogance, over-stressing of routine, superstition.

Virtues to be acquired: Realization of unity, wide-mindedness, tolerance, humility, gentleness and love.

Is it possible for an individual to invoke a ray energy for a specific purpose or is only the Hierarchy able to do this? (July/Aug. '83)

No, it is not possible for an individual or even a group to invoke a ray energy for any purpose. Even Hierarchy can only invoke these energies in accordance with the Plan issuing from Shamballa and the Council of the Lord of the World. The rays have a cyclic manifestation, but from time to time, for specific short-term stimulus, a ray may be invoked by Shamballa and Hierarchy for this purpose.

I wonder if I am right in assuming that as a new ray strikes humanity the positive side predominates, then as the time approaches for another ray to manifest, the negative side predominates, tying in with the rise and fall of great civilizations? (July/Aug. '84)

No, it is not as you suggest. It takes a long time for the incoming ray to manifest relatively purely through humanity. The crystalization of the previous civilization takes considerable time to dissolve, as it were, and disappear, so that in the beginning it is mainly disharmony that the incoming ray creates. This gradually changes to a more stable situation as the new ray overcomes the crystallized patterns of the previous time. Towards the end of the cycle, of course, the new forms become crystallized in their turn.

As more 7th ray souls incarnate, will this cause friction with a mostly 2nd ray humanity? (June '84)

Friction is not quite the right word to use, but certainly the bulk of present day humanity will have to learn to adapt to 7th ray type of work and procedures, moving from a mystical to a more practical and scientific mode of approaching and understanding reality. The incoming 7th ray will make its impact on all in incarnation and gradually change these modes.

Ray Relations Between Nations

Each nation, like each individual, is governed by two rays: a soul ray, which is sensed and expressed by the initiates and disciples of the nation; and a personality ray which is the dominant mass influence and expression. At present, most nations act in their own separative interests rather than in the interest of the world community as a whole, and are therefore expressing their personality ray. From time to time, however, through the activity of the initiates and disciples of the country, the soul ray may be given expression and the true quality of the nation can be seen. As an example, in Germany's aggressive militarism (between 1870 and 1945) we see an expression of its 1st ray personality; whereas, through the work of its great composers—Bach, Beethoven, Handel, Wagner, Schumann and Brahms; its philosophers Hegel and Kant; its poets Goethe and Schiller; its painters Durer, Holbein and Grunewald—the beauty of its 4th ray soul is manifested. The German racial strain is ancient but the nation is young, astral and mediumistic, and therefore responded readily to the powerful 1st ray force, materialistically focused, of its dictator, Hitler (a medium himself), and of von Bismarck, who had three 1st ray vehicles in his make-up. The Master D.K. has prophesied that one day, when its soul ray is dominating, Germany will give to the world the blueprint of a correct (that is, spiritually oriented) hierarchical form of government. Germany's national motto (from the esoteric angle) is: "I preserve," but the effort so far has been to preserve an impossible racial purity.

Two rays, above all, are at all times conditioning humanity: the 2nd ray of Love-Wisdom, and the 4th ray of Harmony through Conflict. It follows, therefore, that those nations which have these two rays as dominant influences, whether on the soul or the personality level, must be influential to humanity as a whole. Of the major nations, only Great Britain and the U.S.A. have the 2nd ray on the soul level, while Brazil has a 2nd ray personality and a 4th ray soul. (There is a close connection between the 2nd and 4th rays.) India and Italy have 4th ray personalities and Austria a 4th ray soul.

India's soul ray is the 1st, which is the personality ray of Great Britain and links closely the destinies of these two nations. Great Britain's outstanding characteristic is its governing faculty, which it owes to this 1st ray influence. Britain's national motto, "I serve," will be implemented when the wisdom aspect—loving understanding—of its 2nd ray soul is put at the service of the race. In the British Commonwealth, Britain has given to the world a first blueprint of a federation of autonomous nation states, while the United States is doing a similar service in blending together people of many countries into one federated nation.

At the moment, the 6th ray, with its fanatical separative tendencies, conditions the personality expression of both the U.S.A. and Russia and prevents their correct response to world need. Each is so sure that its own way, capitalist or communist, is the only way for all mankind that they fail to grasp the world picture or hear the cry for justice from the developing world. Russia's soul ray is the 7th, and is responsible for the desire for order imposed by its leaders. The fault lies not in the order but in its imposition from above. The world awaits the expression (as in the Marshal Plan after World War II) of the love aspect of America's 2nd ray soul. Then the idealism of both the American and the Russian people will find a common ground, and will open the way to a new world order and eventual brotherhood.

For centuries France maintained the light of civilization for Europe. Her soul ray is the 5th, while her personality is on the 3rd ray. The brilliant French mind has contributed much to European history, but always France has been her own main concern and interest. Her problem is that she has responded to the separative action of the 5th ray of lower mind combined with the materialistic, manipulative tendencies of the 3rd. When her response is to the revealing function of her soul ray, dominating the personality, France, the Master D.K. has prophesied, may have the glory of revealing, scientifically, the fact of the soul.

The interplay of forces between the nations, conditioning their actions, is endless, and this is only the briefest hint of their complexity and interest. It is not by accident, for example, that so many people from Italy and Russia have made their homes in the United States. The common bond of the 6th ray has brought them together. This is also true of certain other large national groups now residing in the U.S.A. but whose rays are not given here. The fact that Russia and Spain have both 6th and 7th rays has made each a major battleground of ideas in this century; their inner conflict is inevitable.

Much more could be written about the gradual transmutation of the nations' personality characteristics by the ray of their soul. They proceed exactly as does the individual, only more slowly. The fact that individuals do change and develop into world servers is the guarantee that the nations will do likewise. Under the stimulus of the Christ and the Hierarchy, this process will be speeded immeasurably. (Mar. '83)

The Rays of Nations

The Master D.K., through Alice A. Bailey, has given the rays of various countries in *The Destiny of the Nations*. However, in a number of cases the rays were not given, the reason being that the countries in question were undergoing a period of changing of rays. My Master has now made good some of these omissions and added further countries with their rays. These are indicated by asterisks.

	Soul	Personality
Africa (the continent)*	6	7
Argentina*	1	6
Austria	4	5
Australia	2	7
Belgium*	5	7
Brazil	4	2
China	1	3
Canada*	2	1
Egypt*	1	7
France	5	3
Germany	4	1
Great Britain	2	1
Holland*	5	7
India	1	4
Indonesia*	6	2
Italy	6	4
Japan*	6	4
Norway*	2	4
Russia	7	6
Scandinavia (4 nations)*	3	2
Spain	6	7
Sweden*	3	2
Switzerland*	2	3
U.S.A.	2	6

In *The Destiny of the Nations* by Alice A. Bailey, we find that the 1st ray energy in its early phases inevitably leads to destruction. Especially, the 1st ray energy causes the death of those material forms and organized groups which prevent the free expression of the life of God and do not accept the new culture. In reading this, I was thinking of th=e many Jews who were killed in the second world war. The Jews did not recognize the Christ and, thus, denied the new culture. Is this an example of 1st ray energy and, if so, is it not strange that the powers of evil, working through the Nazi leaders, in a curious way helped to realize the plan of God?

How can we distinguish between the powers of evil and the destructive force of the 1st ray energy? I understand that the 1st ray aims at unity, while evil causes separatism. How do I know when destruction is producing unity or separation? (June '85)

While it is true that the Jews did not recognize the Christ in Palestine 2,000 years ago, this does not mark them out for the destructive power of the 1st ray. If this were the only criterion, then all non-Christians—Hindus, Moslems, Buddhists, Taoists—would be candidates for such destruction, and this is obviously not the case. Although some six million Jews died in the Nazi horror camps, they were not alone in suffering this fate. Millions of Poles, Russians, gypsies and many others, Christians and non-Christians, suffered likewise. The Jews, however, are 'chosen' in the sense that they are a microcosm, representative of humanity, having within themselves all that is good and all that is bad in mankind. Their fate under the Nazis therefore is a demonstration, as it were, of the Nazis' (or rather the forces of evil who worked through them) hatred for all mankind.

It is important to understand that the first aspect of God has two phases, one creative, one destructive; one evolutionary, one involutionary. The forces of evil are, of course, on the involutionary arc, while we are on the evolutionary arc. The overriding determining factor in relation to all energy is the motive behind its use. The energy itself is impersonal. There is no simple rule in being able to discriminate between creative and destructive energies except through their effects. Such discrimination is gradually acquired through experience. The problem for mankind, of course, is to see how destruction of forms can lead to a greater unity in life terms. Destruction is always painful and frightening for us, but from the point of view of the creating Logos (and also of the Masters) it is inevitable and beneficial when directed by Divine Purpose.

Are there elements in the world responsible for all human vices? (July/Aug. '84)

A vice is an attribute of a ray improperly expressed. All rays have virtues and vices particular to their energy. The soul expresses only the virtues of the ray while the imperfect personality expresses, more or less, the vices. The evolutionary aim is to transmute the vice of the ray into its higher (virtue) aspect. If the questioner really means are there forces of evil in the world, the answer is yes. The evil of this (as yet) imperfect planet is inherent in matter itself.

You have mentioned the fact that nations express both a soul ray and a personality ray; does a nation sometimes die out before the soul ray succeeds in its manifestation? (Feb. '84)

Yes, especially in ancient times when many nations disappeared from history before the soul ray became manifest. As people, and therefore nations, evolve, this becomes rarer. The expression of the soul ray (through the work of the initiates of the nation) is often spasmodic, however, and nations will go through cycles in which either the soul or personality ray tends to dominate.

What causes a country to change rays? (Feb. '84)

A nation has cycles of change in its personality ray which correspond to the successive incarnations of the individual. In each case, the soul ray remains the same. The reason for this change is to do with the evolutionary pattern of the nation as a whole, under the impact of the soul ray energy as focused by the nation's initiates and disciples. In this way, the soul of the nation seeks a broader and richer expression of its purpose in successive cycles or 'incarnations.'

When a country has the 7th ray as its soul ray, is that country predisposed to totalitarian government? (Apr. '85)

I assume the questioner is thinking of the Soviet Union, which is the only country (in the lists given) with a 7th ray soul. Having a 7th ray soul would predispose a nation to create order, standardized structures, but not necessarily through a totalitarian form of government. After all, there have been (and are today) many totalitarian governments of nations with quite different rays. For example, Germany under Hitler was extremely totalitarian. Germany's rays are: soul, 4; personality, 1. Italy, totalitarian under Mussolini, has a 6th ray soul and 4th ray personality. Spain, which was a dictatorship under Franco, has a 6th ray soul and 7th ray personality. Argentina has a 1st ray soul and 6th ray personality.

There are other forms of totalitarianism, too, besides political. Any imposition of a form or denial of freedom is totalitarian. Hence, for example, we have economic totalitarianism in the U.S.A. (rays: soul, 2; personality, 6), and religious totalitarianism in the Catholic Church (Christianity is a 6th ray religion).

The Russian Constitution (like that of the United States) upholds the rights of the individual and aims at functioning under democratic principles. Unfortunately, as in the United States and elsewhere, the ideal is seldom manifest. The time will come, however, when the aspiration of the Russian people, under the influence of its 7th ray soul, will bring into being the embryo of the new world religion. The present oligarchy in Russia has a limited tenure.

Do you really believe that a majority of Americans, with their love of consumption and possessions, their stubborn self-righteousness and their religious dogmatism, will make the changes Maitreya advocates? If so, why?

I should perhaps make it clear that this question comes from an American! The answer is yes, I do. The opposite side of the coin of American materialism, "stubborn self-righteousness and religious dogmatism" (all demonstrations of America's 6th ray personality glamours) is an intense idealism and capacity for self-sacrifice. The world is really waiting for the demonstration of America's 2nd ray soul nature (love), and when this does manifest, under the inspiration of the Christ, that idealism and capacity for self-sacrifice will sweep through the United States and galvanize it into changing direction. Of course, I am not suggesting that this will happen overnight or be painless, but painful or not it must happen. America, like the rest of the world, has no other alternative except self-destruction.

Do institutions and organizations have their own soul and personality ray structure? (June '83)

No. Every institution or organization is the creation of people with various ray structures. They will tend to reflect the rays of the dominant people involved.

The Rays and Planets

Is it possible that in our 2nd ray solar system there are World Teachers who belong to other ray types? (Dec./Jan. '83/'84)

Yes. They are not always on the 2nd ray. For instance, Hercules and Rama were 1st ray souls. Although They did not hold the office of World Teacher in Hierarchy—that is always on the 2nd ray—They were, for humanity, major teachers for Their time.

Since there are Seven Heavenly Men and twelve planets, is there a Heavenly Man ensouling more than one planet at the same time? (July/Aug. '84)

No. Each planet has its ensouling deity or Heavenly Man. The Seven Heavenly Men are the "Seven Spirits before the Throne,"—the Logoi of the seven sacred planets—Who focus the energies of the seven rays. These planets are: Vulcan, Jupiter, Saturn, Mercury, Venus, Neptune and Uranus. The other five, including Earth, are still non-sacred planets.

Are there solar systems constructed with more than seven rays? (June '86)

Despite the fact that some groups talk about twelve (or more) rays, and notwithstanding the young American I once met whose group had been "bringing in the tenth ray," there are only seven rays spiralling through Cosmos, which are the expression of seven great Lives, and whose interaction creates the visible universe. Given the vices or glamours of the rays (their imperfect expression), I am quite happy to settle for seven. The mind boggles at the possible glamours of the Eleventh Ray of Mediocre Endeavour, or the Twelfth Ray of New Age Fantasy!

Can you tell us about how the ray energies enter life on this planet through the zodiac and the sacred planets? What about the energies coming from non-sacred planets? (July/Aug. '83)

Each of the seven rays (each of which is the expression of a Solar Life) expresses itself through three constellations of the zodiac or through a triangle of energies. It is this relation which forms the basis of the Science of Triangles and of astrology itself. It relates our planet to the solar system and the solar system to the larger whole. The rays are expressed by and transmitted through the constellations as follows:

Ray 1: Aries—Leo—Capricorn
Ray 2: Gemini—**Virgo**—Pisces
Ray 3: **Cancer**—Libra—Capricorn
Ray 4: Taurus—**Scorpio**—Sagittarius
Ray 5: **Leo**—Sagittarius—Aquarius
Ray 6: Virgo—**Sagittarius**—Pisces
Ray 7: Aries—Cancer—**Capricorn**

The constellations in bold print are the controlling factors—today—in the triangles. The rays use the planets as transmitting agents. In this world cycle each planet transmits the following energy:

Sacred Planets
Vulcan—1st ray
Mercury—4th ray
Venus—5th ray
Jupiter—2nd ray
Saturn—3rd ray
Neptune—6th ray
Uranus—7th ray

Non-sacred Planets
Mars—6th ray

The Earth—3rd ray
Pluto—1st ray
The Moon (veiling a hidden planet)—4th ray
The Sun (veiling a hidden planet)—2nd ray

The sacred planets are those in which the planetary Lord of Life (planetary Logos) has taken the cosmic initiation corresponding to the third initiation in man, the Transfiguration. The Heavenly Men ensouling the non-sacred planets have not yet reached that stage of evolution, and Their body of expression, the planet, expresses and transmits the particular ray quality with less purity than do the sacred planets.

Can you give the planets in order of their evolution? (July/Aug. '86)

In order of evolution, the sacred planets are: 1) Uranus; 2) Mercury; 3) Vulcan; 4) Venus; 5) Jupiter and Neptune; 6) Saturn. The non-sacred planets in order of evolution are: 1) Mars; 2) Earth; 3) Pluto and a hidden planet; 4) a hidden planet.

The Rays and the Individual

In the appendix is presented for the first time (except in *Share International*), a list of the rays governing some of the major world figures, both historical and recent, whose thought and action have created our culture and civilization.They have been the means whereby the Plan has been implemented. The energies at their disposal through their ray structures have conditioned our life and sensibilities and brought us forward, during these last two thousand years, to the readiness for a tremendous expansion of consciousness and the preparedness for the new revelations and relationships.

A study of this list will show how certain rays and combination of rays incline the individual towards a certain kind of activity and line of service—his line of least resistance—through which, in any particular life, he can best serve the world and carry out his personal destiny.

Of crucial importance, of course, in understanding an individual's world service is a knowledge of his or her point in evolution. For the first time, the initiatory degree attained by these disciples in that life is given in the list. Many of them, of course, are long-since Masters, and as such continue their service to the Plan. The list gives the major rays in the following order: soul, personality, mental body, astral body and physical body.

The 1st ray is the ray of Power, and this becomes evident from the chart: every major statesman or political leader was strongly influenced by this ray. Mao Tse Tung (1-1-1-2-1) and Abraham Lincoln (1-2-1-2-1) (both disciples of Shamballa rather than Hierarchy) had four and three sources of this energy respectively, and most of the others had it as a major influence, either as souls or personalities, or both.

It is interesting to see, too, how many of the great figures of world history had this ray governing their mental body. Through it they could powerfully influence the thought of their circles and time. It provides breadth of vision and the fearlessness necessary for world service. For example, the soldiers von Hindenburg and Paul Kruger share the structure 1-1-1-6-7 with Charlemagne, Prince Metternich, and Juan Peron, while Bismark was 1-1-1-6-3.

The Master D.K. has written (through Alice A. Bailey) that artists are to be found on all the rays, yet it is obvious from the list of initiates that the 4th ray of Harmony or Beauty has a special role in artists in all fields, as painters, sculptors, musicians and writers. All the great artists have this ray strongly influencing their lives and work, from Praxiteles (4th Century BC), one of the greatest sculptors of ancient Greece (4-4-4-6-1), to Gustav Mahler (1860-1911), the great Austrian composer and conductor (4-4-4-6-3), besides Donizetti (4-4-4-2-7), Puccini (4-4-4-6-7), the French composer Milhaud (2-4-4-4-7) and the Italian painter Modigliani (6-4-4-4-7), and a host of others. The 4th ray confers on any painter a feeling for colour, and gives a composer the gift of melody. It is no accident, therefore, that the great masters of melody were strongly endowed with this energy. Mozart (4-4-4-4-3) had four 4th rays and Hector Berlioz (4-4-4-6-3) three.

The Master D.K. has also written that the combination of the 4th and 7th rays makes the highest type of artist. Almost every major artist or composer had both these rays in their structure. Incredibly, Leonardo da Vinci (4-7-7-4-7) had only these rays, and Rubens (4-7-1-4-7) had them on four levels.

Connections between different individuals and their ray structures are endless. The rays of Richard Strauss were 1-6-4-4-7 while those of Wagner, whom he so much admired and emulated, were 1-1-4-4-7.

One of the more interesting of these relationships is provided by the famous musical trio, Cortot (piano), Thibaud (violin) and Casals (cello), formed in 1905. Cortot's rays are 4-2-4-2-3, while those of Thibaud are 2-2-4-4-3 and of Casals 2-4-7-6-3. Casals was a second degree initiate, while his colleagues had yet to take the second initiation. This fact, and the presence of his 7th ray mental body, makes it likely that Casals, also a conductor and music festival organizer, was the dominant influence in that famous trio. Not only that, but it was he alone who took a very positive and committed stand in relation to political and social world events.

Another famous musical virtuoso of the time, Fritz Kreisler, had the ray structure 4-2-2-4-3, while Stradivari, whose instruments both Thibaud and Kreisler no doubt played, was 2-4-2-4-7. The composers Brahms and Benjamin Britten had the same rays: 2-4-4-6-3, as had the writer George Sand and the painters Mark Rothko and Ben Nicholson.

Readers may be interested to know that Mozart, whose rays, as already mentioned, were 4-4-4-4-3, was in his next life an obscure violin maker. In that life his rays were more practical, 4-4-5-2-3. He is now a Master.

The name of John Dalton (1766-1844) may be unfamiliar to readers, but he was a second degree initiate and one of the greatest of chemists. The practical, scientific 5th ray is strong in his make-up: 2-5-5-4-3, as it is in the Dutch scientist and inventor of the microscope, Anton van Leeuwenhoek (1632-1723) 3-5-5-2-7; in Brunel, the great 19th century engineer: 2-5-1-6-5; and in Richard Arkwright, inventor of the revolutionary weaving machine, the "spinning jenny," 2-1-5-4-5.

It is no coincidence that the rays of the great Swiss religious reformer, Huldreich Zwingli (1484-1531): 6-6-1-2-3, are exactly the same as that of his great German contemporary and fellow reformer, Martin Luther (1483-1546). They are also very closely related to that of several other major reformers of his time; for example, John Knox (6-6-1-6-3), John Calvin (6-1-6-6-3), George Wishart (1-6-6-6-7) and Hugh Latimer (6-6-6-2-3); while the rays of the biblical scholar, Miles Coverdale, and the English translator, William Tyndale, also contemporaries, were 6-6-7-6-3. Furthermore, the rays of the German mystic, Meister Eckhart, were also 6-6-1-6-3, and those of Charles Taze Russell, the founder of the Jehovah's Witnesses, were 6-2-1-6-3.

In each case, these are the rays of the zealot. This combination of two or three 6th rays with the 1st or 7th gave precisely the kind of one-pointed (not to say fanatical) power to carry forward the Reformation, one of the most influential movements in our history. Chambers Biographical Dictionary has this to say of Knox, for example: "Knox is the pre-eminent type of the religious Reformer—dominated by his one transcendent idea, indifferent or hostile to every interest of life that did not subserve its realization." A very accurate description of the 6th ray type.

The 6th is also the ray of sacrifice, and Wishart was martyred and burned to death for his 'heresies,' while Zwingli died on the field of battle, fighting for his faith.

It is not by accident that all the Christian saints have this ray powerfully present in their ray structures. St Catherine (6-6-6-6-7) had four vehicles on this ray and St Francis (6-6-6-2-3) three. Such a structure gave all the requirements for devotion and self-sacrifice.

It is interesting to note how few people on this list have 7th ray souls. This will change as the new age develops and the 7th ray energy waxes. One of these few was Edvard Kardelj (7-6-7-6-1), almost unknown in the West. He was President Tito's 'right- hand man' and was responsible for the Yugoslav Constitution. A second to third degree initiate (2.5), he exerted enormous influence behind the power of the President who was of the same degree but on the power line: 1-1-1-4-1.

These endless parallels and possible relationships cannot be by chance. The ray structures given by the soul have exerted their influence and guided the disciple into his or her chosen field of service and expression. Thus is determined the nature of that particular life, influencing society to a greater or lesser extent, depending on the degree of initiation attained.

Hazel Hunkins Hallinan, although practically unknown even to writers on feminist concerns, was for seven decades a stalwart and tireless fighter for women's rights. She was born Hazel Hunkins in Aspen, Colorado in 1890, but made London, England her home from 1920 until her death in May 1982.

A second degree initiate, she studied chemistry at college, but upon graduating found that it was impossible, despite her determined efforts, for a woman to be employed as a chemist at that time. It was the frustration of this realization that brought her into the women's rights movement.

Her ray structure (3-4-1-6-7) provided her with ample equipment for her task. As a second degree initiate she was polarized on the mental plane, and her powerful 1st ray mind, giving her great breadth of vision, enabled her to influence large numbers of women for 'The Cause.' Her 4th ray personality, under the influence of her 3rd ray soul, gave her the characteristic 4th ray elan and enthusiasm (when fired by a cause).

She was only five feet, one inch in height but was utterly fearless—and indomitable—in her many confrontations with authority. In her fight for women's suffrage, she underwent the sufferings and indignities of prison and force-feeding many times. This same 4th ray (and her broad viewpoint) brought a sense of humour and proportion to her activity which might otherwise, through the influence of her 6th ray astral body, have been marred by fanaticism.

Through her 7th ray brain, her 1st ray mental body found perfect and practical expression. She was able to organize and inspire in equal measure, and to channel the broadest idealistic concepts into practical political approaches.

Her 3rd ray soul made politics, and particularly political struggle for the betterment of women and of all humanity, a natural field of service.

Helen Adams Keller was remarkable by any standards. Her story is well known, extraordinary, and enduringly inspiring.

Born in Tuscumbria, Alabama in 1880, she became deaf and blind at the age of nineteen months. Cut off from sensory contact with the world, she grew to be almost like a wild animal. Her behavior demonstrated tremendous frustration, not surprisingly when her ray structure is known. As an initiate (1.7-8) with a powerful 1st ray soul and 1st ray personality, the inner tensions must have been unbearable. This same 1st ray equipment, however, provided her with the power of will to overcome her handicaps.

There entered her life another, almost equally remarkable, woman, Anne M. Sullivan (Mrs. Macy). This woman of unbelievable patience and perseverance took the wild animal and taught it to speak. By the age of 24, Helen Keller had so mastered her difficulties that she was able to take a B.A. degree. She lived to be eighty-eight and gained distinction as a lecturer, writer and scholar.

Her outstanding characteristic, of course, was will-power but her 4th ray mental body, in which her soul was focused, brought a highly intuitive faculty and great imagination to bear on her task and her later work. Her 5th ray brain provided the methodical approach and insight necessary to the scholar, and to tackle the enormous difficulties of learning in the first years.

Her relatively purified 2nd ray astral body gave her an emotional serenity without which, no doubt, her task would have been all but impossible.

Here is a clear illustration, one might think, of a karmic situation, traumatic in its nature, but in which the soul has provided the ray equipment to overcome it.

Questions on the Ray List

In the given ray list of initiates (in the appendix), not a single initiate with a 3rd ray soul (except Confucius) has reached the third initiation. Have there been so few 3rd ray souls in incarnation over the past few centuries, or is it more difficult for them to evolve? If so, why? Are there other reasons? (Dec./Jan. '83/'84)

It is important to remember that the given ray list is not necessarily representative nor does it necessarily, despite attempts to do so, give a balanced view of the world's disciples over the centuries. I am an artist, and I know the work of more artists—painters, sculptors, musicians, poets, writers—than of disciples working in other fields. There must be a great many very advanced people working (perhaps largely anonymously, in groups) in scientific, educational or political and economic fields, of whose presence I am unaware.

Another factor may be that I have dealt only with people no longer in incarnation. It could be that if one were to include living disciples in the above fields many would be found to have taken the third initiation. It should be remembered, however, that there are in incarnation only between two and three thousand people who have taken the third initiation.

A further and important factor may be this: Master D.K. does state that it is more difficult for 3rd ray types to correctly grasp the spiritual dimension of Reality, focused as they are on the form aspect. (This focus on the material world is that which makes the left-hand path more of a temptation for the 3rd ray type than for others.) However, once this type has responded to the inner spiritual life he is quicker in putting that revelation into effect in his life. The 3rd ray type, moreover, suffers less from glamour than from illusion. He therefore finds the third rather than the second initiation the major difficulty.

How is it possible that only a few philosophers in the list of initiates have a 3rd ray personality or mental body, while above all the 3rd ray gives someone philosophic capabilities? (Dec. '84)

For one thing, the list makes no claim to being complete. While it is true that not all the philosophers on the list have strong 3rd ray influences in their structures, many of them do, either from the soul, mental, or physical brain levels. The 3rd ray—when it is correctly expressed—gives the capacity for abstract thought. It also gives its exponent a powerful sense of the world of form and the ability to express experience on the physical plane. There is more than one approach to reality by philosophic means, and other rays are required to give this variety of approach. How sad for the world if Bertrand Russell's 'Humanistic Positivism' (he had three 3rd rays) were the only philosophic approach available. He said that the next logical step in his thinking would be to accept that God exists—but that that was not a step he was prepared to take!

Why was the degree of initiation omitted from several names on the list? Was it intentional, or an oversight, or was the information not given? (May '83)

The information was given but the omission was intentional. All the people concerned were Avatars and not from the human evolution. It was simply out of courtesy to Them, as honoured guests of this planet, so to speak, that I withheld the information. I did this in consultation with my Master Who, of course, gave all the information on the names.

Is there anything to be gained by studying the lives of the great initiates who may have expressed in their lives the

higher qualities of their rays if, as is likely, we are expressing more of the lower aspects? (Feb. '84)

I would think most certainly. Few people, even great initiates, are totally rounded out and balanced in the expression of their ray structure, and much can be learned through a study of their rays and of how the initiate in question coped with (or failed to cope with) inherent strengths or weaknesses in his make-up. Also, perhaps above all, such a study, as of the lives of the Saints, can be a great source of inspiration. A knowledge of the rays, of individuals and nations, throws an entirely new light on psychology and history and provides a fascinating and enlightening field of study.

In the Alice A. Bailey books the rays of some individuals (e.g. the Buddha, Hercules, Napoleon) are given, and are sometimes different from those you have given. Can you explain the reason for this? (Apr. '85)

Unfortunately, in giving rays of people (or animals) the Master D.K. (through Alice A. Bailey) omitted to say whether He was giving the major or sub-rays. In this list, my Master has given the major rays of the initiates. It is my information that D.K. gave the most *influential* rays governing the people under consideration—whether they were major or subsidiary. It is quite often the case that the sub-ray is more influential than the major ray.

Perhaps at some future date, if my Master has the time (and the inclination), He will give the sub-rays of the initiates on the list, showing which were the most influential rays, major or subsidiary.

Major Rays and Sub-Rays

Of what significance are the sub-rays in the ray structure? Do they generally point to things to come, attributes currently being formed? (Dec. '85)

The function of the sub-rays is to qualify or (if the same) to reinforce the major ray. Very frequently, the sub-rays represent the major influences of the immediately previous life still affecting the person, which influences the major rays will eventually absorb and diminish. Very often the sub-rays are more potent than the major rays, thus representing the task for that particular life—that is, the overcoming of these influences, and the establishment, clearly, of the major ray.

When the sub-ray is more influential than the major ray, why is it not then the major ray? (Mar. '86)

The sub-ray is the sub-ray of the major ray in each case. While it may be more influential now, that is not to say that the major ray will not become dominant in the course of the life. The sub-rays qualify the qualities of the major rays.

Are the sub-rays of an individual those rays that are on the wane from a previous life,or are they a ray influence that will appear stronger in an ensuing life? (Sept. '86)

Sub-rays are very often influences still affecting the individual from a previous life (when they very likely were the major rays), but they can also be the demonstration (not necessarily for the first time) of an influence which will be stronger in an ensuing life. The former is more frequently the case.

What is the purpose when the major and sub-rays are the same? (Mar. '86)

When the sub-ray is the same as the major ray, it strengthens and reinforces the quality of the major ray.

How do we know the difference between major rays and sub-rays? (June '85)

It is difficult to know which are the more influential, major or sub-rays. The usual procedure is to tackle the major rays first, have these confirmed, and then set about finding the sub- rays, which will either qualify or reinforce the major rays.

Concerning sub-rays within a personal ray structure, if, for instance, the personality ray were 6th ray with a 2nd sub-ray—does this mean the 2nd sub-ray of the 6th ray or the 2nd sub-ray of the 2nd ray? (Nov. '85)

It means the 2nd sub-ray of the 6th ray.

Do people's minor ray influences ever change during a specific incarnation? For instance, the ray of the mental or astral body? (July/Aug. '83)

No. The rays remain the same for the whole of the incarnation.

Personal Ray Structure

How do we set about finding out our personal ray structure? (June '83)

Study the virtues and vices of each of the seven rays until you have a firm picture of each ray as it expresses itself through these qualities, and, as honestly and objectively as you can be, relate them to yourself—as a soul, and as a personality with three vehicles, mental, emotional and physical. Try to allow your intuition to function and try not to make value judgements about, or show preferences for, particular rays. These prejudices will inhibit the functioning of your intuition.

In my experience, most people want to be powerful, loving and effective, and therefore tend to see themselves as having the 1st, 2nd, and 7th (because it is the incoming ray) rays in their makeup, whether this is so or not. Many people see themselves as having 1st ray power when in reality they are demonstrating 6th ray zeal and fanaticism.

The emotional conflicts through which all people go (especially between the first and second initiations, when the effort is being made to control the astral elemental) are not necessarily an indication that the person is on the 4th ray of Harmony through Conflict. Certainly, this ray is never far away from the human evolutionary path, but these conflicts occur on all the rays. Discrimination, intuition and honesty are therefore prerequisites for finding one's ray structure, but this is neither so difficult nor so easy as might be thought. It does require work.

Certain teachers tell—or even sell—people their ray structures. Quite apart from the fact that there is no guarantee that they know the correct structure (in my experience this is certainly not the case), the real value in knowing one's rays lies in knowing oneself—which requires effort and objectivity. Simply to be told one's rays, if correct, denies one this valuable growing experience and, if incorrect, only serves to confuse and delay progress.

What is the best way to ascertain the origin of a recognized quality, i.e. how do we find out if that quality is the result of, say, the mental body or the personality ray? (June '83)

The personality ray gives the general tone of a person, the mental ray gives the cast or quality of thought. Study the books for the ray attributes and, holding the quality in the mind and imagination, try to sense and *intuit* which vehicle it pertains to. This sounds difficult but in practice (and with practice) it is not so difficult. It is really through a combination of direct perception and intuition that we find out.

Is there a formula for calculating rays? (Mar. '84)

No. It is necessary to study the qualities, the virtues and vices associated with each ray and relate these to oneself or others as objectively as possible. With practice, it certainly becomes possible to recognize the ray influences and expression.

How can we distinguish the differences between 1st and 6th rays?

The vices (which are the glamours) are similar. In my experience, many people confuse the two. Almost without exception, 6th ray personalities, when they are studying their ray structure, imagine themselves to be 1st ray personalities. This is because of the similarity of the glamours (or vices) of each. But one is to do with the glamours of will, and the other with the glamours of desire. The 1st ray is the ray of will, or power; the 6th ray of devotion is based on desire. For instance, anger is a vice of both rays, but stemming from different causes. Desire to control others is a 1st ray vice. It comes from the domineering power of the 1st ray. The desire to control others is also, I would say, a glamour of the 6th ray, but it is for a different purpose. It is the fanatical belief in, and adherence to, one's own ideal that leads to the desire to control others. It is not coming from the will, it is coming from 6th ray desire, absolutely locked in its own righteousness, devotion to its ideal and itself, and determination to impose that ideal on everyone.

The rays with the major glamours are the 1st, 2nd and 6th. The glamours of the 1st and 6th rays are more alike because the desire principle in the 6th ray reaches its highest reflection, or correspondence, in the 1st ray. Desire pertains to the personality; then it is will for power, whereas when will comes from the soul it is essential love. I am not saying that the 1st ray personality is more ensouled than the 6th ray personality, not so. But the 6th ray characteristic is working through the desire principle, whereas 1st ray will is working through the desire principle only when it is a glamour. When it is from the higher aspect, we see demonstrating, in the case of the 1st ray, the will and power of the soul whose qualities include strength, courage, steadfastness and singleness of purpose, and in the case of the 6th ray abstract idealism, intuition, devotion, tenderness and one pointed singleness of purpose. The virtues and vices of the 6th ray are diametrically opposite. The virtues are turned into the very opposite of themselves. That is what the vices and glamours really are—the quality of a ray wrongly expressing itself.

You mean the 6th ray vices and virtues are more dramatic in contrast?

Exactly. The difference between the virtues and vices of the 6th ray are more dramatic than in any other, and hence the particular difficulty in dealing with the problem of glamour. In my experience the 6th ray is the most glamoured of all the rays. Why? Because it is focused on the astral plane. It comes through the solar plexus, which is the vehicle for astral energy, and the problem for the 6th ray exponent is to bring down his or her ideals from the astral plane onto the outer physical world. However, the 6th ray soul is as perfect as any other soul. The soul qualities of the 6th ray are marvellous: abstract idealism and devotion, sympathy, love, intuition and reverence. What I would like added to the Master D.K.'s list is self-sacrifice—one of the major qualities of the 6th ray soul.

How does one distinguish between the ray of the mind and that of the brain (where does one end and the other begin)? (June '83)

The ray of the brain is the ray of the physical body—which might make it easier to recognize. Each ray creates a rather specific type of physical body which is quite recognizable even with different racial and national types.

Is it possible to describe the different emotional and mental types according to rays? (Apr. '86)

Yes. It is precisely the rays which give the different qualities of the various types.

How is it that despite having certain rays people don't show their characteristics? For instance, 2nd ray personalities are not necessarily loving—why? (June '83)

The reality is that the rays only give one the potentiality for certain attributes. So, for example, having a 2nd ray soul or personality does not necessarily mean that the 2nd ray qualities of love and wisdom, empathy, etc. will be demonstrated. On the contrary, they may well have to be built in. The soul has provided the *possibility* of this taking place through the 2nd ray influence.

Why is it that people whose rays should make them gentle, quiet and reticent, for example, appear to be far more forceful, etc. than could be expected simply from ray structure? (June '83)

Again, the answer is the same as for the previous question. The sub-rays, too, might be altogether different. There is also the possibility that quite different rays from previous incarnations are still strongly influencing the person's expression in this incarnation. This brings in another influence which can only be discerned by a Master.

In the ray list of initiates, only six persons have a 2nd ray physical body. Besides that, most of them died very young (Chopin was 39 years old, Giorgione 33, John Keats 26, Schubert 31, and U-Thant, as an exception, was 65). Is this common for 2nd ray physical bodies and can you tell more about it? (July/Aug. '86)

It is true to say that it is not the most powerful physical body in the world, but that does not mean that people with 2nd ray physicals necessarily live only short lives. On the contrary, especially if the sub-ray is 7 or 3 or 5, a person with a 2nd ray physical body may well live to a ripe old age. It simply means that it is a specially sensitive type of body and tends to suffer therefore from the impact on the nervous system of its hypersensitivity.

Is it possible to describe the different physical types according to rays? (Dec./Jan. '83/'84)

Yes. Each ray produces a distinctive physical type which seems to cut across individual family, national and racial characteristics.

The 1st ray type tends to be tall, strongly built and large-boned with a general air of power, natural authority and physical fearlessness. They are often rather fat (from over-indulgence rather than glandular disturbance) but as often lean, hard and 'durable.' Military men and policemen are often 1st ray. Among athletes, heavyweight boxers, weightlifters and shot-putters tend to be 1st ray physical.

The 2nd ray physical type is usually (but not always) small and delicately made, with a sense of fastidious refinement and sensitivity. He or she will not be the natural games player, except perhaps with cards and other mental games requiring sensitivity and intuition.

The 3rd ray physical type (with the 7th ray the most common) comes in all sizes and shapes. A large number of athletes are of this type, which is characterized by an impression of physical co- ordination and adaptability (when healthy and fit). They have the ordinariness of 'the norm' since we see them everywhere—large and small, fat and thin. They tend, except when particularly large, to have average-sized features.

The 4th ray physical type seems to me to have some of the characteristics of both the 2nd and 3rd ray types: some of the delicacy and refinement of gesture of the 2nd plus some of the basic energy (but more febrile) of the 3rd. They tend to be rather small. Charles Chaplin had a 4th ray physical ìbody.

The 5th ray physical type gives a somewhat stiff, set appearance; a tendency to clumsiness and awkwardness rather than physical co-ordination. They are often squarish in shoulders and head, with rather deep-set eyes under square brows.

The 6th ray physical types tend to be large and run to fat. They have a rather soft, flabby appearance with broad faces. They seem to be somewhat rare in Europe (our list has only two), but are more common in the U.S.A..

The 7th ray physical type can be tall or short but is usually thin and rangy. It is an extremely durable type, very athletic, especially in sports demanding stamina—the long distance runner rather than the sprinter. Elegant in movement and pose, with clear-cut, well-proportioned features. They often give a somewhat leathery impression.

Are well-known sports figures often 1st ray physical? (July/Aug. '83)

No, except in heavyweight sports such as boxing, wrestling, or weightlifting. The best physical ray for sports appears to be the 3rd ray. This provides the co-ordination and adaptability required in sports. The 7th ray, too, is often found, especially where stamina is a major need. The 1st ray physical type seems to be favoured by politicans, providing them with a powerful brain, physical presence and resilience.

Is the ray of the physical body the result of heredity—that is, the group that one has incarnated in—or are there more subtle reasons? (Nov. '85)

The soul determines the rays of its vehicle—mental, astral and physical. These may or may not bear some relation to one's parents' ray structure. Frequently, the physical ray of the parents is shared by all members of the family, but this is by no means always the case.

If you can see yourself expressing the lower, negative qualities of a given ray can we bring in other ray qualities to offset this and overcome it; and if so, can we do this in one life? (Feb. '84)

Yes indeed. A study of the ray biography of Gandhi (see *Share International*, December '83/January '84 issue) will show this: the inclusive 2nd ray qualities are used (consciously or unconsciously) to offset the separative tendency of the 6th ray, although he never overcame the fanatical aspect of that ray. Of course, the aim is to build in the virtues of the rays, but certain weaknesses, e.g. the timidity and lack of confidence which often occurs in 2nd ray personalities, can be strengthened if there also exists a ray on the 1-3-5-7 line whose stronger quality can be brought to bear. The success or otherwise in ìachieving this balance in any given life depends, naturally, on the effort made.

Does one ray influence help to cause the right use of another ray? For instance, would the 4th ray energy help to offset 6th ray fanaticism? (Dec. '84)

Yes. The secret in understanding the rays is to know how to use the quality of one ray to make up for the weaknesses or to offset the glamours of another. To my mind, the 5th ray of concrete mind would be more successful in offsetting 6th ray fanaticism than the 4th ray. Or failing that in the make-up, the second, which is inclusive and magnetic.

Do people of the same ray 'set up' tend to gravitate to each other and seem to 'like' each other? Are there some rays which tend to repel each other? (May '83)

It is true that people of the same ray structure will tend to understand each other's viewpoint and general approach to life and so will gravitate together, but it is also true *on the personality level* that we dislike people who are too like ourselves. It is a truism that we most dislike in others our own faults.

2nd ray people tend to be repelled and frightened by the manifestation of 1st ray power, while 1st ray exponents often dislike the sentimentality of the 2nd ray type. Of course, on the soul level, there is no repulsion; all souls can work together in harmony whatever the ray—hence the necessity of approaching people as souls and finding contact with them at that level.

Do twins who are very much alike have the same rays? (Apr. '84)

No, not necessarily. They can be and often are quite different.

Do people living together absorb each other's ray energies to the extent of appearing to express the rays of the other

person rather than their own? If so, is it good? (July/Aug. '83)

No, people do not absorb other people's ray energies to such an extent. Where people appear to become like each other we are seeing a case of empathy to the point of imitation, which empathy would be the expression of an existing ray influence, particularly of the 2nd ray. We can really only express that which we already are.

How do the 1st and 2nd rays work together? (Dec. '84)

It depends entirely on the individual. In general, the 1st ray brings strength of will, dynamic purpose and fearlessness, while the 2nd brings loving understanding, intuition and inclusiveness. They therefore complement each other.

Is spiritual pride a characteristic of a particular ray force? (July/Aug. '84)

People on the 1st and 6th rays are most prone to the glamour of spiritual pride.

Must the destroyer aspect of divinity always be wielded by an adherent to the left-hand path? (Sept. '86)

No, by no means is this the case. The destroyer aspect is the 1st ray of will or power. There is no reason to assume that all exponents of 1st ray energy, even in its destructive aspect, would be on the left-hand path.

When we recognize in ourselves the energy of rays not in our personal equipment what can be the reason for that? (Apr. '84)

The main reason will most likely be the influence of a ray powerfully present in the immediately previous incarnation.

The influence of the group in which one is working can also have a powerful effect. Likewise, the ray of one's nation also has a pervasive effect on one's personality expression.

Can we truly understand a ray that is not in our makeup? (Dec. '84)

For most of us this is very difficult. However, the more advanced a person becomes, the more of the qualities of all the rays—synthesized by his own ray—he will have built into his equipment, and the more he will function from the soul level. On that level there is no difficulty in understanding.

When you like very much the music of a certain composer, can you conclude that you have more or less the same rays? (Dec. '84)

Of course it must happen sometimes, but if your taste in music is reasonably wide you will find that this is by no means always the case. Very many other factors are at work in musical appreciation. Also, one's taste and strong likes in music often change over one's life.

The Soul and the Rays

Who chooses the soul ray? (Nov. '85)

The soul itself.

Is it possible for a soul to incarnate with all its bodies on the same ray? (Sept. '85)

Theoretically, yes. In practice this is seldom found. Even then, only along the 2-4-6 line.

Is it possible that the soul would select the same set of rays for two consecutive lives? (Sept. '86)

Although infrequent, this does happen.

I have the impression that when souls incarnate as men they especially take rays from the 1-3-5-7 line, and when as woman from the 2-4-6 line. Is this so? (Dec./Jan. '83/'84)

No. A quick look at the list of initiates and their rays will show that the number of disciples is divided pretty well evenly between the two lines, whether men or women.

Do the even rays tend to produce more introverted people than the uneven rays? (Dec./Jan. '83/'84)

Yes. The line 1-3-5-7 deals with the form, the concrete world, with the function of matter, so that those on that line tend to be extroverted to the outer, formal aspect of life. The 2-4-6 rays are connected with the inner, spiritual life, with expression through the medium of form, with quality, and those on this line are therefore more drawn to the inner soul quality through introversion.

It would appear that those upon the 2-4-6 line or ray activity are vertical and horizontal transmitters of energy, whereas those upon the 1-3-5-7 line would be more activity oriented, the actual physical changers. Is this the case? (Jan. '86)

To put it in the terms used by the questioner, I would say the 2-4-6 approach is more vertical while the 1-3-5-7 approach is more horizontal.

Do the rays which are present at the time of birth remain the same in the life that follows? (Mar. '83)

Yes. The rays of the personality and its vehicles, mental, emotional and physical, may (and usually do) change from life to life, but remain the same for the duration of each particular life. The soul ray remains constant from life to life, and changes only at the beginning of a new world cycle, which of course is very rare.

When the first and second initiations have been achieved in a former life (or lives), what happens when the individual next incarnates with a different ray structure? Does the soul impose control quite easily or is it a struggle? (June '83)

It depends on the individual. Speaking broadly, the period between the first and second initiations provides the field of major struggle between the soul and its reflection, the personality, which often strongly resists the growing soul control. The second initiation is said to be the most difficult one to take for this reason. Usually, once the second initiation has been achieved the progress is rapid. This tends to be the case whatever the ray structure, which in any case is chosen by the soul itself.

Are there clear stages in learning to work with the rays, and is the path of initiation one of the final stages? (June '83)

The path of initiation (on which there are five major stages) is precisely the learning to work with and to control the forces, which are the ray forces, underlying all appearances. Every incarnation provides the possibility of a purer expression of the underlying (soul) ray quality. This begins to be achieved by the third initiation, at which time the ray of the monad (divine spark) makes itself felt. The Master of the fifth initiation expresses the monadic ray in its purity and has control on all planes.

If a disciple were a 2nd ray soul, is it conceivable that he could have a Master on one of the other rays? (July/Aug. '85)

No—unless he were 'loaned' to another Master for some particular purpose or training. This happens frequently.

Since all 6th ray and 4th ray initiates must transfer to the major 2nd ray, can we assume that Jesus is now a 2nd ray soul even though He is the Chohan of the 6th ray? (Oct. '85)

No. At the third initiation the initiate aligns with the Monad or Spirit aspect which is always on rays 1, 2, or 3. Those whose souls are on the minor rays (4, 5, 6 or 7) must find at that time, their *correspondence* on one of these three major rays, or rays of aspect as they are called. That is not to say that one changes ray. The Master Jesus is still on the 6th ray, although a 2nd ray Monad, and is the Chohan of the 6th ray—head of the major 6th ray ashram.

Group unity without the Piscean type of leadership can be quite a problem, especially when numbers increase. Are there any useful guidelines as we attempt to build the foundation of New Age groups? (Nov. '84)

This is a common problem which will obviously grow as more groups are formed along lines different from the past. If we can take for granted that most group members are equally sincere and dedicated to the purpose of the group, that is a good start. Most division within groups stems from different ideas on procedure and policy. This is inevitable, given the different ray structures within the average group. The world at this time is saturated with 6th ray energy (the energy of Pisces) with its tendency to exclusiveness and fanaticism. Whether they realize it or not, most members of most 'new age' groups are exponents of 6th ray energy, which of course accounts for their idealism, but also for their difficulty in working *with*, and not only *for*, a group. The only way to overcome these problems is to foster a strong love relationship between group members and to learn to recognize, and work from, the soul level of each. Whatever its ray, the soul is altruistic and inclusive. Learn that in groups, personality desires and differences do not count. Avoid mutual criticism and foster self-sacrifice for the greatest good. Remember that this is a period of transition in which difficulties are inevitable. Everyone is learning, more or less, the same lessons.

Soul Focus and Polarization

In connection with ray structures, what is the difference between 'polarization' and 'soul focus'? Do they both change or shift from life to life? (Nov. '84)

By 'polarization' is meant the plane on which the individual's consciousness is habitually focused—physical, astral, mental or spiritual. Each race has had the evolutionary goal of achieving consciousness on a plane and of perfecting the appropriate vehicle of response. For example, the third root race—the Lemurian, the first truly human race—had the aim of perfecting the physical body and achieving full physical plane consciousness. The fourth root race, the Atlantean, had the goal of achieving and perfecting astral consciousness, man's sensory feeling response to outer stimulus. Ours, the fifth, Aryan race has the goal of perfecting mental plane consciousness. All of today's humanity has physical and astral consciousness and some degree of mental consciousness.

To have consciousness on a plane is not at all the same thing as to have control on that plane. Thus, control on the physical plane (actually control of the tiny devic lives which create the substance of the physical body) is only demonstrated when the first initiation can be taken. When the astral elemental is controlled the second initiation becomes possible, and the third initiation demonstrates control on the mental plane. The focus of consciousness thus shifts upwards as evolution proceeds. Even today, the majority of humanity are polarized on the astral plane; they still retain Atlantean-type consciousness. This astral polarization continues until a point about half-way between the first and second initiations. There is then a period in which the polarization oscillates between astral and mental until full mental polarization is achieved and the second initiation can be taken. The state of mental polarization continues until about half-way between the second and third initiations, when spiritual polarization begins and the intuition gradually takes over the functions of the lower mind. This is fully achieved by the fourth initiation.

By 'soul focus' in connection with the ray-structure is meant the body or vehicle—personality, mental, astral or physical—through which the soul is focusing its major stimulus in any particular life. This focus can and does change from life to life as the soul—for its own purposes—gives special stimulus to a particular ray governing a particular vehicle. The shift in polarization, on the other hand, takes place slowly, over many or several lives.

What is the real value of being mentally polarized? (Sept. '85)

Being mentally polarized allows the soul to work through the mental body and destroy the glamour of the astral plane activity. Every act of the mind that correctly controls the emotional body and relegates it to its proper place is an aid to eventual mental polarization.

How would one see the difference when the soul is focused in the mental body or in the personality? For instance, does it affect the type of activity chosen or the way of application? (Dec. '84)

The way of application. The heightened stimulus given to the ray of the body in which the soul is focused increases the activity and overall influence of that body in the structure.

(1) Can one be a 1st degree initiate and still be soul focused in the emotional body? (2) At what point can we be focused on the mental and can this take place during one lifetime? (May '86)

(1) Yes. (2) This question shows a common confusion (dealt with earlier) between the terms 'soul focus' and 'polarization'.

This soul focus in any given life can be on any of its vehicles: personality, mental, astral or physical. Polarization is the level—physical, astral mental, or spiritual—at which the consciousness is habitually concentrated. This polarization shifts upwards through the evolutionary process.

There are usually many (average 6-7) lives between the first and second initiations. With the beginning of mental polarization at '1.5' the process speeds up, and the second initiation may well be ìtaken in that life.

Within one incarnation can the soul change its focus from one body to another, for example, from mental to personality or vice- versa? If so, under what circumstances does it occur? (July/Aug. '85)

The soul, we must suppose, could change its focus but in fact it does not, under any circumstances. Evolution, from the soul's standpoint, is not to be hurried; it has no awareness of time and proceeds purposefully, intelligently, and carefully. For long ages the response of its reflection—the personality—is slow indeed.

I read that the personality ray changes according to cyclic differentiations. Can this happen in one lifetime? That is, could one start life with one personality ray dominant and end with another? (Sept. '85)

The personality ray would not change in the course of one life, but if the major and sub-rays were different one of them might gain the dominance, especially if the soul focus was on a vehicle of similar ray, and thus stimulate the personality ray, major or minor.

Why would the soul choose to focus itself in the astral body as against the mental? (Sept. '85)

To stimulate a particular ray. To bring out certain qualities of feeling (not necessarily emotion) and by this means to correct an overstimulation of a ray from the previous incarnation. For example: a mentally polarized person might, in the process, have become rather cold and isolated in relation to others. The soul might then focus itself on the astral vehicle, along the 2-4-6 line, to invoke the warmth and love nature into the equipment.

Can you have two rays the same and they still not be the dominant influence? (Dec/Jan. '83/'84)

Yes, this frequently is the case. For instance, if the soul ray is one of these two and not controlling the personality then they would not be dominant, especially if the other was the ray of the physical body. A person might have the same rays for the mental and physical body but be powerfully focused in the astral body. In this case, the ray of the astral body would be dominant. A further case might be where a ray is given twice to bring in an influence as yet only potential.

How strongly do the mental, astral and physical rays ìin-fluence the personality ray? Is this a matter of where we are polarized, or is it a blending of the body rays with the power where the soul is focused? (Dec. '84)

The influence of the mental or astral rays on the personality ray depends on the point of polarization—whether mental or astral. But if the soul focus is on the astral or physical bodies in someone mentally polarized, then the major influence will come from the astral or physical ray. The soul will quite often place its focus on the mental body in someone focused on the astral precisely to bring about the necessary shift in polarization from astral to mental.

More Individuals—Their Rays and Initiations

I would be interested to know the true feelings of Pontius Pilate when judging Jesus. Is there anything you can say about this and can you reveal his ray structure? (Apr. '85)

He felt a certain sympathy for Jesus, but thought that there was nothing he could do in the circumstances without upsetting the Jewish Elders, so he took the line of least resistance, even against his better judgement—and nature. He was an initiate of the first degree (1.4). His rays were 2-6-3-6-7 (sub-rays: personality 6, mental 3, astral 4, physical 1).

Can you give the ray structure and point in evolution of the late Indira Gandhi? (Apr. '85)

Indira Gandhi was a second degree initiate. Her rays were 1-1-7-6-3 (sub-rays: personality 1, mental 1, astral 6, physical 3). With four 1st rays in her make-up she wielded power with ease. One could say she was born to rule. Her soul focus was on the mental body (in particular through the 1st ray sub-ray) and being a second degree initiate she was mentally polarized.

Her real achievement was in unifying (at least to some degree) the diverse peoples and forces of India. Her 1st ray soul with its synthesizing breadth of vision could with ease work through the powerful 1st ray personality and mind. The 6th ray astral (reinforced by the sub-ray) tended to work in the opposite direction, however, giving her at times an extraordinary blindness to the realities around her, and an over-exclusive concern for what she saw as India's interests. This reduced, somewhat, the influence for good in international affairs which might otherwise have been hers. She had, of course, the typical fearlessness of the 1st ray type.

What were the rays of Hermann Hesse? (Dec. '84)

His major rays were: 4-4-3-6-3 (sub-rays: personality 2, mental 6, astral 6, physical 4). He was a second degree initiate (2.1).

Could you give the ray structure and level of initiation of Nicholas Roerich? (Oct. '85)

His ray structure was: 7-7-7-6-7 (sub-rays: personality 4, mental 1, astral 4, physical 7). His point in evolution, in precise terms, was 2.1 degree initiate.

Since he has just died, can you give the ray structure and point in evolution of the painter, Marc Chagall? (May '85)

He was on the verge of the second initiation, in fact, 1.9. His rays were: 2-4-4-6-7 (sub-rays: personality 7, mental 2, astral 4, physical 3). He was, of course, mentally polarized; his soul focus was on the personality, rays 4 and 7. With three 4th rays and two 7th rays he was well equipped for his vocation.

Since he has just died, can you give us the ray structure and the degree of Krishnamurti? (Apr. '86)

His rays were: 2-2-4-6-7 (sub-rays: personality 6, mental 4, astral 2, physical 7). He was a fourth degree initiate.

Can you give the ray structure and point in evolution of Olof Palme who was assassinated recently? (Apr. '86)

3-6-7-4-7 (sub-rays: personality 4, mental 4, astral 6, physical 3). He was a 2.1 degree initiate.

Is Bhagavan Swami Brahmananda Saraswati Guru Dev, the teacher of Maharishi Maheshi Yogi, a Master? If so, when did he become a Master? In his last life? On what ray? (Apr. '86)

Yes, Guru Dev is a very highly evolved Master, having taken the Ascension Initiation. He is therefore a sixth degree initiate. He is on the 6th ray of devotion or abstract idealism.

Could you please give the ray structure of Guru Nanak, 14th century Hindu reformer?

6-6-1-2-3 (sub-rays: personality 7, mental 4, astral 2, physical 7).

Is it possible to give the rays of Baha'U'llah? (Apr. '86)

The founder of Bahai, Baha'U'llah, was an initiate of the third degree. His ray structure was: 6-6-6-4-7 (sub-rays: personality 6, mental 6, astral 4, physical 7). He was mentally impressed (not overshadowed) by Maitreya with the Bahai teachings, but was in fact a disciple of the Master Jesus. He thought that he received the teachings direct from 'God' and believed himself to be the Christ. He informed the Pope of the time and world leaders to this effect. He was eventually beheaded as a 'heretic' by the Arabs.

The Mahikari movement is based on the transmission of light and its purpose is the purification of the world and mankind. (1) Is it a beautiful way of service to mankind? (2) Does the light come directly from God or from the astral level? (3) Is this way of working in tune with the way described in *Esoteric Psychology* Vol. II, by Alice A. Bailey, pp.607-610? If not, what is the main difference? (4) Can you give us the ray structure and the degree of initiation of its founder, Yoshikazu Okada? (Apr. '86)

(1) Yes. (2) The highest astral. (3) Yes. (4) 6-6-6-4-3 (sub-rays: personality 4, mental 3, astral 6, physical 7). He was a 2.1 degree initiate.

Was the late L. Ron Hubbard, founder of Scientology, influenced or guided by a Master or disciple? What was Hubbard's ray structure and initiate status?

He was influenced by a Master, not outwardly or consciously but subjectively, on the inner plane. His ray structure was: 3-7-1-6-3 (sub-rays: personality 4, mental 6, astral 4, physical 7). He was 1.8 degrees initiate.

What were the rays and point in evolution of Erich Fromm? (Sept. '86)

6-2-4-6-7 (sub-rays: personality 4, mental 6, astral 6, physical 3). He was 1.6 degree initiate.

Animals

Do all the animals come under the same ray? (Dec./Jan. '83/'84)

No. The rays of only the domesticated animals have been given. On page 260 of *Esoteric Psychology* Vol. 1, the Master D.K. gives the following: elephants—1st ray; dogs—2nd ray; cats—3rd ray; horses—6th ray. On page 164 of the same work a different set are given: elephant—2nd ray; cat—4th ray; dog—6th ray. This discrepancy results from the fact that in the second enumeration above it is the sub-ray of the major ray which has been given.

Are animals only influenced by rays on the physical level—or also on higher levels? (Dec./Jan. '83/'84)

The animal kingdom is influenced mainly by the 3rd ray of active intelligence (actually far more potently than is man) and by the 6th ray of devotion. This 6th ray stimulates the astral nature of the animal kingdom, while its incipient mental equipment is stimulated by men's minds (5th ray). This is especially true, of course, in relation to the domestic animals. Eventually, the control of the animal kingdom will take place through the controlled, focused mind of man.

CHAPTER VII

REINCARNATION

Life after Death, and Rebirth

One of the great tragedies of our present outlook on existence is our attitude to that recurring event which we call death. We approach it, for the most part, with fear and loathing, seeking by every means to resist its call, prolonging, often beyond its usefulness, the activity of the physical body as a guarantee of "life." Our dread of death is the dread of the unknown, of complete and utter dissolution, of being "no more." Despite the vast amount of evidence gathered over the years by the many Spiritualist groups that life *of some kind* continues after death; despite the intellectual acceptance by many that death is but an awakening into new and freer life; in spite of the growing belief in reincarnation, and notwithstanding the testimony of the wisest Teachers down the ages, we continue to approach that great transition with fear and trepidation.

What makes this attitude so tragic is that it is so far from the reality, the source of so much unnecessary suffering. Our fear of death is our fear that our identity will be obliterated. It is this which terrifies. Did we but realize and *experience* our identity as an immortal Being which cannot die or be obliterated, our fear of death would vanish. If, further, we realized that after so-called death we enter into a new and clearer light in which the sense of our identity is altogether more vivid, that there are yet higher aspects of our Being awaiting our recognition of which until then we are unaware, our whole approach to death would change for the better.

We would see death and physical-plane life as stages in an endless journey to perfection, and death as the door into far less limiting experience on that road. Freed from the confines of the physical world, our consciousness would find great new vistas of meaning and beauty hitherto denied it. In the time immediately ahead, the Masters and Their disciples will teach the truth of that experience we call death and open up for all a great new freedom. We will learn to accept death for what it is: restitution of our vehicles to their source—"ashes to ashes, dust to dust"—and liberation into new and meaningful life.

We shall come to understand that the single, momentous event we now call death is an orderly succession of stages whereby the soul withdraws, each in turn, from the vehicles it has created.

The process of death begins when the soul withdraws its energy from the dense physical body. This can take place over a longer or shorter period of time. A series of heart-attacks or an illness which becomes steadily graver could be the sign that the soul is beginning this process. As soon as death takes place, the subtle bodies—the astral and the mental bodies within the etheric vehicle—withdraw from the dense physical body. This, too, can take place quickly or more slowly, but the Masters advise that one should wait for three days before burial or (preferably) cremation to ensure that the etheric body has completely withdrawn from its physical counterpart.

The individual consciousness is then left in the etheric body, which in its turn will also be discarded. The particles of substance making up the etheric vehicle will then stream back into the ocean of etheric energy which surrounds us. The speed of that disintegration process depends upon the individual's karma.When the etheric vehicle has been cast off, the astral sheath gives the person consciousness on the astral plane, where he will remain for a time on one or other of the seven astral planes which best corresponds with his astral nature. There he will once again have to deal with his desires carried over from his earthly life and often remains enmeshed in these.

For most people, the greatest fear of death exists in their expectation of loss of identity and consciousness, of loneliness and cessation of contact with family and friends. Far from experiencing such a loss, the dead man, freed from the limitations of the physical vehicle, finds that his conscious awareness is heightened immeasurably. He sees both ways: the world of forms which he has just left and the new world into which he has come, with familiar people around him ready to welcome him into that more liberated state. At the same time, he can still tune into the feelings and thoughts of those left behind. Far from being a traumatic experience, death for many is so gentle and smooth that they do not realize they are dead, requiring the help of those whose task it is to acquaint them of this fact. There are disciples, initiates and some Masters active on the astral plane, protecting people and making them aware of their death.

On the astral plane one does what, normally, one would have been doing in incarnation on the physical plane. If the consciousness is very much focused on the astral, with very little mental focus, such a person could remain on the astral plane for a long time—'long' to our way of thinking, for outside the realm of the physical brain there is no such thing as time. Although life on the astral plane is a fact, as it is a fact on the dense physical plane, it is nevertheless only an illusion. All our hopes, fears and aggression, our hatreds, jealousies and vices, form powerful thought-forms which must, sooner or later, be dissolved. Therefore, the only hell which exists is that which we ourselves have created on the astral planes. The hell which we encounter is the hell of our own desires, our atrocities, our own separation and our own grudges and fears which inhabit the astral realm. This is the principle behind the advice of the Masters: that we learn to control our thoughts and emotional reactions.

For that reason also, it is important to raise the consciousness as high as possible at the time of death, using the final nerve reflex to drive the consciousness through the astral and the lower mental levels onto higher mental levels as far, as fast, and as consciously as possible. There should be deliberate preparation for death, therefore, and in the future people will be taught how to die consciously in order to do this.

After the death of the physical body, the individual concerned remains on those astral planes which correspond most closely to the point of development attained by him in physical life. On those subtle levels our faculties of perception become freed from the process of thinking and reasoning which function through the physical brain. All knowledge and experience can be directly seen, heard, felt and known in their full significance. There is instantaneous perception, knowledge and beauty, and a type of joy and liberation such as we cannot know on the material plane.

On the higher astral levels this direct experience is of a more ecstatic kind, of a higher, more refined emotional nature corresponding to the higher astral levels of the heart centre. A person who has attained a certain level of development before death experiences an almost constant ecstasy and joy on those levels, a sense of beauty and splendour which is the reflection on that plane of buddhi, or love-wisdom. Buddhi is actually a state of rapture which can be expected on the physical plane when a high degree of buddhic contact is achieved during meditation.

The experience on the mental plane is of an entirely different kind. Here it is less a matter of rapture than of knowledge or wisdom; not only rapture, but the great significance and meaning underlying it can be known on that level. Someone sufficiently evolved, intuitively aware, understands this and the Purpose and Will of God.

For more advanced people, existence on the mental plane would be the last experience before coming into incarnation once again. But it is possible that the mental body in its turn might be dissolved, after which the individual concerned would live in a state of *pralaya*, in *devachan*. This is a non-mental, non-astral, non-material state of existence somewhere between death and life. It is a state of Being, out of incarnation, where the life impulse is in abeyance. It is a state of unending bliss, an experience of perfect peace. To live in *pralaya* does not mean that one is unconscious, but no conscious learning process takes place prior to taking incarnation again. It is a state of being taken up into the Absolute, from whence one returns, under law, when group need demands it.

In *pralaya* the soul lives in its own realm with no other purpose than to be the soul. Because there are no lower vehicles in this state of existence, the soul will not gain any experience, as it does on the other levels. Progress of a specific kind can be made only on these other levels. The soul comes into incarnation directed by the Logos in accordance with group purpose and the Plan. It is a great sacrifice for the soul to descend onto the physical plane and take incarnation, which takes place under its own self-sacrificing will. This self-sacrificing power of soul-will is a great driving force. In *pralaya* there is no will to incarnate. It is possible to remain in *pralaya* for a few dozen to countless thousands of years, until such time as a group of souls is sent out of *pralaya* into incarnation because the time is right and the circumstances suitable. The soul body, or causal body, gains experience in this manner. The causal body receives more soul-knowledge, soul-consciousness, as its vehicles become more refined.

This refining process of the soul vehicles (the etheric, astral and mental bodies) takes place by means of the so-called 'permanent atoms.' These are atoms of physical, astral and mental matter around which the bodies for a new incarnation are formed. The permanent atoms retain the vibratory rate of the individual attained up to the moment of death. If that person has made great progress, his or her bodies in succeeding incarnations will be more refined, akin to the vibration of this permanent atom and, due to the magical working of the soul, will increasingly attract matter of a sub-atomic nature. In this way, the permanent atoms will spiral up to reach increasingly higher frequencies. Because a body attracts to it matter of a similar vibratory rate, each advancement through each life will create a more refined body of increasingly higher vibration. The permanent atoms are, therefore, nuclei which attract the atomic particles from which first the mental, then the astral, and subsequently the etheric-physical bodies are formed—after which the dense physical body 'precipitates.'

The permanent atoms of an individual are connected to the soul's causal body and are not influenced by experience when out of incarnation. The causal body is located on the highest of the four mental levels, and is a kind of reservoir or storage of all perception, all knowledge and all experience of the physical, astral and mental realms. A 'silver cord' connects the soul and its body with the three permanent atoms. Consciousness is continuous in this cord, so that when it is time for the soul to reincarnate once again, particles of matter of like vibration are magically attracted to form around the permanent atoms. The permanent atoms still vibrate at the same frequency as in the previous life and are permeated with the consciousness, the energy vibration, of those levels.

At the beginning of subsequent incarnations, when the vehicles are ready, the soul forms its mental, astral and physical sheaths. The accumulated knowledge and experience, gained over a succession of previous lives, flows down from the soul level to the physical brain, which retains as much as it can consciously absorb, use and know. This knowledge cannot really be tapped until the brain centres have been sufficiently awakened to be used in this way. Where this does occur, we have what we call 'a genius.' In the soul are mirrored the Monad or Spiritual Will, Buddhi, spiritual intuition, and Manas, the higher mind. A genius is able to attune him or herself to the soul level and to that of manasic or buddhic consciousness, or thinking. This is the source of that higher knowledge and superior talent held in store from experience in previous lives. A genius, therefore, is someone who has a close and instantaneous contact with the soul, and can bring the wisdom and knowledge from that level down into the physical brain because the brain centres, which in most people remain unused, have been opened. (Oct. '82)

I am disturbed by information that I read in *Share International* and would appreciate a clarification. In the article by Aart Jurriaanse (Vol. 5, No. 3) I read that the personality "will disintegrate and be absorbed into the etheric world at the death of the form" (body). If the part that now identifies as 'Me' is to dissolve, and be no more, why should I put forth effort in spiritual practice that will benefit a soul that intends to dissolve 'Me,' along with the body, at death? (Apr. '86)

This question points precisely to the major reason for people's fear of death: the thought of dissolution, the fear that 'I' will be no more, and is the result of identification with the 'wrong' or limited part of oneself. The personality is not the self, but a temporary reflection of the Self or soul, changing at each new incarnational experience until it truly reflects the soul nature. In fact, at death there is a greater, more intense sense of the Self, a greater freedom than is possible for anyone without continuity of consciousness, that is, with no break in consciousness between the life-death-life states.

How does the soul maintain its identity throughout the various incarnations? Or does it, in any ordinary sense of the word? (Apr. '85)

The soul is the consciousness aspect in the threefold Being (spirit-soul-personality) that we call man, and is the source of the sense of identity. However, it is only on the personality level that the sense of separate, personal identity pertains. The soul has no sense of separation but is conscious (although in a totally impersonal way) through its vehicle, the causal body, of each incarnational endeavour and achievement or non-achievement.

How do we (our souls) make sure that we do not 'lose ground' or slip backwards when out of incarnation and return less evolved? (Mar. '86)

The physical, astral and mental vehicles each have one permanent atom, which becomes the nucleus of the new body on each plane. The soul magically forms around the permanent atom bodies of matter—physical, astral and mental—whose atoms vibrate to the same frequency as the permanent atoms. This ensures that we start a new incarnation at exactly the point reached at the end of the previous one.

How do our souls occupy their time while we are in incarnation? (July/Aug. '84)

It is the soul, not the personality, which is in incarnation. On the soul level, time does not exist (so the soul has no need to occupy itself, or to keep busy to avoid boredom!). Cyclically, the soul meditates on That of which the soul is a reflection—the Monad or Spirit—and, again cyclically, it turns its attention on its own reflection, the human personality.

Your answer to the previous question, which is a very deep one, reminds me of an answer given by the Source of *A Course in Miracles* which, when asked if reincarnation is a fact, answers in an indirect manner: Since there is no time (on a higher level), there cannot really be reincarnation (though the Source goes on to say that the concept is not harmful if it reminds people of the continuity of existence). I interpret your answer to mean: Souls live on a timeless level. Incarnation is a reflection or projection of soul on a time plus personality basis. But, if that is so, I cannot fit

the first sentence of your answer: "It is the soul, not the personality, which is in incarnation"—nor am I quite sure how karma works. Am I right in thinking that the soul absorbs karmic influences during a lifetime, then between two lives 'processes' these, as it were, to enable it to do its next choice properly.? (Jan./Feb. '85)

It is true that I believe that the soul lives on a timeless level, an ever-present Now. Nevertheless, its body of manifestation, the causal body, which exists on the highest of the four mental planes, is the receptacle for all the experiences of its reflection—that is, the man or woman in incarnation—throughout all lives. It is this total experience which eventually becomes open to the physical brain around the time of the fourth initiation, when the causal body is shattered, it being no longer needed. By "it is the soul, not the personality, which is in incarnation," I mean it is the soul which makes the conscious choice of reflecting itself downwards onto the physical, astral and mental planes, working through the personality, and which is the conveyor of the life principle and consciousness to that personality. When the body dies, it is at the decision of the soul, which then withdraws that life force. The soul, as I understand it, is aware of the action of karma—cause and effect—but it is in fact the *Lords of Karma* who make the decisions about how that karmic law actually works out in any given life. To this the soul responds co-operatively, so to speak, by arranging the life situation, etc., of its various incarnational periods. Time, as you know, is a concept of the physical brain and has no existence outside the physical plane. It would appear that our most advanced physicists are coming to this conclusion too.

Why does the spirit of the deceased sometimes 'float' around for years before it reincarnates? The best example of this is given by citing one of your own teachings, that Jesus of Nazareth died in 9 AD and in the year 16 AD rein-

carnated as Apollonius of Tyana. Thus, Jesus was spiritually adrift for approximately seven years. What did his spirit do during this seven-year interval? Was Jesus seen in spectral form by any human bystanders (or any of his followers) during these seven years? (July/Aug. '86)

I am afraid there is a misunderstanding of what I wrote about Jesus of Nazareth and His reincarnation as Apollonius of Tyana. Jesus was out of incarnation for approximately seven years, but was not, as you put it, "spiritually adrift." In the previous article I attempted to show the various levels of experience in which a person can be involved after so-called death. Jesus, then a fourth-degree initiate, was not "adrift" in any sense at all, but worked closely with his Master, the Christ, and his fellow initiates on the inner planes during those seven years. For a part of that time he was in *pralaya*—a kind of equivalent to the Christian idea of Paradise, a state of constant bliss. He was not seen in any "spectral" form by any humans during those seven years because he did not walk the earth. Ghosts or "spectral" forms are the exception rather than the norm, and they occur only with relatively unevolved individuals, tied to the physical plane by some strong desire or emotional experience such as violent death, etc. The 'normal' thing is for people to leave the physical plane completely soon after death.

Where is the information of our previous incarnations stored? (Jan./Feb. '85)

In the causal body, the vehicle of the soul, to be found on the highest of the four mental planes.

Why is it that normally we do not remember our previous lives and what is the mechanism which prevents us? (Jan./Feb. '85)

It is because we do not possess continuity of consciousness (that is, from 'life' through 'death' to 'life' again). For a few weeks or months (depending on the individual child) the baby does indeed remember its previous life, but this quickly fades as the impressions of the outer world impinge more and more on its consciousness. Although it is by no means always the case, by the time the third initiation is being taken, continuity of consciousness is beginning to be established. Eventually, at the fifth initiation, total recall of all past experiences is achieved.

When out of incarnation do we have total recall of past life experience? (Apr. '84)

Momentarily, yes. There is a point in which the personality consciousness finds itself face to face with the Angel of the Presence, the Solar Angel, the soul. In that brief encounter (seen from our time experience) the whole of the past life is seen in terms of its value to the soul and whether the soul's purposes have been fulfilled or not.

From many accounts of death and dying it would appear that the dying seem to 'see' deceased relatives or friends (invisible to others present); is this hallucination or wish-fulfillment? Do they in fact see anyone? (Oct. '85)

There is no reason to believe that this phenomenon is simply hallucination or wish-fulfillment. The dead are indeed met and greeted "on the other side of the veil" by those loved ones who have preceded them. There is every reason to believe, therefore, that the dying do see these friends in advance of their death.

Why is it that the spirits of the dead sometimes make appearances in a spectral form which is similar to the physical form of the previous incarnation? For example, someone reports having seen (at a seance) the 'ghost' of Winston Churchill several years after his death. Please explain this. (July/Aug. '86)

What you call the 'spirits of the dead'—in other words 'ghosts'—take the physical form of the previous incarnation through the power of the thoughtform of their personal physical identity. This is true in every case. In fact, the Masters Themselves, in building Their body of manifestation, the *mayavirupa*, do so in the thoughtform of Themselves in the incarnation in which They achieved Masterhood.

With regard to the 'ghost' of Winston Churchill being seen several years after his death, this is completely erroneous. Winston Churchill was a third degree initiate in that life, and in no circumstances would he appear as a 'ghost' at any seance. On death he would immediately rise to the higher mental planes, inaccessible to a seance. (These seances are fraught not so much with fraud as with illusion.)

Is there any value in praying for the souls of the departed, for example to uplift them onto a higher plane if their destiny is on a lower one? I doubt it because the Bible says we are judged "according to our measure," and "as we reap so shall we sow." But again it says, "pray for one another." Is this meant to include departed souls? (May '85)

To my understanding, there is no way we can influence the destiny of a departed soul once death has occurred (at least after three days have elapsed). The value of prayer is for persons remaining on the physical plane. Prayers for and with a person about to undergo transition, however, can be helpful to focus his or her attention on the soul level and so increase the spiritual tension required to reach the higher planes. Praying for "one another" on the physical plane is always beneficial.

If someone cannot be healed and they are in great suffering and pain, do they have the right to end their physical suffering by suicide? (June '85)

Yes, they certainly have the right. That is not to say it would be a wise thing to do. Who is to say what the next day will bring in relief?

The Laws Governing Reincarnation

The important factor in relation to the incarnational process is that we incarnate, not individually, but in groups. While, of course, individual incarnation does take place, it is only incidental to the greater event of group rebirth. Group rebirth proceeds cyclically, according to certain laws governing the manifestation of energies or Rays, and connected also with the point in evolution of the groups involved.

The question is often posed about the length of time between incarnations, and a great deal of information has been published on this, much of it erroneous and necessarily speculative. The fact is that there are enormous differences in the length of periods out of physical manifestation, both of individuals and of groups. Some souls have an extraordinarily rapid cycle of incarnations and 'pralayas,' while others spend aeons between each incarnational experience and the next. There is no 'average' time (remembering always that we are speaking about physical-plane time; outside the physical brain, time does not exist). However, it is possible to give a generalized picture which (with many variations) accounts for the incarnational pattern of three main groups within humanity, under the impact of three Laws.

The masses today are, largely, focused in the emotional-astral vehicle—their consciousness is still mainly that of the Atlantean or fourth root race, whose evolutionary goal was the perfection of the astral body. Many millions now in incarnation were part of the Atlantean race and still demonstrate powerfully the emotional tendencies of that race.

For them, the less advanced, the period out of incarnation is usually short. Being 'young,' as egos, they still have much to learn, and are drawn magnetically into physical-plane life by the thought-forms which bind them to the earth plane and by the karmic ebb and flow which has arisen on earth. They do not have much say in the matter themselves, but, under the Law of Evolution, they are cyclically impelled, again and again, to incarnate, to learn, to experience, and by trial and error, pain and suffering, to make eventually the free choice: the conscious return out of matter back to spirit and liberation.

Those who are somewhat more evolved tend to stay for a longer period out of incarnation, owing to the fact that they have not created such strong earthly ties and are more flexible, freer, with more mental focus. Also, they need more time to absorb and assimilate (because of their richer personality experience) that which can only be taken up and assimilated on the higher planes, out of incarnation.

As I have already said, more evolved egos spend a greater or lesser period of 'time' in *pralaya*, a state of existence between death and rebirth in which there is no impulse to incarnate again. *Pralaya*, or the experience in *devachan*, corresponds to the Christian idea of paradise. There these souls will wait, sometimes for short periods, sometimes for untold ages, until the need arises for the presence of that particular group on the physical plane.

All souls are on one or other of seven streams of energy—the seven rays—and as these rays come into manifestation, so too do groups of souls on these rays. These more advanced egos do not come in individually, nor are they swept in blindly under the Law of Evolution as are their less advanced brothers. They incarnate under *group law* for a certain purpose, under the influence of a specific ray energy, and in connection with some aspect of the Plan. Each generation brings into incarnation a group equipped with the knowledge and ability to deal, more or less, with the problems of that period. In this way, the Plan is gradually developing and unfolding through the work of successive groups coming into incarnation again and again, groups who may well disappear out of incarnation for aeons at the end of an era.

There are never more than four rays in manifestation at any given time, so that in any period we may look for four different ray types in incarnation. For instance, the majority of individuals now in incarnation are 2nd, 3rd, 5th, and 6th ray souls. The 6th ray of devotion or abstract idealism is fast moving out of manifestation so that 6th ray souls will also gradually pass out of physical plane life and enter *pralaya* until 'required' again. An increasing number of 7th ray souls will take rebirth over the next 2000-year period, because the 7th ray of ceremonial order will prevail during the coming era. These groups become channels for, and exponents of, the particular ray energy and so can work easily in response to its stimulus.

There is another group which comes into incarnation very quickly: the most advanced individuals, the disciples and initiates. Neither the Law of Evolution nor Group Law governs their return, but another law impels them to rebirth: the Law of Service. They choose consciously to incarnate of their own free will. Because they know and wish to serve the Plan, they decide, under the assignment of their own personal Master or not, how best they can serve. But because they are initiates, the Master, who knows the path which will lead them to their goal, watches over them and advises when they should return into certain environments and circumstances. The initiate will also want to return then to continue where he or she left off, in order to be of further service. They repeatedly and quickly take incarnation to work through the last few steps of the Path of Initiation. The aim of the initiate is to work off karma rapidly and so become free and equipped for service. The soul impresses its vehicle with this desire during incarnation and so obviates any desire of the disciple for the bliss of *pralaya* in *devachan*.

Another reason for rapid cycles of incarnation may be the necessity of 'rounding out' the disciple's equipment by concentrating one-pointedly for several lives on acquiring some quality otherwise lacking, or to contribute some special quality, perfectly developed in him, to the work of a particular group or nation.

Every soul incarnates and reincarnates under the Law of Rebirth. Groups of souls come in together in order to work out karma created in the past. Hence, this law provides the opportunity to repay ancient debts, to recognize and work with old friends, to accept ancient responsibilities and obligations, and to bring to the surface for re-use talents and qualities acquired long ago. What beauty and order there is, therefore, in this law which governs our appearance on this plane.

To summarize, we can say that reincarnation depends on the particular destiny of the individual. If he or she is not sufficiently developed, there is no destiny as yet; the individual is simply drawn back into incarnation. When the man or woman has progressed somewhat further, his or her destiny becomes a group destiny. In the case of a disciple or initiate, however, the cycles of incarnation are governed by individual destiny and, above all, by the desire to serve. (Dec. '82)

How does the soul make its choice as to where, when and to whom it will be born? (Apr. '85)

It depends on the evolution of the soul. Under the Law of Evolution, unevolved souls are drawn magnetically to the prepared bodies through karmic necessity; they have little choice. More advanced humanity, coming in under Group Law, are attracted to particular family and national groups (with which they have karmic connections) according to the world's need for such groups' energies at a particular time. Initiates enter under the Law of Service and choose (with the help of their Master) the family, conditions, etc., which will allow them best to serve in their special way.

Did we choose our families as babies in order to be put into a situation in which the desire to serve would grow, because of that particular situation, say, having been born to alcoholic parents, etc.

The soul is not so much concerned with the parents' mode of life in which it chooses to incarnate. What it is concerned with is ray structures, that is, energy patterns, position in society, and above all, their points of evolution. The family chosen provides the field of experience for a soul at a given point in evolution, with particular purposes and also with particular limitations determined by his own ray structure. All of this is taken note of by the soul in choosing a family.

The family relationship is not so crucial for the masses, but with advanced units of humanity it begins to be much more crucial. With the most advanced, the disciples and initiates, it is absolutely crucial. With advanced individuals, the soul is aided by the Master in choosing a family.

How do disciples and initiates choose their parents for incarnation?

The major factor in that case is the point in evolution of the soul seeking incarnation, and of the parents. The parents will provide a body of a particular vibrational rate which that soul needs to perform his service activity in the world. There would be no possibility of a third degree initiate taking incarnation with parents who were relatively unevolved. There has to be a degree of similarity of vibration. Also, what would be the point of a third degree initiate incarnating among the least evolved of humanity? He has a gift to give. He has the experience as a soul and the radiance as an initiate to give out to the world. If he tried to do that in unresponsive circumstances, the whole purpose would be lost. So the crucial thing is the point in evolution.

Is one always karmically related to all the members of one's family? (Apr. '85)

Usually, but not always. From time to time 'new blood' is brought into most families. Of course, new karmic ties are being formed all the time.

Why must reincarnation be so incestuous—for instance, "You are my husband now, last time you were my mother," and that kind of thing?

For many people, rebirth takes place under group law. It is this which accounts for the fact that close family relations, with permutations, are repeated again and again. This provides the opportunities to repay karmic debts, right old wrongs, renew working partnerships and so on. The fact that relationships are so "incestuous" shows the need for harmlessness in all relationships.

If souls incarnate in groups, does one choose parents who have the same soul ray as one's own? (Jan./Feb. '85)

It is usually the case that parents and children have the same soul ray but this is by no means always the case.

How does the mechanism, if any, work which decides that one is to be born as a boy or a girl? (Mar. '83)

It is the soul which decides. According to its purpose in any particular life, the soul creates its vehicle of expression on the physical plane in all respects. We really are an expression of our soul. On the soul plane there is neither male nor female, and the division of the sexes on this level is but a reflection of the polarities of the Father-Mother God whose union brings us as souls into being. Through repeated experience as both male and female, we eventually bring both these aspects into equilibrium.

In an age of surrogate mothers and sperm banks, is the soul's job made more difficult to discover its desired parents? (Jan./Feb. '85)

No. An advanced soul, at least, will choose to be born only to those parents with whom it has karmic connection.

Can we consciously choose our parents, sex, country, etc., for our next life? (Jan./Feb. '85)

No. These choices are made by the incarnating entity, the soul, in accordance with its purpose(s).

Can a parent obtain an indication of his or her child's soul purpose for the current lifetime by studying the astrological rising sign and aspects to that position? (Jan./Feb. '85)

No. What can usefully be learned from such a study are the particular forces likely to be influencing the soul in that life. Of course the relevance of that information when applied will depend on the point of evolution of the child.

Do some incarnating souls change their minds shortly after birth, thus accounting for some of the sudden infant deaths that occur among seemingly healthy children? (Jan./Feb. '85)

It is not a question of the soul "changing its mind" in such cases, but of the personality refusing the new experience, perhaps because of a particularly strainful incarnation immediately before.

What happens to a soul that doesn't develop over several lifetimes? (July/Aug. '85)

It may need, and receive, some special karmic stimulus. We live in a cyclic Cosmos, a cyclic world; we create in cycles, live our life in cycles. Likewise, the soul manifests itself cyclicly. It does so in such a way as to get the best result for its intention and purpose. When its reflection, the personality, is not making very much progress, perhaps for a number of incarnations, the soul may place its vehicle into a situation of adversity, of limitation. This would then generate tension, and therefore the needed progress, because there is never progress without tension. Advance is always the result of spiritual tension. Spiritual tension is that motivating force which leads to release and renewed activity.

Do we tend to be born in the same country or continent again or are we migrating? If so, are we doing so in groups as well? (July/Aug. '85)

There is no general rule, except that we incarnate in groups. A person or group may be born in the same country or continent again and again and then have a series of incarnations in many different locations.

There seems to be something contradictory in your statement that souls incarnate in groups (or families or races) and reports from people who remember former lives, for instance during regressive hypnosis. These people often declare that they remember lives in which they have been a white man or woman, an African, Chinese, Indian, etc. (Mar. '83)

There really is no contradiction. While the tendency is for family groups to incarnate more or less in the same area of the world for many centuries, this is by no means always the case, and much to-ing and fro-ing takes place. For instance, the Master D.K. has stated that the British people are largely reincarnations of the Romans, and that many present day British were Indian in former lives while many present day Indians were British in former lives.

Why is it that some people seem to carry their physical or racial characteristics from previous lives so clearly in their present physical vehicle; for example some people, although white Europeans of British stock, look very oriental? (June '83)

While it is possible to carry physical characteristics over from previous lives it is really rather rare. There are no pure races today. The races and the nationalities are made up of an unbelievable admixture which has been created over long periods of time. When we see Europeans with oriental characteristics we are usually seeing the result of racial mixture, rather than the result of previous incarnations. The rare cases occur when very advanced disciples incarnate, perhaps for the first time, in situations quite different from a long series of incarnations elsewhere.

In a specific life as a Westerner, could it still be visible that one was from Asia or Africa in a previous incarnation? (Jan./Feb. '85)

In physical characteristics, no, but in ways of thought, general approach to the world, yes.

Is it possible to incarnate without one of the bodies or vehicles—etheric-physical, astral or mental—and if so how can we ensure the cohesiveness of the physical activity? (Mar. '86)

No, it is not possible to incarnate without all the lower vehicles. At the stage now reached by humanity, all the vehicles would be present—although their levels of development might be different.

What determines how much time there is between incarnations? (July/Aug. '85)

Karma and destiny. In a word, the Plan. It depends on one's point in evolution and soul ray. Not all rays are in manifestation at any one time.

Now that evolution is being stepped up, is the time between incarnations being shortened: (1) for disciples; (2) for the general populace? (July/Aug. '85)

(1) Yes. (2) Not yet.

Is there such a thing as reincarnation in the deva world as well? How does procreation in the deva world take place?

The deva evolutions are not in dense physical manifestation so there is no incarnation (and therefore reincarnation) as such, but successive waves of activity and rest. Also, devas are either sub-human, and therefore not individualized, or super-human and conscious, individualized entities. Myriads of elemental and devic lives make up the body of expression of an oversouling Devic Lord. Procreation, or rather, creation, takes place by the action of the oversouling Deva.

Christianity and Reincarnation

During Biblical times, was reincarnation widely accepted? (July/Aug. '85)

Yes, this would appear to be so. (See the article, "Reincarnation and Karma in the Bible" in the special issue of *Share International*, Vol. 4. Nos. 1/2 p.16.)

Since we know that the idea of reincarnation has been around for a long time, how did it get lost? Christian churches seldom teach it. (June '85)

Of course this concept has never been lost in the Orient. In the West, however, it would appear to have been commonly accepted until the 6th century AD. Many of the early Christian teachers and theologians, Origen (185-253 AD) in particular, laid great emphasis on this basic law of rebirth. It was the Emperor Justinius who forced the Church Fathers at the 5th Ecumenical Council in 553 AD to proclaim this teaching anathema. This ban has, unfortunately, become part of the established church teachings.

What effects do you foresee the acceptance of reincarnation having on the Western world? (Sept. '85)

It seems obvious that a true realization of the implications of reincarnation (and not simply an intellectual acceptance) will transform the whole Western approach to reality. The idea that life is not short, brutish and arbitrary; that there is purpose and plan; that we are undergoing a process of gradual perfectionment; above all that the great Law of Cause and Effect governs our existence, must change our viewpoint. The need for right human relationships, for harmlessness, will become abundantly clear.

Reincarnation, Karma and Past Lives

[This article is an edited transcription of a talk given by Benjamin Creme at Ubbergen, Holland, 16 February 1986.]

In the world today, there are really three approaches to the idea of reincarnation.

A two-fold one in the West, where the idea itself is almost non-existent: either a belief in the transmigration of souls—that you could be a human being in one life and an animal in the next, and therefore that there is great danger in swiping flies and treading on ants because it could be your grandmother—or simply an interest in past lives. That is almost the sole interest in the concept of rebirth in the West.

In the East, broadly speaking, people do believe in reincarnation. And, correctly, in relation to the Law of Karma. Unfortunately, even in the East, the Law of Karma is seen from an erroneous point of view. Of course, here and there, both in East and West, there is a correct interpretation and approach to the idea of rebirth, and its close connection with the Law of Action and Reaction, Cause and Effect.

In the Orient, most people believing in the Law of Karma accept that they are who and where they are because of their actions in a previous life—which is true; but unfortunately they think they can do nothing about changing their particular situation—which is not true.

In the West, we tend to think that we are totally in control of our destiny (we are to some extent), but that there is no greater law governing our destiny, which is not true. There is a misunderstanding, East and West, about the Law of Karma and its working out through the Law of Rebirth.

The Westerner tends to reject the idea of a future life. It is an idea which is only just beginning to engage people's minds. If he thinks about it at all, he really thinks about it in terms of "if I have a future life, I must have had a past life; and if I had a past life it is interesting to know who I was." The popular

"if I have a future life, I must have had a past life; and if I had a past life it is interesting to know who I was." The popular literature in the West about reincarnation is almost exclusively about previous existences. There are now many techniques—authentic or otherwise—advertised and used to take people back into an experience of their past lives: hypnosis, rebirthing, and so on. Of course, there is much serious research on the subject going on in several countries. The work of Professor Ian Stevenson and others is adding much evidence pointing to the likelihood of the fact of reincarnation. But is it so desirable to know our past lives? I think if most of us really knew our past lives there are one or two things we might be a bit ashamed of, and maybe would prefer not to know.

There is a little-known law that when we become truly aware of our past life we enter into the karma of that time. Most of us have a heavy enough load of karma to deal with in this life without an unnecessary load from some previous one, which happily we are not yet called upon to resolve.

Needless to say, you will always find clairvoyants. The channel, the sensitive, is only too happy—for a price—to look into your past and to tell you your previous lives, but how do you know if they are right or wrong? In what possible way can you verify what any so-called clairvoyant tells you? It is better for you to keep your money. If you are told that in a previous life you were important and powerful (it is usually some king, queen, priestess), a priestess in Egypt, say, how can you prove this? And are you, today, at least the equivalent in importance, influence and power in the world, contributing something original and creative to life?

It is also the easiest thing in the world to be mistaken in our own 'memories.' Let me illustrate with an instance from my own experience which rose in my consciousness during a profound meditation lasting about five hours. I saw myself (it did not look like me now but I recognized myself nevertheless) as a minister of religion during religious persecutions somewhere in Europe around the 1650's. My church looked on to a square. I stood on the steps outside the church listening to the shrieks and cries of pain and terror. I knew what it meant: the Protestants were being set upon by the soldiery and put to the sword. From a road at one corner of the square the people came running, screaming, chased by the soldiers. Diagonally across the square and into the church they ran, seeking sanctuary. I stood in the church entrance, a very tall, broad figure in a long black cassock, urging the terrified people into the church. The soldiers came up the steps, stabbing and laying about them with their swords. I was not at all afraid (I looked, as I remember now, to have had a first ray physical) but held my arms out sideways to block their passage. I said: "This is a holy place." To my surprise, they were not the least impressed and one ran me through with his sword. I can see it vividly now—this tall, broadly built man and the sword through his chest. I fell and can still clearly feel the sensation of the hard, cold stone on my cheek as I lay dying on the steps of my church. For years, I believed I had remembered in total clarity, like a film, my last minutes of a previous life and it was not until about ten years ago that I learned from my Master that the experience was real, had happened, but not to me. It was nothing to do with me; I had never lived near that town or been the minister in the black cassock. It was a clairvoyant experience of the death of someone closely related to me on the soul plane. So how do you know what you are picking up? How can you be sure?

Eastern people have a different point of view. They are not so worried about *who* they were in their past life. They believe that if they are poor, hungry, miserable, indebted to the landlord, with hardly enough to feed their family, they were someone really terrible before. They believe it is the Law of Karma, because they were so bad, nasty, horrible, such low-grade human beings in their past life, they deserve the misery they are in now. They believe that; it is the teaching. And they believe, because it is the Law of Karma, that there is nothing they can do about it. They accept it totally, fatalistically, as their due according to the Law. They also believe that if they accept their lot meekly and try to be 'good' they will be rewarded with a higher status next time round. If there is one thing which has kept the Orient down, in terms of its living standards, its social happiness, social democracy and equality, it is the acceptance of the Law of Karma on that basis. There is nothing to prevent the untouchables of India from transforming their lives except the acceptance that their untouchability is due to their misdeeds in former lives. Some kind of balance has to be reached, both from the Eastern and Western viewpoint, in approach to these two great laws: the Law of Karma, Cause and Effect, and the Law of Rebirth, its corollary.

The Law of Cause and Effect is the basic law governing our existence in this solar system and is the outcome of the action of the energy of the 'alter ego' of our system, the constellation Sirius. Just as our personalities are acting out, more or less well, the intentions of ourselves as souls, so this solar system acts under the intentions of Sirius as its 'soul.' To put it more succinctly, the relationship between Sirius and this solar system is the same as the relationship between our soul and its reflection, the personality. Every thought, every action that we have and make, sets into motion a cause. These causes have their effects. These effects make our lives, for good or ill. We are now, have been, and will go on, making our lives from moment to moment. Sooner or later, the causes set into motion by our thoughts and actions will produce effects which will rebound on us; and we will experience that as 'good' or 'bad' karma. When it is uncomfortable we call it bad karma. And when it is good karma, when life is comfortable, easy, we do not notice it. We take it as our right, our due, because that is what we expect life to be like. People really only talk about karma when they mean bad karma. It is important to realize and remember that we have more 'good' karma than 'bad' karma.

Like all laws, the Law of Karma is under the control, the jurisdiction, of certain entities—in this case, the Lords of Karma. The Lords of Karma are like cosmic judges. They look at this action and reaction of causes and effects which we set in motion, and they regulate this according to our needs as evolving souls. Our souls incarnate in a personality with a given structure of energies, rays, which relate to the karma and the possibilities of that particular incarnation. The souls co-operate with the Lords of Karma to decide, you might think, what pain or pleasure we will suffer in any particular life. That, of course, is precisely the wrong way to describe what happens. The soul is not at all interested, nor are the Lords of Karma, in our pleasure or our suffering. These are simply psychological reactions to events. What they are interested in is the working out of the Law, the cosmic Law of Cause and Effect. Also, the soul has its own purposes for every given incarnation. It provides itself with a vehicle, the personality, with mental, emotional and physical bodies which will provide the possibility for its intentions being achieved in that particular life. That purpose might not be achieved, but the soul provides the possibility. The soul lives ever in hope!

The ultimate aim is to live life in such a way that we make no personal karma. We can do that either by being perfect or by being dead. Since being perfect is much more interesting than being dead, most people accept the premise of trying, more or less, to achieve the soul's purpose and staying to the last possible moment to do so. Thus, we work with this burden of karma which we have ourselves created in the present and past lives. We try, consciously or unconsciously, to become perfect. We have no control over the events of life. The only thing we can control is our reaction to these events. So the aim is to achieve such a measure of detachment from events that we can control ourselves.

In this way we cope with the burden of karma in any given incarnation. This is not a case of sitting in a catatonic stupor, so that we do nothing and therefore create no karma. What we can do, in every event, in every situation, is distance ourselves from that event. Looking at the event as being out there, with ourselves here, and not react. In this way we gradually create an impersonality in relation to life, a detachment in relation to events, where we become indifferent to whether our karma is 'good' or 'bad.'

Correctly seen, evolutionary life is a gradual renunciation of the lower for the sake of the higher. As a soul in incarnation, a high level of divinity has incarnated at a lower level of divinity. The journey to perfection, the evolutionary goal, is the gradual renunciation of these lower levels by embodying, at these lower levels, the higher; becoming more and more what one essentially is as a soul. The soul makes its journey into incarnation over aeons of time, and then back, out of the need to incarnate. The path of return for the soul is the gradual release of itself from the limitations of the physical, astral, and mental planes. This is done by infusing its vehicles, physical, emotional and mental, with its energies and qualities.

Two things are going on at the same time in this process. One is the gradual spiritualizing of the vehicle by the soul. The other is the burdening of the vehicle, intentionally, by the soul, to burn up ancient karma. As the soul progresses in its incarnational experience, so its reflection, the man or woman in incarnation, receives a heavier and heavier burden of karma. Until in the last incarnation of all, but one, in which the person will be a fourth degree initiate, the burden is at its heaviest. It is for this reason that the fourth initiation is called in the West, the Crucifixion; in the East, the Great Renunciation. In that experience everything, all the lower aspects, are being renounced in favour of the higher spiritual reality. That is why the life of the fourth degree initiate is usually, from the world's point of view, painful, heavy indeed. People imagine that, as a man or woman progresses in evolution, he or she should become freer and freer of karma. The opposite is true. Not only that, but as a man or woman becomes a disciple, becomes initiate, a world-server, he or she takes more and more of the weight of world karma. They are the upholders of the world. Their shoulders are, and need to be, broad. Imagine a bridge over a river, and the river is the world and its karma. The disciples and initiates are the pillars of the bridge, and the spaces in between are the masses of people. Where there are spaces the water flows easily through, the pillars of the bridge take the force of the flood, of the water. In a very real sense, the disciples and initiates of the world support the world. That is one reason why the life of the disciple is, from the average man's point of view, a very difficult life to lead. But of course he is governed by the great Law of Service.

Under this Law, disciples and initiates come very frequently into incarnation to serve world need and to finish off this earth experience as quickly as possible. Not to get it over with, but to serve the better. The more advanced a person is the more he can serve, the more useful he can be to the world. When a certain level is reached—that of third degree initiate—the relationship to the Law of Cause and Effect changes. Gradually the law is manipulated by the person himself. As a conscious divine soul, working in the world, he becomes really the pilot of his own plane. He may have a co-pilot, his Master, but he is the pilot. It is not an automatic thing, but gradually this point is achieved. He takes an active part in his own evolution, consciously working with the Law of Karma, under the control of his soul. Then it may come to pass that his previous lives will open up before his inner eye. As this happens, the karma of that time becomes open to him on the physical plane, which, of course, increases the burden of the initiate. The aim is that by the time the person is ready to take the fifth initiation and become a Master, all karma will have been resolved, burned up, taken back to the source from which it came.

How do you get rid of karma, how do you deal with it? You cannot give it away. It is too heavy, nobody wants it. There is no sale for excess karma; everyone has enough of their own. So what do you do, how can you cope with this burden that limits your activity, your joy, your happiness? There is a very simple method. It is called service. Service is the way 'par excellence' for getting rid of karma. Of course it does not get rid of it, but it burns it up. The process is something like this: as you serve you draw to yourself energy. By giving out energy, you get energy back; that is the law. Basically, it is the Law of Love, which governs our nature, without which the universe would not exist. It is of course, in another sense, the Law of Cause and Effect itself. As you give love, you set in motion a cause, the effect of which is the return of love.

The Law itself sets in motion its own fulfillment. As we serve, we demonstrate love. As we demonstrate love, by law, we get love. That strengthens and potentizes the individual in a way in which he can deal with his own karma. As the person progresses in love, in service, he is automatically distancing himself from the effect of events. The events take place, but they have less and less effect on his psychology. In the East they say: "it's my karma." In France they say: "c'est la vie." Gradually we have to develop an attitude of "c'est la vie." If it is good, easy, c'est la vie. If it is hard, difficult, painful, c'est la vie. We really have to live with that attitude.

To return to the subject of past lives. Is it of *value* to know our past lives? After a certain point: yes. Before that point, not only is it not of major value, it can actually be dangerous. And it is irresponsible for so-called clairvoyants to tell people about their past lives, even if they are correct. If they are wrong, people will still create thought-forms around that incorrect image of themselves. That makes for glamour, illusion. If they are right, the people involved become subject to the karma for which they may not yet be prepared.

There are occasions, in certain illnesses of a mental nature, which cannot be handled in any other way, in which it may be useful to go back to a previous life. These are relatively few, and the way is through hypnosis. The whole subject is fraught with danger and complexity. When our past lives enter spontaneously into our consciousness, they will do so under Law. It is actually more important to understand the Law as happening now, not in the past. Of course it is useful to know that you were a road-sweeper in the last life; it gives a sense of proportion. The more important thing is to know that at every moment we are making karma, we are creating our next life right now.

The Law of Karma is a great binding Law, but it is benign. Nobody receives more karma than their soul, and the Lords of Karma, know they can *usefully* handle. Some lives for some people are very hard, very painful, very limited indeed. From the point of view of the soul, this is probably intentional and useful, productive. The soul knows that by the burning in this way of a burden of karma from the past, greater progress can be made. What holds us back, what limits us, is our karma, our load of karma on our back. The efforts made in dealing with the karma pave the way for periods of growth. Our development proceeds thus in cycles.

The Law of Karma is not a mechanical law of punishment. If you hit somebody on the head, it is not inevitable that you will be hit on the head. It is not a question of an eye for an eye and a tooth for a tooth. It is simply the energetic outcome of previous causes set in motion by ourselves; all that we do will inevitably come back in some way or another. However, we *can* do something about it. The untouchables of India *can* change their lives. They are not bound by karma to be untouchables. That is a social structure, a class system, which binds people to particular stations in life. It is totally artificial and man-made. The poverty, the squalor, the degradation and the misery of people in the Third World is not necessary. It is not a result of karma, but of our greed. And we have the major responsibility to help them change these conditions and enter true living.

People think of karma as always from the past life, but what about yesterday's karma, or the day before, last week's, last month's karma? It is this succession of moments of action and reaction which today we are coping with, which tomorrow and in our next life we will cope with. Until we come into right relationship with each other and with the Whole of which we are a part, we will go on making bad karma. It is more important, more useful, to realize the benefit of right relationship, thus handling the Laws of Karma and Rebirth correctly, than to know our past lives. (July/Aug. '86)

Recall of Past Lives

Is there any use in knowing your former lives? Is there not a tendency to escape from difficulties in the present life to easier-to-cope-with former lives? (Jan./Feb. '85)

There is value in knowing former lives, if this can be done without getting lost in glamour. It can be illuminating and conducive to a sense of proportion. It gives a longer perspective to the evolutionary journey than mere theoretical belief in reincarnation.

I really do not think that a knowledge of previous lives provides a means of escape from present life difficulties. Someone who tries to escape from the present difficulties (probably most of us at some time or other) is going to do so whether past lives are known or not. And what if the remembered life was fraught with great difficulty and suffering? Would it then be a basis for escape?

I do believe, however, that in the West the new interest in reincarnation has centred almost exclusively in recall of past lives, with the harmful ensuing glamours which that has released. The important life is the one in which we find ourselves now.

People talk a lot about so-called deja-vu experiences. Have they necessarily to do with incarnational memories? (Jan./Feb. '85)

Sometimes these deja-vu experiences do indeed relate to previous life memories but as often as not this is not the case. There are many reasons for this sensation; very often it is the result of a lapse, and then regain, of attention when some person, place or happening makes a strong impression; in other words a 'memory' of a very recent event.

Is regression to supposed previous existences under hypnosis reliable? (Jan./Feb. '85)

No, not absolutely. Sometimes it would appear that the contacted experiences are true and provable (but not necessarily having happened to the person under hypnosis). At other times they have been proved not to have been possible in the manner described. So the question remains: what are we dealing with in these 'regressions'—reliving of previous lives, or clairvoyance and telepathy? I suggest it is sometimes the one, and sometimes the other.

If hypnosis works through relaxation, why would we not have spontaneous knowledge of former lives during the relaxation of sleep? (Jan./Feb. '85)

Indeed, spontaneous recall of former lives does sometimes take place during deep sleep, but, as with hypnosis, it is not reliable. The major content of dreams comes from the activity of the lower mind in light sleep phases. Hypnosis works not only through relaxation but, as in meditation, through a withdrawal of the attention from the outer world of the senses and a refocusing of the attention inwards (and, in meditation, upwards).

Is it advisable or even helpful to attempt to regain memories of past lives from reliable psychics? (Jan./Feb. '85)

It is certainly possible to attempt it but to my mind not advisable. After all, what is a 'reliable' psychic, and which recalled memory can be proved to be authentic?

Can some current fears and phobias—with seemingly no reason to exist—be better understood by knowing previous life experiences that originated them? (Jan./Feb. '85)

If the fears do originate in a previous existence then, of course, it would be of value to understand the circumstances of their arising. But the vast majority of our fears originate in this lifetime, whether or not we can see, consciously, their basis.

How can we be sure that even very clear and vivid images from a supposed former life are indeed real? Is it not very easy to be mistaken or misled here? (Jan./Feb. '85)

The simple answer is that we cannot be sure. It is very easy to mistake clear and definite images for one's former existences when they are, for example, being picked up telepathically from someone else. (I spent years believing that certain clear 'memories' received in deep meditation were recalls of my former lives until told quite otherwise by my Master.)

There have been stories of late about people who have 'slipped into another time frame.' Also about people who have suddenly vanished altogether. Would you comment please? (June '85)

If the questioner means, do I believe these stories, the answer is no. There is no such thing as 'another time frame' into which to 'slip.' Time is relative. It is an experience of the physical brain only and people can and do experience time differently or as non-existent—which is the true nature of 'time.'

What I do believe is that people believe the fantasies and formulae of science fiction (however interesting they may be) too readily!

Is it coincidence that people who do seem to remember former lives (apart from those who make up the memories themselves) have often been violently killed in that previous incarnation?(Jan./Feb. '85)

No. The shock of violent or sudden death frequently provides a source of tension which drives the memory downwards to the brain.

At which level of evolution would we definitely be aware of our previous lives? Even the third degree initiates (Churchill, Mao) do not seem to have done so. (Jan./Feb. '85)

Certainly by the fourth degree some previous lives would be recalled. The fifth degree Master has total recall of all past experience.

That third degree initiates like Churchill and Mao do not (we presume) recall past lives, or perhaps do not even believe in reincarnation, is not unusual. These 'men of action' are frequently so extroverted in their life activity that such soul knowledge would not be helpful to them. General Patton of the United States army, on the other hand, was both a man of action and a firm believer in reincarnation and claimed to remember previous lives (also as a soldier!).

Is it possible to know future lives? If so, does this imply that everything is, after all, pre-ordained? (Jan./Feb. '85)

Yes, it is possible to know future lives. Those who are familiar with Alice Bailey's *Discipleship in the New Age*,will remember the frequent references to the following lives (and ray structures) of certain disciples, and my Master has already given me my ray structure and indicated the general area of work in my next incarnation. Clairvoyance or pre-vision is not, of course, the monopoly of the Masters, but this whole area of clairvoyance is so saturated with glamour and illusion that I personally would believe only that of a Master.

Is everything, thus, preordained? In a sense, yes. Everything co-exists in the eternal Now (the Master and the soul see both ways, so-called past and so-called future). All possibilities exist in the eternal Now, but our acts, decisions and thoughts determine which of these possibilities precipitates, thus setting in motion the Law of Cause and Effect (or Karma).

How highly evolved do we need to be before we will be able to foresee one or more future incarnations? (July/Aug. '85)

Although this is by no means always so, a disciple between the second and third initiation may be able to see or be given an inkling of a future incarnation. This would not be possible at a lesser level.

Have some of us known the Christ in previous lives? (Nov. '82)

Yes, and He Himself has said as much in some of the Messages. Many have worked with Him before in previous lives, some when He manifested through Jesus. People will find they recognize Him—not His physical appearance, but His qualities. (In Palestine, He worked through the Master Jesus, but He does not look like Jesus.) There is no doubt that there are many in incarnation now who worked with the Christ before in Palestine or in India when He appeared as Shankaracharya and Krishna. Many will recognize certain qualities and, in fact, be drawn to Him because of that ancient karmic link. This will happen in both East and West.

Karmic Effects

Is there any way of telling whether suffering is caused by our karma or otherwise? (July/Aug. '85)

All suffering is the result of the action of the Law of Cause and Effect, and therefore karmic. By karmic, I think the questioner probably means stemming from long past action and this is frequently the case. But most of our suffering comes from our thoughts, actions and reactions of the present and immediate past. Our hatreds, fears, jealousies, envy, frustrations and (thwarted) ambitions cause us to suffer, moment to moment. This, too, is the action of karma. We misuse energy—soul, mental, astral and etheric—and so we suffer, through the Law of Cause and Effect, by such misuse. The desire principle has us in its grip, and only by controlling the desire principle—through the mind—can we overcome suffering. Most of our suffering is therefore self-inflicted and unnecessary. We share, however, in the karmic suffering of humanity as a whole, but that is something else, the human inheritance.

What is the function of the Lords of Karma? How do they work?

The Lords of Karma (there are four in our system) manipulate the Law of Cause and Effect. They determine the effects of that Law in our lives according to our individual karmic needs at any given time. Every thought and action that we make sets in motion a cause; the effects of these causes make our lives. We are reaping as we sow. Everything that happens to us is the result of the actions that we ourselves have taken, thoughts that we have had, in the past. This process is not haphazard but works out according to the action, the judgment, of the Lords of Karma. They are not judges in the legal sense of the word; they exercise judgement in the manipulation of the Law.

They do not inflict punishments, because no punishment is involved. They work with the the Law of Cause and Effect and simply manipulate the energies which are governed by the Law of Cause and Effect in such a way that—in total justice, not as punishment—the effects of our actions work out in our lives.

The Lords of Karma also work in relation to the planet Saturn, which governs this Law and is called, therefore, the Planet of Opportunity. Astrologically speaking, it provides the situations, which allow opportunities for learning experiences (which karmic reactions are), and therefore for renewed growth.

They also work very closely with the Lord of the World and the Hierarchy of this planet. When someone asks to be placed on my Master's healing list, the Master will sometimes say, "There is a karmic situation with which I cannot interfere. But it may be possible to appeal to the Lords of Karma, and I will do so through the Christ or the Buddha." I think the Masters must know in advance the likelihood that there is a good chance that some mitigating energy may be used on behalf of the person. Then the word comes back that divine intervention, perhaps by the Buddha or the Christ, may be made, which allows the healing to be given, or a situation changed in that person's life which would not otherwise be the case. Occasionally, the word comes back, "It is a case where the Law must govern and there is no way either the Lords of Karma or the Christ or the Master may interfere in the situation. The karma must go forward, and no healing can at present be given."

The Law is, I would say, both beautiful and just. It works under the Law of Love. Love is in the justice; justice is in the Love. There is beauty in that if we could but see its action, and how they manipulate it with the greatest Love. Perhaps, when we are Masters, we will see the beauty of it. At the present, all we can do is be thankful that the Lords of Karma exist, and remember that there is always more 'good' karma than 'bad' karma.

Does the same Law apply to humanity as a whole in the same manner?

Yes. And to the planets within a system, and to systems within the galaxies, and so on. As above, so below. There are greater Lords of Karma on a galactic level who manipulate the karma governing the galaxy, and the individual solar systems, and then of course, at our level, the humanity of this particular planet.

As Avatars, the Christ and the Buddha may be able to manipulate the energies functioning under the Law of Cause and Effect in such a way as still to carry out, in the long term, the plans, the purposes, the Will, of the Logos. If they were to allow too much interference with that Law, the Purpose of the Logos would not be carried out. The Logos of our planet must therefore work in accordance with His knowledge of the Plans of the Logos of the solar system. And the Solar Logos must work in relation to the Plans of the Logos of Sirius (the alter-ego of our solar system). And so, in some respects, the hands of the Lords of Karma are tied too. If an action created a change in the gradual working out of the Purpose of the Logos, that of the Solar Logos, and of the Logos of Sirius, it would not be allowed.

Obviously, small as we are, our actions would need to be colossal to affect such Plans. But they are dealing with the karma of 60 billion souls (there are 60 billion Monads on our planet). The effect of the action and reaction of these, together, is colossal. We are a reflection of the reflection of the Logos, and everything that we do and do not do, everything, every thought, every action, however small it is, adds up in total to an action on the part of humanity as a whole. It therefore affects the karma of humanity as a whole, and the infringement or otherwise of the Laws governing the evolutionary purpose of our planetary Logos. This relates to the evolutionary purpose of the Solar Logos, and the Galactic Logos, and so on. Everything we do, therefore, every thought and action, has a reaction, a reverberation somewhere in Cosmos.

How does karma work in relation to Hierarchical healing?

In a given situation, a Master can use a certain amount of energy under Law. In some cases, perhaps in a child, this will be enough to provide a total or partial cure. In other older or more severe cases, it may only prevent the worsening of the condition. When the karmic situation (which is dynamic) changes once more, more energy becomes available and is administered, with greater or lesser effect, as the case may be. This process is repeated until the patient is cured, or the disease alleviated to the degree that the total karma permits.

Is misfortune always retribution for past lives or can it be purely an opportunity for spiritual growth through overcoming suffering? (Jan./Feb. '85)

We are so used to functioning under the pleasure-pain syndrome that we tend to consider all painful experience as misfortune and as necessarily retribution for past misdeeds. The Law of Karma is not about retribution, but about cause and effect. Our life proceeds in cycles, some painful—representing opportunities for growth through understanding and gaining of detachment, and others relatively pleasurable, evolving easily on the gain of the previous struggle.

(1) Whatever can be the soul's gain or purpose to incarnate in the body of a mongol? (2) It is said that it is the parents' karma to get a mongol child—is it not as much

the karma of the child itself, or a matter of combined karma? (Jan./Feb. '85)

(1) In taking the body of a mongol child the soul seeks a limitation of its life to fit in with karma.

(2) This question reminds me of the question of the Disciples to Jesus about the blind child: "Did this child or its father sin that it was born blind?"—a clear implication of the acceptance of the doctrine of reincarnation at the time of Jesus. The karma pertains to the child itself, not the parents.

(1) Are physical handicaps always the result of karma? (2) Is it possible to use physical handicaps as a means to evolve faster, while there is no karma involved? (3) Is it inevitable for all of us to live, in one or more lives, with such physical handicaps—or are there other ways to deal with karmic debts? (Jan./Feb. '85)

(1) No, physical handicaps are quite frequently the result of straight-forward accidents at birth. Karma is not only reaction but action. New causes—which produce the effect, karma—are continually being set in motion.

(2) Yes. The effort involved in overcoming handicaps has often a great character-forming role, thus aiding evolution.

(3) No. There is no law which says we must all experience physical handicaps. Where they do have a karmic origin, however, they are frequently, though not always, the result of physical cruelty to others in the past.

Does the soul provides its vehicle with physical handicaps for a particular purpose?

There are certain limitations which the soul quite definitely seeks in incarnating. It might even seek a body with very severe handicaps in order precisely to limit it for that life, and in so doing burn up a burden of karma accumulated from previous lives, which may be holding back the evolution of the individual. It is often the case that, as the result of the tension generated by the overcoming of the limitations, the next life is one of great progress and development.

Since we are responsible for all our actions, including our thoughts, are our dreams creating karmic results as well? (July/ Aug. '84)

Yes. Dreams are the result of our lower mental and astral/emotional activity still active during sleep. They are very often, as you know, expressing unconscious desires and inhibited thought activity. These self-created thought-forms inevitably produce effects of some kind—and hence karmic reaction.

By punishing or disciplining ourselves can we work off karma?(Apr. '84)

No. We have to distinguish also between discipline and punishment. Self-punishment does nothing more than increase a sense of guilt which is a major obstacle to acquiring a heart pure and unclouded, able to experience love and joy. Self-discipline, on the other hand, is necessary to create the integration of the vehicles preparatory to initiation. A disciple is someone who is disciplined. The way to 'work off' karma is by service, altruistically undertaken.

It is said that we come into incarnation to improve previous relationships, and that we are related to the same people again and again. If so, should we not try to keep married no matter what happens? A divorce might help this time, but then we would have to undergo the same experience with the same person in another life. (Jan./Feb. '85)

Marriage is a man-made institution and its laws and customs vary from country to country. There is no karmic reason why a marriage should be kept intact "no matter what happens." It is the relationship, involving as often as not karmic ties, that matters, not the marriage as an institution. Karmic relationships do not necessarily involve marriage—otherwise we would all marry many more times than the average film star! The choice to marry or not is always made in this life by the people involved—it is not a karmic necessity. Similarly with the decision to end a marriage.

You have said that our present 'life situation' is due to our past karma. Is not then the present 'life situation' of the starving millions due to their past karma? Have they not been placed in that starving situation by reason of past misdeeds? If not, it would seem that the Law of Karma was not operating justly in this case. (Sept. '83)

I think we would all agree that no-one understands the working of the Law of Karma better than Maitreya, the Christ. Yet He has said: "These people die for no other reason than that they have the misfortune to be born in one part of the world rather than another." They are not "placed in that starving situation by reason of past misdeeds," but are brought into incarnation under group law. The family and tribal groups to which they belong have for centuries, probably, lived in these areas. They starve because we, the developed nations, usurp and waste three quarters of the world's food—because we can afford to pay the market price. Many developing countries export food, needed by their hungry citizens, to earn the 'hard currency' to pay for essential imports of oil and machine goods. Moreover, since most of the capital for development comes from abroad, most of the profits created by their developing industry likewise goes abroad. They can never catch up since the rich nations dictate the rules of international commerce—in their own favour. So the fault is not in their 'past misdeeds' but in our greed and lack of sharing, whereby we in the West are generating a great burden of karma for the whole world. Karma is an active, not passive process in which we all share responsibility.

Why may not the Masters use Their supernatural powers to save from starvation vast masses of humanity in the drought-stricken areas since you have said that the prevailing hunger and suffering are not the result of their bad karma. (May '85)

The saving from starvation of millions in the Third World requires only ordinary 'powers' and is the responsibility of humanity as a whole. For the Masters to use 'supernatural' powers to end the starvation would be an interference with our free will, and against the karmic law. Any reader of *Share International* will realize that the starvation in Ethiopia, for example, is unnecessary—foreseen and warned against for years by the aid agencies, and is the result, not simply of drought (an 'act of God') but of poverty and political machinations. Humanity must learn to identify with all branches of the human family and act as brothers, through sharing, to save itself.

Are there ever exceptional circumstances in which one person by free will or otherwise can pay off the bad karma of another? (Sept. '84)

Broadly speaking, no. However, there are times in which an Avatar directly, or working through a disciple, can indeed 'take on,' or in other ways mitigate, the karma of another.

Do animals have karma? (July/Aug. '85)

Yes, not personal or individual karma (they are not individualized), but they share the group karma of the animal kingdom.

It has become widespread to put an animal 'to sleep' by injection for humane reasons. Does this abrupt termination of life influence in some way the animal's karma and/or the owner's karma? (June '85)

No. If done humanely and without cruelty or ulterior motive, no negative karma is involved.

Abortion

At which moment during pregnancy does the soul ("life") enter the body of the unborn child? (Mar. '83)

Around the fourth week the soul puts down a thread of energy through which it vitalizes the prospective vehicle. Around the fourth month the soul really 'grasps' the foetus and activates powerfully its physical life. This is the 'quickening' which every mother experiences. From then on, the movement of the child is very pronounced.

What effect does abortion have on the reincarnating soul? (Jan./Feb. '85)

Obviously, it prevents incarnation! This might well be a good thing in preventing the premature incarnation of an immature soul. It is important to remember that many (too many) souls are drawn into incarnation ahead of time by the magnetic attraction set up by the (over)production of bodies. This overproduction is, of course, the result of man's mishandling of the sex function. The Masters do not support abortion but each case must be considered separately. To Them, abortion is *sometimes* the lesser of two evils. An unwanted, unloved child brought into incarnation might suffer more than the effect on it of being aborted.

What karmic liability does having an abortion create for the parent? (Jan./Feb. '85)

It depends on the purpose of the incarnation. Not all incarnations have the same value for the world. If the incoming soul is very or rather advanced, more harm is done. Therefore the greater the karmic liability.

Is this (karmic) liability increased or diminished relative to their level of evolution, i.e. the more spiritually developed the greater the responsibility and thus the greater the liability? (Jan./Feb. '85)

Yes. Precisely.

Does miscarriage signify that the soul drawn into possible incarnation has 'changed its mind' as it were? (Oct. '85)

No. The vast majority of miscarriages occur because of technical factors—the state of health of the woman involved, the introduction of drugs, or some other physical cause. There remains a small percentage of cases in which the incarnating entity resists incarnation and aborts the pregnancy.

Organ Transplants

What is the karmic effect of organ transplants? Is it a good thing to do?

Basically, it is not a good thing to do. Every cell of the body contains within it the vibrational rate of the point of evolution of the person involved. It is the individual's body, his experience, and the culmination of all his incarnational experiences to that point. When that is transplanted into another body, which may be at a completely different point in evolution, and have a completely different vibrational rate, it sets up an antagonism. The transplant may well be done physically, but the karmic effect would be considerable. It should not really be done.

If an attempt is being made to prolong the life of the physical body (and this is not always a good thing to do) as in the case of an accident, or depletion of the function of some particular organ in a young person, the case for transplanting might seem to be proven. However, the emphasis should be on finding a way of producing alternative, artificial organs, not the transplanting of existing, living organs from a dead person into a living one. As the organ of the other individual is absorbed, the vibrational rate of the cells and tissue, and some part of the karmic situation which pertains only to that person is also absorbed. Each person's karma relates only to himself. One's lives and deaths, one's illnesses and health, are the direct result of one's own karmic activity. That should not be transferred to somebody else. When you transfer physical plane organs, you are really contributing to the karmic complexity of the individual who receives the organs. Each of us has enough karma to deal with, without being involved in somebody else's.

Do blood transfusions also create karmic problems?

Precisely the same situation pertains to blood transfusions as to organ transplants. That is not to say that one should never receive blood in an emergency. But the same principle holds. The donor might be giving blood with the greatest goodwill in the world, but however much goodwill is given with the blood, the karmic picture within the blood pertains to the individual who gave it, and not to the individual who is receiving it.

The blood carries the life of the individual. It flows through the blood, which has a vital function in carrying the soul purpose through the body. The transfusion of blood confuses the karmic issue. It muddies the stream of karma between two individuals. It brings together, karmically, individuals who have no karmic relationship other than the sharing of the blood, or the organ. There is no karmic intention that these two people should come together in that way. One may also receive blood from dozens of individuals who have contributed, so the karmic stream may be muddied many, many times.

However, in the case of blood transfusion, this condition is temporary, because the persons's own blood always replaces that of the donor's in due course.

It might be interesting to quote the Master D.K.'s more symbolic statement on blood transfusions (*Esoteric Healing*, p.345): "Blood transfusion is symbolic of two things: First, that the blood is the life, and secondly, that there is but one Life permeating all forms, and therefore transferable under right conditions. It is also a synthetic act of service."

I do not think that these two statements are mutually exclusive but rather represent approaches from two different perspectives.

What about people, like hemophiliacs, who have to have complete blood transfusions every so many days?

An artificial blood compound should be found. Such a compound is not beyond the ingenuity of science to evolve. We have just never set our sights on doing it, because we have never seen the karmic situation that lies back of blood transfusions, organ transplants, and so on. We should be putting creative and research energies into finding the means of producing artificial blood and organs (a step is being taken now in artificial hearts).

In your answer on blood transfusions, you used the phrase "no karmic intention that these people should come together ..." This appears to imply that some relationships

are within a 'karmic scenario' while others are not. Could you elaborate on this please?

Together with what might be called Cosmic Opportunity, two laws govern reincarnation: the Law of Karma (Cause and Effect) and the Law of Rebirth. The Law of Rebirth itself functions as the Law of Evolution, Group Law and the Law of Service. For a large number of more advanced human beings, their incarnational cycles are governed by Group Law. It is the interaction between the Law of Karma and Group Law which creates family units and clan and tribal relationships. The 'knots' of karma created between people (through action and reaction) set up a magnetic pull which draws them into incarnation together (under Group Law) again and again. They come together, not only as part of a group incarnating under the Plan as exponents of particular energies, but also to resolve the karmic debts formed in previous lives. Karma, however, is dynamic, not static, and this process continues until, through harmlessness and right relationship, we cease to make personal karma.

In organ transplants and blood transfusions, the relationship (the sharing of the organ or blood and therefore of the vibrational frequency) is quite haphazard and due to chance. There is no *karmic* reason for the relationship.

Is it a progressive or regressive move for humanity to be involved with genetic engineering? (Sept. '84)

I believe that it is both progressive and regressive. It is progressive in that it shows man's growing control of the processes of nature, leading eventually to control of the energies of the universe. This will make man a co-worker with God. It is regressive in that it is a further example of our (present) lack of understanding of the laws governing rebirth and of the karmic effects of the genetic experiments.

Other Individuals and Teachings

Sai Baba

In the book by Samuel Sandweiss, *The Holy Man and the Psychiatrist*, I read on page 177/178 that Sai Baba says that he himself is the Christ who, Jesus predicted, would come again. This contradicts what you say, that Maitreya is the Christ and is living in London since 1977. Please explain these differences. (June '83)

With respect, Sai Baba does not say that he is the Christ. If you will refer again to these pages you will find him saying something even more extraordinary; that he is the one who *sent* the Christ, and that the Christ meant that he, Satya Sai Baba, would come again!

The Christ, Maitreya, and Sai Baba each embody the same type of energy (the Love Principle) but at different levels: Maitreya at the planetary and Sai Baba at the cosmic level. Both are Avatars. Sai Baba does not come out of our earth evolution but is a cosmic visitor, so to speak. He is a Spiritual Regent. Just as a regent 'stands in' for a king, so a Spiritual Regent 'stands in' for 'God,' the King, Sanat Kumara, the Lord of the World in Shamballa. He may well have been involved in the decision to send the Christ, 2000 years ago, in Palestine.

Maitreya embodies the energy we call the Christ Principle and holds the office of the World Teacher in our Earth Hierarchy. These two great Beings, one Cosmic, one Planetary, work together closely for the regeneration of the world.

Where, in the Bible, does it say that Sai Baba will incarnate? (Dec. '85)

I do not believe that the Bible does say so at all. The Western Bible is a work (correctly interpreted) of great esoteric wisdom, truth and prophecy, but is not the sole repository of such wisdom, truth and prophecy.

Is Sai Baba the creator of the Cosmos? (Apr. '86)

No. Sai Baba is an Avatar—a representative of Divinity on the planet.

You say that the Lord Maitreya was Krishna. Yet Sai Baba seems to indicate that he was Krishna. Can you explain this, please? (Oct. '83)

I believe that Krishna was a previous manifestation of Maitreya, but Sai Baba is also correct (if I may say so) in claiming to be 'Krishna.' It is a question of the level of the energy associated with Krishna, namely, love. Sai Baba is a Cosmic Avatar and embodies that energy at a Cosmic level while Maitreya, a planetary Avatar, does so at the planetary level. Each is a manifestation of the Love of God. Maitreya's individual consciousness, however, manifested through Krishna by overshadowing (in much the same way as in Palestine through Jesus) while Sai Baba identifies with the Cosmic Krishna, or Christ Principle.

If Maitreya was Krishna, can we take it that the Bhagavad Gita gives a reasonable indication of His teaching at that time? (June '83)

Yes. Despite the discolouration which has occurred by its dissemination over the centuries, it remains a fairly accurate allegorical statement of His teaching for that time.

Besides Krishna and Jesus are there any other manifestations or major overshadowings by Maitreya known to us in history?

He also manifested Himself as Sankaracharya.

If God is here in the person of Sai Baba why must we look for a Christ? (Feb. '84)

Even if we accept that Sai Baba is an Avatar, a divine incarnation (I do, but many obviously would not), he has a different function from the Christ. He comes, indeed, to help Maitreya in His work. It is not a question of one or the other, but both. We are doubly blessed.

If Sai Baba is a Spiritual Regent, does He influence millions of people who are definitely not His devotees in any sense of the word? (July/Aug. '83)

Yes, very much so. He embodies Cosmic Love and that energy flows from Him into the world. People respond to it from where they are, according to their capacity to respond.

Has Sai Baba also a task when someone takes an initiation? (Dec. '84)

No. Sai Baba has no direct part to play in the five planetary initiations, but has an indirect role in stimulating the love nature of humanity in general, which opens the heart centre in those nearing the first initiation.

Does Sai Baba come from Sirius? (Nov. '84)

It would be better to ask Sai Baba. But since I am asked the answer is, no.

How is it that Sai Baba lacks the ability to speak any languages other than his own native Indian dialect, while Maitreya can converse in any language through His telepathic abilities? (Sept. '84)

Languages have to be learned, even by the Great Ones. Maitreya can indeed converse in many languages—but not in any language. His overshadowing of humanity on Declaration Day will result in our brains translating His message (given telepathically) into our own language. I have no doubt that, if necessary, Sai Baba could do likewise.

Kali Yuga

What specifically does Hindu tradition say about the return of Krishna in this cycle? (Feb. '84)

As I understand it, Hindus expect the return of Krishna at the end of Kali Yuga (some sects expect a further incarnation of Vishnu as Kalki Avatar, also at the end of Kali Yuga, the dark age). Opinions vary as to when Kali Yuga will end but there seems to be a consensus between Sai Baba, Swami Premananda and my Master that Kali Yuga is now ending.

Besant says that Kali Yuga was the last 5000 years. Buddhism had always said 200,000 years. Which is correct? (Feb. '84)

Besant is correct. To be exact, my Master says it is 4,700 years. The Buddhist figure of 200,000 years refers back to the major decline of spirituality in late Atlantean times which led to the destruction of the Atlantean land-mass and civilization nearly 100,000 years ago. This can be seen as the beginning of a 'dark age.'

Agni Yoga Teachings

Can you comment on the role of the Agni Yoga teachings in the Reappearance of the Christ? Also, what specifically is the Master Morya's world task at this time? Do the transmissions given to Helena Roerich still describe current conditions (even though given in the 1920's and 1930's)? (Nov. '84)

To my mind, the Agni Yoga teachings constitute one of the major attempts of Hierarchy to prepare humanity for the new age. They are entirely relevant to the present—and future time. The first book of the series, *The Call*, was given by Maitreya Himself, and was intended to alert disciples to the fact of His imminent return. The Master Morya, as I have said elsewhere, is one of the first group of Masters to be seen by humanity, and is the stimulus behind the occult groups of all kinds. His immediate task is to regenerate and purify the teaching of these groups.

How were the Agni Yoga Teachings originally given? (Oct. '85)

By mental telepathy through Helena Roerich (a disciple of the Master Morya) in Russian.

You stated that Maitreya had given the first book of Agni Yoga Teachings (*The Call*). Did He write any of the others? (Oct. '85)

My information is that *The Call* is His sole personal contribution to the Agni Yoga series. I do not believe that this is generally understood by the *Agni Yoga Society*, who seem to attribute all the books to the Master Morya. *The Call* is also titled: *Leaves of Morya's Garden*, I.

Is it true that the Master Morya was formerly the Emperor Akbar of India? (Nov. '85)

According to my information, no.

H. P. Blavatsky

According to *Letters from the Masters of Wisdom*, 1925, the Master K.H. wrote in 1885 that *The Secret Doctrine*, when ready, will be the triple production of Morya, H.P.B. and Himself. However, you say in your book that *The Secret Doctrine* was given to H.P.B. by the Master D.K., which is implied by certain passages in A.A.B.'s books. This upsets some Theosophists. What is correct? (Oct. '83)

My information (from my own Master) is that the broad general outline and scope of *The Secret Doctrine* was conveyed verbally to H.P.B. by the Masters K.H. and Morya, while the bulk, the esoteric lore, was given to her telepathically by D.K.. She herself gave the correspondences between the esoteric science and the exoteric science of her day. It was in fact a group work.

Why, in *Isis Unveiled* by H. P. Blavatsky, is the concept of reincarnation avoided or not explained, as it is in *The Secret Doctrine*? Was this because the Masters thought that the Western world was not ready to deal with the idea? (July/Aug. '86)

Yes. Remember that the Western world was still trying to grapple with the idea of 'survival' after death as introduced by the Spiritualist Movement. One big idea at a time!

Alice A. Bailey

How clear a channel was Alice Bailey? Could one say she was infallible? (Sept. '84)

No, nor, I think, would she have claimed to be infallible. Not even the Masters claim infallibility. But I think we can be assured that if a Master of Wisdom (D.K.) continued to work through Alice A. Bailey for thirty years, He must have been well content with her accuracy as a mediator.

St Patrick

According to C.W. Leadbetter in his book, *The Masters and the Path*, Maitreya was living in a Celtic body, and David Anrias states that he was in the etheric body of St Patrick. Did Maitreya incarnate as St Patrick? (June '83)

According to my information, Maitreya has never used a Celtic body, St Patrick's or anyone else's. Nor did He incarnate as St Patrick. The latter was only a second degree initiate, while Maitreya took the third initiation (He was the first of Earth humanity to do so) way back in Atlantean times, and is long, long since a Master, at the moment a seventh degree Master—a Planetary Life.

In St Patrick's *Confession* in Old Latin (its authority is accepted by Celtic scholars world-wide) he heard a voice say: The one who gave His life for you is "speaking in you." You say Maitreya did not incarnate as St Patrick. Is this Confession then a fraud? (July/Aug. '84)

No, the *Confession* is not a fraud, nor is it wholly accurate either. No doubt St Patrick thought and believed that the Christ (or Spirit) was speaking in him, whereas in fact the 'voice' he inwardly heard was that of his Master, the Master Jesus, Who overshadowed St Patrick, and who "gave His life." Neither

Maitreya nor the Master Jesus incarnated as St Patrick, who, as you will see from the List of Initiates and their Rays was not more than a second degree initiate. That degree was relatively very advanced, of course, in the 4th and 5th centuries AD.

Lao-tse

Could you outline the relationship between the "way" of the *Tao-Teh-King* by Lao-tse, and the "way" of Maitreya, the Christ, today? Is Lao-tse still connected with Hierarchy? (Feb. '83)

My information is that Lao-tse is no longer on this planet although he keeps a long-standing connection with our Hierarchy. Each teacher gives his teachings for a particular time and place. Fundamentally, all the different teachings embody the one truth; they vary only in emphasis and relevance for specific times, places and peoples. The common denominator is their revelation of the Oneness of all life. This is as true for Tao as for the teachings of Krishna or the Buddha, the Christ in Jesus or of Maitreya today. The "ways" merge in the principle of love.

Krishnamurti

What role will Krishnamurti, who was previously proclaimed as the medium of the Lord Maitreya, play or is playing at the moment now that the World Teacher has reappeared? (July/Aug. '83)

Krishnamurti is, of course, a teacher, one of the most influential of the many teachers today. At one time he was indeed being prepared, along with a few others, by overshadowing, as a possible vehicle for the World Teacher. When the Lord Maitreya decided to manifest Himself by means of the self-created body (*mayavirupa*) in which He now lives among us,

Krishnamurti began his present teaching work, which presumably will continue.

John the Baptist and Mother Mary

Was John the Baptist ever overshadowed by Maitreya? (Nov. '85)

No.

You say in your book, *The Reappearance of the Christ and the Masters of Wisdom* that John the Baptist is long-since a Master and is no longer in the world. Where is He? (Oct. '84)

He became a Master in the second century AD and immediately went to Sirius. (There is a direct relationship between Sirius and the Hierarchy of this planet. "The Path to Sirius" is one of the seven ways of "the Higher Evolution" which governs the evolution of the Masters.) There He awaits His return to this earth as an Avatar in about 500 years time.

If Masters take on a male body in Their last incarnation, did the Mother Mary come back after her ascension? (Apr. '84)

The question implies that Jesus' mother Mary was a Master which is not the case. Her 'ascension' was a construction of the Church Fathers, some centuries after her death. She was, as was her husband, St Joseph, a second degree initiate, and therefore came into incarnation again several times before taking the fifth initiation of Mastery. 'She' is at present not in incarnation.

Prince Gautama

You say that the Master Jesus, who was the vehicle for the Christ, is now in Rome. Where is the Prince Gautama who was the vehicle for the Buddha? (June '84)

My information is that the Prince Gautama is no longer on this planet, nor even in this solar system, but is now a member of the Great White Brotherhood on Sirius. Our Hierarchy is a branch of the Brotherhood and many Masters go directly from this Earth to Sirius if that is Their chosen Path on the Higher Evolution.

Others

I am interested in Guru Nanak, the 14th Century Hindu reformer who became the first Sikh guru. Is he now a Master and do we know him in any other incarnation? Could you give his degree of initiation and rays? (Sept. '85)

He is now a Master of the sixth degree but is not in incarnation. He achieved that degree in the 18th Century. None of his other incarnations are known to us. His rays as Nanak were: soul 6; personality 6, sub-ray 7; mental 1, sub-ray 4; astral 2, sub-ray 6; physical 3, sub-ray 7.

I recently heard about your work as 'heralder' for the New Age 'Messiah' known as Maitreya. Is this the same 'Messiah' who the psychic Jeane Dixon says was born on 5 February 1962 when eight planets were aligned in the constellation Aquarius (an event that hasn't happened in over 2,000 years), and on which day she reported the following 'vision,' she describes as "the most significant and soul-stirring vision of my life?" "... I saw a long-dead Pharaoh and Queen Nefertiti at his side striding toward her. The queen was holding out a baby as though offering it to the world... The eyes of the child were all-knowing... full of

wisdom and knowledge... as I watched in fascination. I saw the child grow to manhood, and a small cross that formed above him began to expand until it dripped over the earth in all directions. Simultaneously peoples of every race, religion and colour, each kneeling and lifting his arms in worshipful adoration, surrounded him. They were all as one." Ms. Dixon believes that the Messiah was reincarnated into the world as a babe at the time of her vision. She says he will "bring together all mankind in one all-embracing faith... the foundation of a new Christianity with every sect and creed united... the world as we know it will be reshaped and revamped into one without wars or suffering." Was this, then, the exact date on which Maitreya was actually born (which would make him 23 years old at this time)? Or was Ms. Dixon off on her prediction? (Dec. '85)

It is my belief that Jeane Dixon correctly 'tuned into' an astral thoughtform about the return of the Christ. Where, I believe, she was mistaken was in relating her 'vision' to the 'birth' of the Christ in 1962. The Christ has not been born as a baby, in 1962 or at any other date. He created His body of manifestation—the *mayavirupa*—in the six years previous to July 1977, and appears in the world as a mature, adult man. He will remain with us in that body (which will not age) until the end of the Aquarian Age. He will eventually inaugurate a new world religion which will be not simply a 'new Christianity' but will bring together the approaches to God of both the East and the West.

Do you think Nostradamus glimpsed a vision of Maitreya coming from the Himalayas when he wrote the famous quatrain which roughly translates as "An alarmingly pow-

erful king shall descend from the skies to raise the Jagnerie (peasantry)?" (Sept. '84)

I believe that this 'prophecy' is the result of his own astral imagination and has no validity at all.

In *Seth Speaks* by Jane Roberts, Seth says (pages 370;375) that the Christ entity consisted of three personalities: firstly, John the Baptist, secondly, Jesus, and thirdly, Paul or Saul. The Second Coming, he says, will be initiated by the third personality, Paul, because his role had not been fulfilled. I have never heard of a similar interpretation of the Second Coming. Can you explain this? (Mar. '85)

Certainly these three individuals were deeply involved in the first Coming but had quite distinct functions and did not make up the 'Christ entity.' John the Baptist (who had been Elijah) prepared the way (somewhat) and is no longer in this world; Jesus (now the Master Jesus) became the vehicle for the Christ—Maitreya; and Paul (now the Master Hilarion) spread (and somewhat distorted) the teachings, and consolidated the early Christian groups.

The Master Hilarion is involved in the Second Coming—as are many of the Masters—and will be among the first group to make Themselves known to humanity, but in no sense can He be said to have initiated the Second Coming. This was done, in 1945, by Maitreya Himself.

It is not my principle to comment publicly on the many 'teachings' now available through various mediums but this question does refer to my concerns. Much of these teachings are inspiring and informative to many, but all suffer to some extent from having emanated from one or other level of the astral planes—with the inevitable distortions which those planes confer; the astral planes are, after all, the planes of illusion. 'Seth' is not an individual teacher but a group of disciples communicating (from their various levels of evolvement) from the fifth of the seven astral planes.

Orwell's book *1984* shows the negative alternative before us. Is it coincidence that he chose to set it in 1984 or is this helping in sharpening the "Sword of Cleavage" to facilitate our choice? (Sept. '84)

Orwell wrote his book in 1948 and simply reversed the last two figures of the date—1984. It has no more meaning than that.

What is the place and task of Karl Marx now? (Nov. '83)

He is not in incarnation at this time. He does a great deal of work in connection with that of the English Master and the Master R.

Is Rudolph Steiner in incarnation at this moment? (May '86)

Yes.

Hitler, Mussolini, Stalin, Churchill—what are they doing now? Are they in physical incarnation? (Apr. '86)

None of them is at present in physical incarnation.

If spiritual teachers like the Maharishi and Rajneesh are working within the same Hierarchical plan, why are they stimulating separatism by telling their pupils that only they have the correct teaching and the best techniques? (Dec. '84)

Perhaps they really do believe that they have the only correct teaching and the best technique. Whether or not that is the case, can you imagine the reaction of the average seeker if told "My teaching is not bad but no better than any other guru's. Likewise, my technique is all right but you might get better down the road." How many would 'join up' with such a presentation? I believe it is not the gurus who promote separatism but the followers who have a great inner need to be disciples of 'the best,' or 'the only one.'

How does Lord Maitreya differ from Guru Maharaji, Swami Prabhupadha (of the Hare Krishnas), and other Eastern religious leaders who have come to the West? (Nov. '84)

The various Eastern Gurus who have come to the West are disciples of a certain Master, sent to the West to introduce one or other form of meditation or spiritual practice. The Lord Maitreya is the "Master of the Masters," "The Teacher alike of angels and of men" (as He has been called by the Lord Buddha and St Paul); the supreme Head of our Planetary Hierarchy, holding the Office of the World Teacher, and comes as World Teacher to inaugurate the age of Aquarius.

CHAPTER VIII

MEDITATION AND SERVICE

Meditation and Service in Spiritual Growth

Modern psychology has divided humanity into two main types: the contemplative, and the man or woman of action; the introvert and the extrovert personality. Esoteric psychology also recognizes these differences in people's approach to life, but characteristically, since it aims at synthesis rather than analysis, it sees their eventual integration. To the esotericist, the introvert is one whose attention is focused inwards to the soul, who has good and easy contact with that aspect of himself, for whom formal meditation is attractive as a more scientific and organized means of deepening that contact but whose contact with the outside world is relatively fragmentary and limited, leading to difficulties of expression and functioning on the physical plane.

The extrovert, on the other hand, is one whose contact with the outer world is strong and vivid, who has little difficulty in relating to people and situations, but whose contact with the soul is limited and largely unconscious; his attention is directed outwards.

Life after life, our souls create vehicles, our personalities, through which both modes can be developed and perfected. The evolutionary aim is their ultimate integration: an uninterrupted, direct contact and at-one-ment with the soul; and *at will*, a free-flowing rapport with the outer world of people and events. This is the ideal; its achievement marks the initiate.

The twin ways of the path to this integration are meditation and service. Through meditation, contact with the soul is deepened and strengthened, gradually bringing about the infusion of the personality by the soul. The energies and attributes of the soul—Spiritual Will, Love and Intelligence—manifest more and more through the personality until such time as the fusion of the two is complete.

Through service, the purpose of the soul is carried out. The nature of the soul is to serve; it knows only altruistic service. All that it is of Will, Love and Intelligence it seeks to put at the service of the Plan—the Plan of the Logos of which it is a reflection. In Palestine, the Christ revealed the fact of the soul and instituted the Path of Service as the way, *par excellence*, to God-realization.

This is no less true today. The great illusion of our personality life is the sense of being at the centre of the universe. We are all of major interest and importance to ourselves.

Nothing is so effective in decentralizing ourselves as service. Nothing so helps us to gain perspective and to grow spiritually. As we serve, we identify more and more with "the other," that which we serve, and gradually shift the focus of our attention from our little separate selves. We gain a broader, more inclusive vision of the world and so come into a more correct relationship with the Whole of which we are a part.

Many, today, especially those working in the Eastern tradition, under the influence of one or other of the many gurus now teaching in the West, see meditation as an end in itself. They see no need for service or outer action to change society for the better; see no outer change being possible without an inner change of heart. Many also believe that simply by meditation alone they are doing more good for the world than otherwise they could. No doubt, if they were God-realized Masters that might well be so, but even the Masters work unstintingly in service to the world; none more than They.

Through meditation, one draws on the energies and inspiration of the soul which give life and meaning to the personality expression. Where these are denied their correct outlet in service, a 'damming up' takes place in the personality vehicles—mental, emotional and physical—with unfortunate results. Many of the neuroses and other illnesses of aspirants and disciples stem from this non-use of soul energy and denial of soul purpose.

Meditation remains the royal way to contact with the soul, but once this is achieved, the way forward for the true aspirant to discipleship is through the acceptance, also, of the life of service. The inner and the outer focus must be balanced, and a start made on the Infinite Way, the way of service, which calls all true Sons of God from the lowliest disciple up to, and beyond, the Christ Himself. It is the same need to serve which impels the Logos into manifestation and gives us life. (Mar. '82)

What is the most important aspect of service: why we do it, what we do, or the attitude with which we do it? (Jan. '86)

One cannot place service too high as a path to gain spiritual enlightenment, because enlightenment itself is awakening to the role of service. The Masters call Their work the Great Service, and as we evolve to eventual Masterhood we come to realize that throughout cosmos there is really only one great law governing the whole activity of what we call divinity—that is service. God comes into incarnation, creates the manifested universe, and the units of God, of which we are the reflection, come into incarnation specifically to serve. There is no other motive. It is to serve the Plan, which itself is service. We are, all of us, almost exclusively, bound by our sense of our own independent reality—our separate self. This, actually, is a heresy. It is a myth. It only relates to the brain consciousness of ourselves, the personality awareness of our lives. The whole role of meditation and service is to lead us away from that view into the true reality, where there is no separation, because fundamentally there is no separation.

There is one great Oversoul. We are individualized parts of the Oversoul. Our sense of being separate is quite erroneous and stems from our identifying with the lowest aspect of ourselves, the body. As soon as we come into this realization, we make the first real step of progress toward reality. And we find the very nature of that reality is service.

The Logos of our planet is serving the Plan of the Solar Logos in creating for Himself a body of expression, which we call planet Earth. Everything you see on the planet—the people, the trees, etc.—comes into being as thought-forms in the mind of the creating Logos. He does this in service to the greater Plan of the Solar Logos, who in His turn is doing the same thing on a bigger scale in service to the greater Logos at the centre of the galaxy. The Solar Logos will probably only know a part of that Plan, but does what He does in service to the part of the Plan that He knows.

So really there is only service. As souls we are here to serve. The mechanism is the magnetic pull of karma through the law of cause and effect, but the motive for coming in is to serve the Plan. The all-important thing in service is the motive behind it. It is not what you do. It does not matter what service you do. Everything can be service. Every single action you do can be service.

The way you do it is also important. Service should be impersonal. Personally-motivated service is not service. That is service to the separate self. Impersonal service—it is only service if it is impersonal—altruistic service, should be the aim. This brings in the law of service, and has its result in decentralizing us, whereas service to oneself only leads to the bolstering of the sense of separation. So the motive is absolutely crucial.

How can one balance (in terms of time and energy) the desire to serve humanity in the highest possible way—and

the desire for close personal relationships in one's life? (Nov. '84)

This is a great problem for many people especially if their partners show no similar need for service. What is required, I think, is a sense of the needs of the time and a desire to serve and fulfill that need—plus a sense of proportion. If one has duties and responsibilities as parent or spouse, these must be fulfilled. One has to learn to recognize priorities and even to choose between essentials. Perhaps it helps to remember that true servers of humanity (that is, those who *serve* and not just *desire* to serve) are disciples, whether they realize it or not, and that the disciple belongs not to himself, or his family or friends, but to the world. The true disciple, however, will have a sense of proportion, a strong sense of duty and the ability to accept many responsibilities.

Do you have any ideas as to how to find one's ideal role in this creation (in other words to do the work of Christ)? (Oct. '84)

I am often asked by people: am I where I am supposed to be? Am I doing what I am supposed to be doing? It is as if they picture themselves manipulated by some unseen entities or forces into +specific, ideal roles, actions and places. My answer is usually: what do you *want* to do? Where do you *want* to be? There is a whole anguished world to save, to regenerate, to serve. It seems to me that the important thing is to serve the *necessity*, the needs of the time, with whatever equipment you have available, to the best of your ability. In serving you *find* a role—a purpose.

What is meant by the word 'magnetic' when used in reference to a disciple? Is it magnetic in the sense of drawing more energy or drawing people? (Jan. '86)

The disciple becomes magnetic in both senses. As the disciple advances, he or she becomes more and more radiatory. The aura becomes magnetic, attracting to itself energy of ever higher frequency, thus increasing the radiation. This radiation sets up a magnetic field around the disciple which inevitably attracts those with whom the disciple can work. When the aura becomes sufficiently magnetic the inherent telepathic faculty naturally unfolds. If circumstances require it the disciple may then be contacted by Hierarchy (at some level) and offered some line of service.

Would you please shed some light, practically speaking, on the difference between impulsive behaviour and that which results from intuitive levels? (June '84)

Impulsive behaviour is always the response to some emotional stimulus while spontaneous action of an intuitive kind stems from the soul and is the result of some degree of soul contact. Practically, action which stems from the soul is *always*, under every circumstance, right, and altruistic in nature. Impulsive, emotional behaviour, on the other hand, can range, as we know, all the way from emotional aspiration of an idealistic kind to the most blatant selfishness.

Meditation

Could you please explain what is meant by "holding the mind steady in the light?" (May '85)

Through meditation correctly carried out, the "antahkarana," the channel of light between the physical brain and the soul, is gradually built and strengthened. By means of that channel, the soul light is anchored in the head of the disciple. This is seen as a brilliant light within the head during meditation. With the attention drawn inward and upward in that light, the mind is held 'steady,' that is, without thought or movement of the lower mind. In that condition of thoughtless, focused attention the intuitive levels of the mind can come into play; gradually, this becomes an instinctive, fixed condition, needing no formal meditational 'going within' to bring it about.

Many people believe that any thought or idea that enters the mind during 'meditation' comes from the intuitional soul level and is guiding their actions. This is by no means the case. It is extremely difficult for the average aspirant or disciple to "hold the mind steady in the light" for long enough to invoke the intuition, and the 'guidance' which most people receive is that of their own lower minds via the subconscious.

In the prayer given by Master D.K. (The Tibetan) "In the centre of the Will of God I stand," there is the line, "I, the triangle divine, work out that will within the square and serve my fellow men." What does this mean? (May '86)

The triangle divine is the Spiritual Triad—Spiritual Will, Love-Wisdom, or Buddhi, and Higher Mind or Manas—reflected through the soul. The square is Humanity itself. The line means, therefore: Seeing myself as the divine or spiritual triad (my true nature), I seek to work out that divine will and purpose within, and as part of, humanity and thus serve my fellow men.

I came across this statement in Alice Bailey's *Letters on Occult Meditation*: "Remember always that material gain in knowledge for the individual causes stagnation, obstruction, indigestion, and pain, if not passed on with wise dis-

crimination." (p. 343, Letter xi). Could you elaborate? (Apr. '85)

It is a law that all gain in knowledge must be shared before further progress can be made. Progress itself is a result of the law of service, of which sharing is an intrinsic part. Just as the non-sharing of the resources of the world leads to division, separation, starvation, pain and suffering for humanity, and tensions leading to revolution and war, so the non-sharing of knowledge leads to the various stages of obstruction, indigestion, and so on, if not passed on "with wise discrimination." The last phrase I take to mean that it should be shared with those who are open to and seek that knowledge and not rammed down people's throats.

Is occult meditation being taught anywhere presently? (June '85)

This is not a subject that can be taught, but it can be and is practised by many disciples in different parts of the world and is overseen by the Masters.

Will the reappearance of the Christ obviate the need for meditation? (Nov. '85)

No, on the contrary. The presence of Maitreya and the Masters in our midst will provide a great stimulus to all forms of meditation.

Will there be new meditation techniques given by Maitreya? Will they be different from existing ones? (Nov. '83)

No. It will not be Maitreya's function to give new meditation techniques. That is like expecting the managing director of a large international company to train the office boys in office routine. Meditation techniques are, and will continue to be, taught by disciples of the Masters. As time goes on and disciples become ready, meditation forms will be given by the Masters Themselves, working exoterically.

Is it true that meditation lowers the crime rate as TM (Transcendental Meditation) meditators maintain? (Apr. '84)

I believe it does to some extent. All human action is the result of the response to energies and the ideas embodying the energies. A large group of people engaged in dynamic meditation set up thought waves of a constructive kind which must have some influence on the surrounding mental atmosphere.

What can we do about the problem of tension in the head and also resultant headaches due to meditation? (Nov. '85)

If meditation is done correctly there should be no tension or headaches. The questioner is obviously trying too hard, is too vehement and anxious to succeed. It is important to be as relaxed as possible, especially in the head, neck and shoulders. During personal meditation, there may be the sensation of pressure and of a band around the head—the downflow of energy from the soul—but this is pleasant, even when strong. During a Transmission Meditation, the energies likewise give a sensation of pressure as they pass through the chakras. But in both cases the pressure is temporary and should not result in headaches.

With the flowering of the etheric heart centre often comes discomfort to the physical heart. What, if any, plan of action could be taken to lessen the severity of these reactions? (July/Aug. '85)

With respect, I do not accept this statement. The question comes from the same person who suffers from tension and headaches due to meditation. The problem is one of general tension. Keep the attention *away* from the physical heart. If there is any doubt about the health of the heart, a doctor should be consulted for check-up.

In *The Finding of the Third Eye*, Vera Stanley Alder says (p.134) that an operation producing functions of the third eye belongs in the realm of black magic. But T. Lobsang Rampa, a high Abbot of a Tibetan lamasery, has stated that he went through an operation producing a third eye when he was young. Is such an operation possible without being in the realm of black magic? (Mar. '85)

There is a prevalent but mistaken idea that the third eye is always 'there' and requires only to be opened—by a Master's touch, a magical process, or, as in the 'Lobsang Rampa' book, by an operation. The third eye, in reality, has to be created by the disciple himself, through meditation. It is gradually formed through the interaction and overlapping of the energy fields radiating (eventually) from the pituitary body and the pineal gland. There is no way in which an operation can bring about the function of this purely etheric organ.

Is it possible for the Third Eye to change position? I saw it happening in the case of an acquaintance. It shifted to the right and someone else clairvoyantly saw the same thing happening with me. If this is possible, why does it shift and why to the right? (Dec. '85)

It is not possible for the 'third eye' to shift, either to the right or to the left. I can only put down your perception and that of the 'clairvoyant' to hallucination. The person might see an apparent movement due to the movement of etheric energies above and beyond and in and around it, but the centre itself, the third eye so-called, does not move. Just as a star appears to move when it is seen through the Earth's atmosphere and what we really see is the movement of the atmosphere rather than that of the star, so it is with the 'third eye': it retains its position while the energy around it moves.

Transmission Meditation—Its Vital Role

Humanity's true role is to act as a clearing-house for energies, a kind of sub-station for the energies from above humanity to the kingdoms below us. In the future, we will do this work consciously, scientifically, to stimulate, for instance, the intelligence-factor in the animal kingdom, or (as we already do to some extent) to purify and perfect specific specimens of the vegetable kingdom. We have not even begun to use the creative potential which humanity has in relation to these lower kingdoms, whose evolution is our major responsibility. They evolve through the stimulus which we can give them. Each kingdom grows out of the kingdom immediately below it, the vegetable from the mineral, the animal from the vegetable, the human from the animal, the spiritual from the human. Each kingdom evolves as a result of the stimulus from the kingdom immediately above it. The physical form comes from below and the spiritual stimulus to evolution comes from above. It is obvious that the more of the higher evolutionary stimulus we can apply to the lower kingdoms, the faster and more perfectly they will evolve.

We can work in relation to the lower kingdoms exactly as the Masters of the Spiritual Hierarchy, the next kingdom above the human, act in relation to us. Each kingdom moves into the kingdom above it through the process of becoming 'radioactive,' radiating energy. When the mineral kingdom becomes radioactive, the most advanced minerals are gradually transformed into the vegetable and from the vegetable to the animal and so on, up and up. When a man or a woman becomes radioactive, he or she can begin to move from the human kingdom into the kingdom of souls, the spiritual kingdom. It will be quite obvious from this how important it is to absorb from the kingdom of souls (the Spiritual Hierarchy of the planet, the Masters and Initiates of the Wisdom), all the spiritual energy which It sends to us and through us.

Transmission Meditation is simple and yet it performs a number of different very important facets of work. In the first place, it is an act of service. I know of no other means of service to the world of such potency, such value, such importance, and which is so clearly along the line of evolution of the Plan, which, at the same time, is so simple and easy. To become a saint is really quite difficult; to look after the starving, poverty-stricken millions in Calcutta is quite a task—as Mother Teresa knows. We are not all Mother Teresas. But all of us can give up a few hours a week to sit quietly, absorbing and transmitting the energy of Hierarchy.

It is very simple, and yet I cannot sufficiently emphasize the value of these few hours spent in this way. It helps the world more than we could know, and it is self-fulfilling as well; I know no other method of service which makes for such vast and quick inner spiritual growth. It is a yoga and a field of service given to one 'on a plate.' It is impossible to do this work for any length of time without finding that it enhances any other work we might do. Most people after six months or so of working in a Transmission group find themselves being subtly but quite definitely transformed inwardly, psychologically. It is impossible to transmit these great spiritual forces without being transformed at the same time.

The Masters, when they look at the world and see the aspirants and disciples, do not tune in to their thoughts to know what they are doing and thinking. They look at the state of their centres, they see the light, bright or otherwise, which surrounds that individual. That light, of course, is the result of the vibrational activity of the centres. In Transmission Meditation, the energies stimulate the centres through which they flow and the development takes place automatically, and in a scientific way. There are a great many meditations and yoga techniques which aim at the same stimulation of the centres, and while they may have value they can be dangerous unless they are done under the guidance of a Master. This Transmission work, on the other hand, always takes place under the supervision of the Masters and is perfectly safe.

More and more people are beginning to understand the value of group rather than individual meditation. Group meditation intensifies, potentizes, the energetic value of the meditation. In group Transmission, more energy can safely be placed through the group than could be placed through the same number of people individually. In a very real sense there is safety in numbers. The advantage, too, of Transmission Meditation is that it does not interfere with whatever other kind of meditation one might do. On the contrary, Transmission Meditation will enhance the value of one's own meditation.

All that is required is the determination to make it a regular routine in one's life. Regularity is very important. It sets up a ritual, a rhythm, which has its own value. It is important for the members of the Transmission group to meet regularly, once or twice a week, or whatever, but always on the same day at the same time. In this way the Masters know that at a certain place and time there will be a group ready to transmit the energy from Them to the world. This work, we will find, is a door which leads to a path that takes us directly to Hierarchy. It is part of a process planned by Hierarchy whereby the aspirants and the disciples of the world will work in a co-operative fashion with each other and with Hierarchy itself.

Most people want to approach Hierarchy, whether they are ready for it or not; they would like to meet a Master, work with a Master. Transmission Meditation is not a way to meet Masters, but it is certainly the simplest way to *work* with the Masters. The Masters have been engaged for millions of years, quite literally, in transmitting the energy of which They are the custodians through groups in the world. These groups can be Christians or Jews, Hindus or whatever; they can be specific groups like Theosophists or Rosicrucians, and so on. There has never been an act of worship or service in a church or a temple anywhere at any time, which was not at the same time a transmission of energy. It might have been a higher or a lower powered energy and the activity more, or less, conscious, but the energy would be there. It is the continuous requirement of Hierarchy that there are groups in the world ready to transmit Their energy for the benefit of the world.

In starting a Transmission Meditation, the mantram or prayer called the Great Invocation is normally used, and by this means the energy of Hierarchy is invoked. Many groups also use cassettes of the *Messages from Maitreya*, given through myself between September 1977 and May 1982. As they play a Message, the energy, which was released when the Message was given and is magnetized on to the tape, is re-released. Those who do not have cassettes may read one or two of the Messages together aloud before the Transmission. This has the same effect of invoking the energy from Hierarchy. It is impossible, I believe, to read aloud these Messages with serious intent without invoking the energy from the Christ. The same, of course, applies to the Great Invocation; it was given specifically for this purpose.

An important aspect of Transmission work is the alignment between the physical brain and the soul. Anyone who has done any kind of meditation at all is already doing that. The whole purpose of meditation is to bring about that alignment and then the gradual at-one-ment between the physical brain and the soul. While saying the Great Invocation or the Christ Messages, and throughout the Transmission, the attention should be held at the centre between the eyebrows. This is the directing centre. It will be found that the attention will wander. When this happens, inwardly, mentally, the mantram, OM, should be sounded and the attention will come back to this centre automatically. It is important to be relaxed, physically and mentally.

This is not an act of worship. Many people approach these Transmissions as if they were going to church. It should be relaxed, joyful. (Going to church should also be relaxed and joyful, but it seldom is.) Transmission Meditation is an important, serious and useful activity, but it should be done lightly and relaxedly. We do not meditate on the OM, but use the OM to bring the attention to the chakra or centre. That is all one needs to do—the Masters do the real work. It is important, however, to remain *positive* and *mentally poised*—the opposite of a passive and negative focus. The Masters choose the centres. They choose the energy. They know the amount of energy each person can handle and They send it through the group to where it is needed. We do not direct the energy to any particular place, group or individual.

This is a forcing process, or hothouse situation. In a year of Transmission work one can make the inner growth resulting from many years of other forms of meditation.

How long should a Transmission last? It depends on the experience of the group (three or more make a group) and the point in evolution of its members. It is best to sit for as long as the energies flow. I suggest a minimum of one hour, gradually working up to around three hours. Those who wish to leave should be allowed to do so without terminating the Transmission of the others. (Apr. '83)

[Readers are referred to *Transmission - A Meditation for the New Age* by Benjamin Creme, for further information on Transmission Meditation.]

Transmission Energy

Are the energies which are coming through the Spiritual Push directed towards the media, and will they bring Maitreya forward? (June '84)

[In the Spring of 1984, Hierarchy planned a major manifestation—spiritual push—and all spiritual workers, and Transmission Meditation groups in particular, were asked to make themselves available for the greatest service during the period from the end of March until June—throughout the period of the three Spring Festivals: Easter, Wesak in May, and the Christ Festival in June.]

The energies released during the Spiritual Push are not directed to any special category of people at all. They create, rather, a new atmosphere in which it is hoped better decisions in respect of international relations can be taken. Every amelioration of world tension and conditions facilitates the emergence of Maitreya (by fulfilling the conditions of His reappearance) but one cannot say simply that they will "bring Him forward." This depends more directly on the expenditure (by the media as representatives of humanity) of a certain, symbolic, amount of energy in 'looking' for Him.

From where do the energies emanate for the Spiritual Push? (June '84)

From the Ashrams of the Hierarchy but above all from cosmic sources. The Christ, Maitreya, stands at the centre of a triangle of cosmic energies and transforms them (steps them down) so that we can make better use of them. These come from a cosmic Entity called the Avatar of Synthesis Who is extra-systemic and can come down no lower than the mental plane of this earth; from an Entity called the Spirit of Peace or Equilibrium Who overshadows Maitreya in a very similar fashion to that by which Maitreya overshadowed Jesus in Palestine; and from the Buddha, Who brings in the Wisdom aspect from cosmic levels. These three forces are focused through Maitreya as the centre of the triangle. At Wesak (at the May full-moon), the Buddha adds the Shamballa Force, the Will energy of our major planetary centre. This usually replaces the energy of the Avatar of Synthesis until the full moon in Libra (October), although, in recent years, it has been kept flowing until November or December, when the Avatar of Synthesis takes over again. The energy of the Avatar of Synthesis is similar to the Shamballa Force, but is more broadly based (synthesizing Will, Love and Intelligence). It is therefore safer to use than the dynamic Shamballa energy but slower in its effect.

Will these energies (during the Spiritual Push) carry out the work of destroying the old forms or rebuilding new ones? (June '84)

They are mainly to do with the creation of a new atmosphere and conditions of trust; a sense of global synthesis; and the stimulus of spiritual idealism in the masses of people. All of these endeavours lead to the creation of new forms.

Why is the major Push this year? (June '84)

The Spiritual Push occurs every year during the spring months but this year it is extraordinarily potent, what my Master has called a 'major manifestation.' This is seen as a year of increased tension—because of the '1984' thought-form—and also of opportunity. It is thought (by Hierarchy) that humanity is now able to make certain decisions about its future which hitherto it was not able to do—at least consciously. This could lead to a reduction of tension.

What does Hierarchy do with all these energies? (May '83)

Only Hierarchy could know what They do with them. They send them where they are needed, which might be to a particular country or area in the world, or else simply to 'top up,' as we say, to keep at a high level, the reservoir of spiritual energies in the world. It is very important indeed that people in Transmission groups do not direct the energies. They should leave this to the Masters, who alone know where they are needed and in what particular balance and potency. This is a moment to moment changing situation that only the Christ has the science to understand. So, although there might be a crisis in the Middle East and you might think "what a good idea to send some good energy to the Middle East," you could be doing entirely the wrong thing. The energy being transmitted through the group at that particular time might be just the energy which is not needed in the Middle East; the contrary, perhaps. So one should send it to no group, country, or person in particular.

The Christ is in charge of these energies all the time, from moment to moment. As He looks at the world with all its problems, He thinks about it energetically; that needs stimulus, that needs careful handling, that needs, perhaps, energy withdrawn. Not only that, but all the energies have different qualities. So He does not send one thing we call energy, but the energy of will, or of love, or of organization, or whatever. It is the blending of these which makes the effect in the world. So you can see how useless it is to try to decide for yourself what that energy could do, or should do. It is such a complex and occult science that only the Masters can know.

How much is the transmission of energies actually working? (Nov. '83)

It is not possible for us to know exactly how effective is the transmission of energies, but the fact that Hierarchy sends the energies and encourages the formation of Transmission groups shows the importance that They place on this work. My information is that it is without doubt of primary importance.

Is Transmission Meditation accelerated on the energetic points of the world, for example, at Stonehenge in England? (Apr. '86)

No. I believe there is a misapprehension here. The energies transmitted are not dependent on some outer physical stimulus but on the Plan of the Masters who send them, and on the point in evolution of the people in the Transmission groups. The more evolved the people, the more potent can be the energy safely sent by Hierarchy.

Through which chakras do the energies come in, and through which do they go out? (May '83)

This depends on the point of evolution and also on the ray structure of the person involved, the line of force on which people are, as souls, as personalities, with mental, astral and physical bodies—all of these may be on different rays. So it is not possible to say these energies come through one particular centre and go out through another; it depends on the individual. People vary enormously in the state of development of the individual chakras. So if a chakra through which that particular ray energy would normally flow is not open enough, other chakras can be used by the Masters to transmit. There is a limit to the extent to which that can be done, but within these limits it is done.

Therefore, broadly speaking, people will receive and transmit energies along their own line of force. You know that there are seven ray energies, and people can be along the 2-4-6 line, or the 1-3-5-7 line. A group may be made up of people of all different rays. While the energies are being transmitted, you might find that half the group is transmitting the 2-4-6 ray energies and the other half transmitting the 1-3-5-7 ray energies. And of course there are also some groups which are on one line or the other.

I am a little confused by your answer to a question where you speak of being either along the 2-4-6 line or the 1-3-5-7 line. This appears to conflict with your chart of people's rays. You also seem to speak of the blending of the two lines in groups. Is this part of creating harmony through conflict with the increasing influence of the 4th ray? (July/Aug. '83)

There are only three rays of Aspect: rays 1, 2 and 3. Rays 4, 5, 6 and 7—the rays of Attribute—emerge out of these basic three, qualifying them by adding specific qualities. Rays 4 and 6 have a close relationship to the 2nd, the 7th to the 1st, and the 5th to the 3rd. *As souls*, groups will therefore tend to be along one or other of these two lines of force (1-3-5-7 and 2-4-6). Of course, each individual may have any of the rays governing his lower vehicles, as in the charts.

There is a move in Hierarchy to give each energy-line experience in handling and transmitting the energy of the other line, which is a more efficient method of distributing the energies. It is not specifically to do with the incoming 4th ray.

(1) Would someone who does not possess a certain ray be able to channel that ray in Transmission Meditation? (2) Presupposing they can feel the energies, would they feel it?

(1) Someone who had been working in a Transmission Group for some considerable time would almost certainly be able to channel a ray energy not their own. (2) Most likely, if they were sensitive to energies at all, they would also feel it. It would depend on the individual and the group itself.

During Transmission Meditation, do the energies from the Masters pass through the seven chakras or only the top three—the heart, throat and ajna centres? (Apr. '86)

It depends on the individual's point of evolution and therefore which chakras are open and can be used. With the majority, the heart, throat and ajna are used. With some, the crown chakra is also utilized. With some, more advanced, all seven chakras are used.

If our chakras are insufficiently opened (because of karmic reasons), can Transmission Meditation (1) provoke an amelioration of our general state; (2) lead to an aggravation of our problems; (3) be inefficient; (4) lead to a distortion of these energies; (5) in short, should we and can we all transmit? (Apr. '86)

(1) Yes. (2) No. (3) Yes. (4) No. (5) Yes. The whole process is highly scientific and under the control of Master scientists.

Why do people have the experience that the Transmission energy is different on different nights? (May '83)

I think there are two factors here. One is that the energies themselves may be different, have different qualities, and they have a different effect on you. The other is that people vary from evening to evening, because of work patterns, or pressure of the atmosphere; they are more or less tired, more or less vitalized, and therefore probably absorb, when the vitality is low, less of the energies than at other times. The energy potential is exactly in proportion to the spiritual tension. Obviously, people who are more advanced in evolution will absorb and transmit energy of higher potency than those who are less evolved. They would have greater spiritual tension (I am not speaking of physical tension).

Our own spiritual tension varies from day to day. So, in the same way, we will receive such and such a potency of the energy one day, more or less on another day. Of course the group tension is made up of the sum total of the individual tensions.

Another thing is that the energies themselves are sent from, and are brought down by the Masters to, different levels. The energy one night may not seem strong at all, not because it is not being sent out powerfully, but because it is not being received sensitively—it might be so high that the apparatus of the people cannot sense it. The same energy brought down to a lower plane they feel as 'strong energy,' because they are sensitive to it at the lower level. The lower the plane the more we feel the energy. We only think of, as being 'strong,' what we feel strongly. That is dependent on our instrument. It is really not to do with the strength or otherwise of the energy—it may be, but not necessarily.

If a person is closed to esotericism, can the energetic contact (in Transmission Meditation) be established? (Apr. '86)

Most certainly. This is a scientific process and not dependent on 'belief' or academic knowledge.

What is the best way to harness the primary life-energy of the universe? (May '86)

By becoming a student of the Ageless Wisdom and putting its precepts into practice.

How long should we transmit? (May '83)

Groups vary enormously in the length of time they sit in Transmission—from half an hour to 5, 6 or 7 hours, once, twice or three times a week. I know groups who start at seven o'clock and finish at seven-thirty and then they have tea and cakes and chat and so on, and they are very proud to be a

Transmission group, half an hour per week. Some think they have to start at a certain time and finish at a certain time all together. This is not the case. It is important, and useful, that a group starts the Transmission at the same time, but there is no reason at all why the length of the Transmission should be regulated by the concentration ability of the weakest member. Many group leaders have said to me: "But they won't sit longer, they get tired after half an hour, they want to go home or have tea." So it should be open. Those who wish to stay longer should be able to stay longer, those who want to go, can go.

The greater the number in the group the more the energy can be potentized. The energy is not sent individually through the members of the group. If you have a basic unit of three people, that is a triangle; if you have six people, that makes many triangles possible, and it is through these triangular formations, which can be expanded to stars and various geometric shapes, that the Masters send the energy. This potentizes the energy enormously. So obviously, every time someone leaves the group to go home the group is weakened. But it is still better for the Transmission to go on with fewer people for a longer time than for the whole group to go on for a very short time.

I know people sometimes have to come long distances, and then they want to get together socially afterwards, so they want to keep the Transmission short. But it is more important to give time to the Transmission than to chat with the group. That may be pleasant but it is not service, and Transmission work is service. But everyone has the total right to leave the group meeting quietly at any time and let the others carry on.

I would suggest one hour as a minimum aiming to increase gradually to three or four hours, or for as long as the energies flow.

In connection with the formation of triangles and their function in potentizing the energies, consider the following: the addition of one person to the basic unit of three people increases the number of possible triangles to four. With just two more people, making a group of five, there are ten triangles. Six people make twenty triangles, seven make thirty-five, eight make fifty-six triangles, nine make eighty-four and ten people make a possible one hundred and twenty. And so on. It is obvious, therefore, how much more potent the group's activity becomes with the presence of each additional member—and how much the group is weakened by each member's absence. Through this multiplicity of triangles enormously potent energies can safely be transmitted through relatively inexperienced groups.

Soul Alignment

How important is alignment prior to Transmission Meditation? (Sept. '84)

Very important. Essential. It is the alignment between the brain and the soul which allows the Masters, working from the soul level, to channel the energies through the groups.

Is it necessary to have reached a certain level to profit by and serve through Transmission Meditation? (Nov. '85)

There is a self-selecting process at work in that only those sufficiently evolved to *want* to serve will be attracted to Transmission Meditation. But that provision aside, no special expertise or experience is required to transmit the Hierarchical energies in this way.

Do your thoughts obscure the channel of alignment during the Transmission? (May '83)

Yes, but that does not mean to say that if you are thinking, you would not be transmitting the energies. It is a question of degree. As soon as the alignment between the physical brain and the soul is made the energy can be transmitted. So all you have to do during the Transmission is to hold the alignment. If you can hold that alignment and think at the same time, your thoughts have no effect on the energy at all. The concentration needed is really the concentration of holding the alignment, but if the alignment is there all the time, normally, there is no concentration needed to hold it. What does interfere, of course, is the direction of the thought. Astral thought-forms really discolour the energies. The nature of the lower mind is to think, and so long as you do not follow the thought, do not direct the thought, it does not have any great impact on the energy. If you focus the thought on a particular person, or a group, or a country, you direct the energy to that person, or group or country, which is exactly what is not wanted. So the less you think, the better, but it does not mean that lower mind activity has any major impact on the energy flow. The point is, perfection is best, but it is not absolutely essential.

Are there moods or mental states which prevent one from having useful transmissions? (May '83)

Yes there are. Conditions of anguish, anger, especially anger, fear—in other words, strong, emotional, astral reactions are not conducive to the kind of soul alignment which is necessary for the Transmission. On the other hand, if you can make the alignment despite the emotional disturbance, you will find that the spiritual energies will be very conducive to neutralizing that state of mind.

Is Transmission to be done only by mentally stable and well-anchored people? (May '85)

Transmission should be done, in principle, only by mentally stable and well-anchored people. In specific cases it can benefit somebody who does not necessarily fit into these categories, but in principle unbalanced people should not take part. The energies are too high and there is a danger of over-stimulation.

Isn't it dangerous to say: "Meditate, you don't need to work, the energies will do the rest?" Could we not, in this way, receive negative energies if we don't have the means of differentiating between positive and negative energies? Don't you think that a lot of beginners could be misled in this way? (Apr. '86)

Not at all. I do not say, "You don't need to work, the energies will do the rest." What I say is this: Transmission Meditation is extraordinarily potent but very simple to do because the real 'work' is done for one by the Masters. All the energies which They send in this way are spiritual and 'positive.' What is required, however, is the maintenance of the alignment between the physical brain and the soul. This ensures the continuance of the conduit with Hierarchy and a positive, poised, mental focus.

Does Transmission Meditation strengthen the intuition like 'regular' meditation? (May '84)

Most certainly. Every activity (meditation and/or service) which invokes the soul qualities into the personality life strengthens the intuition. Transmission Meditation is a dynamic forcing process, by which means the nature of the soul is powerfully invoked. During the Transmission, because the centres are activated and galvanized, your mind becomes incredibly clear and creative. Through the alignment between the physical brain and the soul which is necessary to do the Transmission, the antahkarana—the channel of light between soul and brain—is kept open. Therefore it is easier for the soul to enhance the intuition of the individual.

Also, you do get an inspirational activity. Ideas often flow from the soul level into the minds of receptive individuals and many people have very good ideas during the Transmission. But that is not the aim. The aim is the act of service of stepping down the energy so that it becomes useful to a broader section of humanity. The real aim, the true motive, is service.

I understand personal meditation to be an orientation towards one's own soul via the building of the antahkarana. Does this process go ahead during transmission too? Also, is the soul itself being aligned towards Maitreya and Hierarchy? (Apr. '85)

The answer to both questions is yes. Transmission Meditation orients one not only towards one's own soul but to the Kingdom of Souls—the Spiritual Hierarchy, and potentizes whatever personal meditation we might do. Also, basically, the Transmissions take place from the soul level and involve both the soul and its reflection, the personal self.

How can I tell the difference between a Transmission Meditation and my own personal meditation? (May '86)

By the circumstances and the 'feel' of the energy. A Transmission only takes place as a result of invocation, whether in a group or not; it was for this reason that the Great Invocation was given out in 1945. In one's own personal meditation, the energy of the soul, if felt, enters the vehicles—mental and/or astral and/or physical—of the meditator. In a Transmission they *flow through* the chakras into the world.

How and when can we most appropriately transmit our soul energy? (May '86)

Here and now. There are many different techniques for invoking and transmitting soul energy. An example is the conscious use of the will and imagination in meditation.

Can we consciously project our soul energy to help in some world crisis in the news? (May '86)

Yes.

I tend to keep my attention focused on the ajna centre continuously, even during everyday activities. Is this not dangerous? (July/Aug. '84)

This is certainly not dangerous. If you are really holding the attention focused on the ajna centre continuously then you are well on the way to achieving mental polarization. Check what happens, however, to your attention when you find yourself in a situation which would normally stimulate a strong emotional reaction. Does your attention remain at the ajna centre or has it dropped to the solar plexus? Which centre then is active?

While asleep are we in communication or at-one with our souls? (July/Aug. '84)

It depends on the level of sleep. For most people, there are points of very deep sleep in which soul-contact is established and the spiritual batteries are re-charged. These are followed by phases of relatively light sleep during which dreaming takes place—an activity of the lower mind.

In Transmission Meditation, isn't there a danger of creating a hypnotic state in continually sounding the OM if one has difficulty in concentrating? (Apr. '86)

In Transmission Meditation one does not sound the OM continually but only to bring the attention back to the ajna centre (between the eyebrows) when it wanders off. In practice, you will find that the energies themselves help to keep the attention up.

Is it better to use the OM during Transmission rather than your own mantram? (May '83)

I would advise confining the use of your own meditation technique, whatever it involves, to that meditation, which would normally be twenty minutes or half an hour, twice a day. During a Transmission, on the other hand, use the OM. Most meditations using a mantram are 'ingoing' meditations, but Transmission work is a very light kind of meditation—it does not involve 'going in' at all. So I would separate the two. You will find that by the stimulus of the centres the Transmission work will enhance the personal meditation.

In Transmission Meditation can the method of the 'Sacred Presence in ourselves' in the heart, for example, replace the repetition of OM? (Apr. '86)

For some people, yes. The problem is that people in general are unaware of their point in evolution or correct method of meditation at that point. It is safer and usually more valuable to focus attention on the ajna centre and use the OM to hold it there. This is the heart centre in the head, the directing centre, and its use shifts the focus onto the mental plane.

Please explain the difference between using the OM inwardly and sounding it aloud. (Apr. '84)

If you sound the OM aloud, you ground the energy on the physical plane. If you say it inwardly, you are placing it on the upper levels of the astral plane, and if you think it, you place it on the mental planes.

The planes are just states of consciousness, energies vibrating at certain points that make us aware. We have physical plane consciousness; therefore the physical plane is a reality. We have astral (emotional) plane consciousness; therefore the astral plane is a reality. We have (more-or-less) mental plane consciousness; therefore the lower levels of that are a reality to humanity. The higher plane is always more powerful than the lower. People think that the physical plane is the plane where everything happens, but actually the physical plane is the least powerful plane on which the energies operate. The OM correctly sounded inwardly is actually more powerful than correctly sounded on the physical. It does more at a higher level.

At the beginning of the meeting, you may wish to sound aloud the OM in unison. That will immediately raise the vibration of the room. (If you are in a room in which you have an on-going Transmission group, you do not need to do this.)

When you sound the OM aloud, you are really saying A - U - M. As you say A it is vibrating at the base of the spine; as you say U it is vibrating in the heart centre, or between the solar plexus and the heart, depending on who you are; and when you say the M it is vibrating in the head. If you say AUM you are bringing all three vibrations together from the base of your spine to the top of your head. That is the power of the AUM. The inward-sounding of the OM is used not to ground energy, but simply to help send the energy into the world. The OM is used to put our attention at the mental plane level, where the energy can then go out. If our attention is down at the solar plexus, if that is where our focus is, then the energy goes out into the world on the astral plane and all astral thought-forms will discolour the spiritual energies which we transmit. As your attention wanders off, sound the OM inwardly to bring your attention back to the mental plane.

Can mantrams produce bad effects if not sounded correctly? (Apr. '84)

Yes. Mantrams produce their effects in relation to the advancement (that is, state of consciousness) of the user. The more advanced the user of the mantrams, the more powerful and the more correct the effects. The use of mantrams, however, can have a mere hypnotizing effect.

My children, who are four and two years old, say OM when they meditate because they imitate their parents. Do dangers really exist and what are they? (Apr. '86)

No. Children using the OM do so at such an ineffective level that there is nothing to fear.

How much does the tetrahedron instrument improve the Transmission? (May '83)

The Tetrahedron does not itself bring in the energies and it does not in any way improve their reception. It does, however, improve the *transmission* of the energies. These come direct from the Masters to us through the chakras. Then they go from us to the instrument. This instrument is not essential, but it is a very useful adjunct and was given for this work by my Master. There are only a very few of these instruments as yet in the world while there are many Transmission groups—and they do good work. The tetrahedron further transforms the energies, brings them lower than we can, and, at the lowered voltage, it gives them, in the end, a final boost—potentization.

It also ensures that the energies are sent out on the lower mental plane, which is the plane of the instrument itself. Just by being the shape which it is, it automatically transforms the energies down on to the mental plane. If it were a pyramid, it would transform the energies on to the astral plane, which is not the plane we want to stimulate. So, in short, it is not essential but an adjunct, a benefit for the work. I would certainly recommend groups to build one.

Transmission and Lower Psychism

Are the visions and messages people seem to get during Transmission valid? (May '83)

Many people have said to me, "We had a marvellous Transmission last Friday, all the Masters were there, the energies were wonderful, beautiful, and they gave us marvellous teachings." That is nonsense. It is pure glamour, illusion, and should be eschewed at all costs. If you are doing that, stop. They do not give marvellous teachings during Transmissions. They do not give any teachings at all during Transmissions. They simply transmit the energies through the people in the group. And all the 'teachings' and all the 'Masters' around them are in the astral imagination of the people. Because many people come into this more esoteric work from the Spiritualist movement they think it is the same thing, but it is not. It has nothing to do with the 'spirit' world and nothing to do with the teachers on the astral planes. It is a scientific process whereby the Masters, working from the Buddhic level, can transform Their energies down on to the physical plane.

Could people have contact with 'entities' during Transmissions? (June '83)

Yes, mediumistic types may allow themselves to hold a passive, negative focus at the solar plexus, and so open themselves to contact with astral entities. The danger is inherent in all meditation work; hence the necessity of holding a positive, *mental* focus (at the ajna centre).

If people do have contact with 'entities' or 'intelligences' where are these entities likely to work? (June '83)

Without exception on the astral planes and no notice should be taken of such contacts. People have free will but if an individual insists on maintaining such contacts they should be asked to continue their work on their own, outside the Transmission group.

Is it likely that 'entities' are giving suggestions on Transmission work different from your advice? (June '83)

It is possible. There are many mischievous entities on the astral planes who might do that through a mediumistic type. Whatever they bring through should be ignored. It has no bearing on this work which proceeds from Hierarchy.

Is it likely that those entities could influence the energies? (June '83)

No, not at all. The energies are under the complete control of the Christ and His group of Masters.

When a group is transmitting what is to prevent some entity or entities from directing the energies where they wish? Isn't it a glamour to think the Masters are directing the energies? Aren't you in a sense relinquishing your free will? (Sept. '84)

If you are working in a Transmission group it can be assumed, I think, that you will have accepted that the energies being channelled through you come from Hierarchy. Since this is the case, is it not also logical that the Masters send these energies consciously, scientifically, directing them according to potency, balance and destination? This being so, is it not also logical to assume that being Master Scientists and Knowers, They can and do prevent any interference with Their purposes and work? Transmission is an act of service, willingly undertaken. In no sense, therefore, is one relinquishing one's free will.

Are 'spirit guides' an actuality? Are they our souls? (Oct. '84)

There are certainly a great many discarnate entities functioning on the various levels of the seven astral or on the lower mental planes who give 'guidance' through mediums and sensitives on the physical plane. This guidance varies from the most banal trivia to teachings of a highly aspirational and uplifting kind. They are not our souls—which exist on the causal plane, the highest of the four mental planes. It is on this level that the Masters communicate with Their disciples.

Is the soul our guardian angel, or are devas involved? (Sept. '86)

The soul is not the guardian angel but the higher self. The guardian angel is a devic entity which supports and protects the human being throughout its evolutionary experience. In this way it learns to relate to humanity in preparation for the eventual fusion of the two evolutions, human and devic, in the 'divine hermaphrodite,' the human representing the male 'son of mind' aspect and the devas the female 'daughter of feeling' aspect. This will take place in the far distant future.

The Great Invocation

Could you please explain the line in the third stanza, "Let purpose guide the little wills of men." (Sept. '85)

The stanza begins: "From the Centre where the Will of God is known, Let purpose guide the little wills of men." This refers to Shamballa, the Earth's highest spiritual centre. It is in etheric matter, and within it sits the Council of the Lord of the World, Sanat Kumara (the Ancient of Days of the Bible). From Shamballa issues the Plan (of evolution of all kingdoms) which embodies the Will and the Purpose of our Planetary Logos, "The Purpose which the Masters know and serve" as the last line of the stanza has it.

If the Purpose of God, invoked through the invocation, guides "the little wills of men" then the little separate wills of men (and of course women) will come at last into correct alignment with the Divine Will and the Plan of Love and Light will work out. All that we do as a race is in response (adequate or inadequate) to the Divine energies of Will (or Purpose), Love and Light released into the world by the Spiritual Hierarchy of Masters.

Will the sealing of "the door where evil dwells" occur on Declaration Day? (May '86)

No. This is a long-term process. It involves the lifting up of humanity above the level that it can be used by the evil forces, thus sealing them off to their own domain: the upholding of the matter aspect of the planet.

Are there additional verses to the Great Invocation and will any of them be revealed in the future? (May '84)

The Great Invocation as used by humanity today is a translation (by Hierarchy)—into terms that we can use and understand—of an ancient prayer or mantram first used by Maitreya in 1945. Couched in an ancient sacerdotal tongue older than any known on earth, it is only seven mystic phrases long. As humanity advances over the next 2,500 years, newer versions will be released, each embracing more and more of the occult meanings of the original mantram.

Can we use the Great Invocation as an inner prayer, along with, for example, the Lord's Prayer, or would we disturb the Masters if we do that? (Sept. '84)

It is not given as an inner prayer but rather as an invocation of the energy of Hierarchy. Nevertheless, its use would not, I am sure, disturb the Masters.

Now that the Christ is in the world should the wording of the Great Invocation be changed? (Sept. '85)

No. I know that some groups have changed the line, "May Christ return to earth" to "Christ has returned to earth" or something similar. This change is a mistake and does not proceed from Hierarchy. "May Christ return to earth" refers not only to Maitreya, the Christ, but to the Hierarchy of which He is the head. This line should be maintained as given to invoke that group of Masters (some 40 in all) Who will return to the outer world over the next 20 years or so.

For years, several groups have disliked the line, "And may it seal the door where evil dwells" and have changed it. Again, this is a mistake. The wording of this Invocation has been most carefully worked out by Hierarchy as a form—which we can use and understand—of the deeply occult mantram used by Maitreya.

Some individuals and groups claim to have 'received' new forms of the Great Invocation, presumably from Hierarchy. I believe this to be nothing other than the result of glamour. As humanity fits itself for their reception and use, there will eventually be released new, more esoteric forms of this invocation. But, as yet, they have not even been formulated by the Masters. They must relate to the state of Being of humanity at the time and this is still unknown.

When a Transmission group has sounded the Great Invocation is it still possible for people who are late to join in? (Sept. '84)

Most certainly. But try to get them not to be late!

Transmission Work

With the time difference (I live in Australia), I am 'tuning in' to your Transmission on waking in the mornings. But I wonder if I should do this, for I find on page 30 of *Transmission - A Meditation for the New Age*, a warning against doing just that. (Oct. '83)

By all means, you should continue to 'tune in' with us as you are doing. Living as you do so many thousands of miles away there is no possibility of your taking part physically in our Transmissions. The 'warning' in the book to which you draw attention refers to the need for regular *physical* participation whenever possible. Where people are members of a Transmission group mental 'linking up' in place of physical attendance should be the odd exception rather than a regular practice.

Are three people sufficient for a Transmission Meditation group or can or should one aim for more? (May '86)

Three constitutes a triangle—and therefore a potentization of the energies sent—and is the basic unit, but the group should be expanded if possible. More energy can safely be sent through a greater number of transmitters. In short, the more the better.

I hold a Transmission group in my house. When the others leave can I continue transmitting on my own after I have shown them out? (June '86)

By all means continue after the others have gone if you feel like it and the energies still flow. But why do you have to get up to show them out? Let them find their own way out!

Is Transmission Meditation appropriate for children, or is it only for adults? (Mar. '86)

Transmission Meditation is suitable for everyone above the age of 12 years. The centres or chakras of children below that age are not yet completely stabilized.

Can a pregnant woman safely take part in Transmission Meditation even in the ninth month? (Mar. '86)

If the pregnancy is normal and the mother is well, yes.

Why must we always transmit at night and not in the morning when we are at our best? (Sept. '84)

Most Transmission groups meet at night since most people work during the day. But there is nothing to prevent anyone doing the Transmission work in the morning. The energies of the Hierarchy are available at all times. They never 'shut up shop.'

Why must we transmit in the dark? It is so easy to go to sleep. (Dec. '84)

It is not necessary to transmit 'in the dark.' The point is that most people can concentrate better in a subdued light. There is no other reason why you should not transmit in broad daylight, as we often do during Transmission workshops.

Can or should you put yourself under self-hypnosis while transmitting or does this work against what is being accomplished? (Sept. '84)

Some people find it difficult enough to keep awake the whole time during a Transmission without introducing self-hypnosis. What is required is a *positive, mental focus* which entails concentration on the ajna centre (between the eyebrows).

What is the right position in which to transmit? Is it possible to meditate with success lying down? (Sept. '86)

A comfortable seated position (or cross-legged, if comfortable) is used. It is possible to meditate lying down but to my mind not the best position, for it is too easy to fall asleep!

If one is in a Transmission group is it all right to take part in other types of group meditation or study with a particular guru? (Mar. '84)

Yes. Transmission Meditation does not work against any other form of meditation. Indeed, it will enhance the quality and effectiveness of any other meditation you may do.

You have said that Transmission Meditation is compatible with TM (Transcendental Meditation). Does this go for Kriya Yoga? (Apr. '86)

Yes. Transmission Meditation is compatible with all other forms of meditation. It is in fact a form of Kriya Yoga, but the work is done for one by the Masters, totally scientifically and occultly correctly.

While Transmission Meditation is one of the best available ways of serving, is it nevertheless possible for a group member to stop if he feels this is not his way? (Sept. '84)

Yes, of course. Service has to be willingly and gladly undertaken, otherwise it is not service but compulsion.

Are people in Eastern Europe active in Transmission work? (May '83)

The groups I know of are in Yugoslavia, because I have made a lecture tour of that country, and in Poland.

In our private Transmission Meditation are Sai Baba, the Avatar of Synthesis and the Spirit of Peace automatically invoked through the use of the Great Invocation/Messages from Maitreya as in the group overshadowing which takes place at your public lectures/Transmission workshops? (Sept. '84)

No. I am afraid there are misunderstandings in this question. Sai Baba is never 'invoked'—nor are the Avatar and the Spirit of Peace—at the public meetings. The presence of the energies of the Avatar, the Spirit of Peace and the Buddha are the result of the overshadowing of myself by Maitreya (through me this becomes a group overshadowing). The overshadowing by Sai Baba (when it occurs—usually in response to my answering a certain question) is at his whim or decision alone.

Some of us who have been working in a Transmission group would like to send 'healing thoughts' to people in need after the Transmission ends. Would you please recommend some hints, guidelines or methods which are in line with this? (Mar. '84)

A simple and effective technique is the following: holding the mind "steady in the light" (focused in the ajna centre), visualize and/or name the people one after the other. At the same time ask aloud that the healing power of God be directed to those in need. This invocation will find response in certain Masters Who either directly or through Their disciples will carry out the healing (within, of course, the limits of karma).

Is Transmission work particularly important now while we wait for the emergence of the Christ? (Aug. '82)

It is impossible to over-emphasise the importance of the work of Transmission groups—the constant channeling of energies directed by the Christ and the Masters. This is probably the most important work that all of us can easily be engaged in—whatever else, whatever other activities we might have in connection with the Plan or whatever other service activity we might be involved in. At the present it is of vital importance in creating a pool of energy and, in conjunction with meditation and prayer, helping to invoke the Christ into the outer arena of the world, to enable Him to begin His mission in the full open sense of the word.

Is Transmission work valuable only until the public appearance of Maitreya or is it an on-going process? (May '85)

Transmission work will most certainly be essential after the official appearance of the Christ and the Masters. In fact it is a continuous activity, on and on, into the New Age and beyond. The Masters, in Their own high way, are transmitting energies from higher sources 24 hours a day. It is the major work of Hierarchy and knows no end.

If enough people transmit these energies doesn't that serve as a powerful invocation to allow Maitreya, the Christ, to reveal Himself? (Aug. '82)

No, I think not. I wish it were as simple as that. As we made clear in the last issue of *Share International* (July/August 1982) it is the role of the media to locate and approach Maitreya and reveal Him to the world. The transmission of energies may play some part, as do also meditation and prayer. The general invocation by humanity during the world wars brought Him into the world under law. By the same token, a general invocation on the part of humanity can bring Him now into the outer public world.

Do Transcendental Meditation and Zen meditators transmit without knowing it? (Apr. '84)

No, not in the manner of the Transmission groups who invoke and transmit the energies of Hierarchy. In TM and Zen meditation (and all personal meditation), the energy is received from the meditator's own soul.

Is not any gathering for prayer or meditation a form of Transmission? (Apr. '84)

If invocation is involved (prayer is a form of astral invocation) then yes. But simple personal meditation whether individually or in groups does not necessarily involve transmission beyond the participants.

In the past when something bothered me, or a member of my family was ill, or there was famine in Ethiopia, I prayed to God to alleviate this suffering. Through my

study of esotericism I see some things less clearly. My question is: who do I ask for help when there is famine in a country? Is it nonsense to pray at all in this case and is the answer to actually do something? What else remains to me to do if the money I donate to an aid organization is not properly administered? (June '86)

There is real value in prayer. When from the heart, it can and does invoke help from Hierarchy as agents of divinity. But we should not simply pray and leave the problems of the world to 'God.' They are our problems, the result of our own or humanity's actions or non-actions. To grow, and to become truly human (as well as truly divine) we have to accept responsibility for the problems, the sufferings, the anguish of our brothers and sisters in the world. We are not separate from them. So action and prayer can go together. If donated money is poorly administered, change the agency to which you donate!

Is there any point in praying before a meal and if so to whom should I direct my prayer? Can it be to Maitreya, my guardian angel, or to the Master whose name I do not know? (June '86)

I believe we should thank the source of all for the food we eat. You can certainly pray to Maitreya and invoke His blessing. I recommend seeing all food as coming from the female principle—the Great Mother—and as being eaten, with thanks, in sacrifice to Her.

The Overshadowing by Maitreya

If it is harmful for young children to join Transmission groups, is it also harmful for them to be present during the overshadowing by Maitreya at your lectures? (Dec. '84)

No. Since their chakras are still in process of stabilization, in a Transmission group they would have to be continually shielded by the Masters from the full impact of the energies transmitted. This is a waste of the Masters' energy. At the meetings, however, the Christ can easily regulate the amount of energy which each person receives. I am fully aware of the increase and decrease of the potency for each individual I look at during the overshadowing.

Are initiations taking place during the overshadowing by Maitreya at your lectures? (Dec. '84)

In the sense of the major planetary initiations, no; in the sense that every transfer of power is an initiation, then yes. The power released and the stimulus to the force centres (chakras) of the audience which takes place are an initiation of sorts. The individuals in the audience are changed, their vibrational rate heightened, their state of Being altered to the degree that they can respond to, and absorb, the energies.

At your lectures, is it correct to keep our attention on the ajna centre during the overshadowing by Maitreya? (Oct. '85)

If you are not a member of a Transmission group, yes. If you are, the crown chakra should be the focus.

At a group Transmission, when you are present and being overshadowed by Maitreya, I understand our attention

should be on the crown chakra; otherwise, transmitting on our own, should it remain at the ajna centre? (Oct. '85)

Yes.

I have heard that touching each other can transfer lower vibrations from one to the other. Why, then, when you preside at a Transmission Meditation, do you ask people to hold hands?

If it is true that by touching each other we can transfer 'lower vibrations' from one to the other, then it must be equally true that by touching each other we can transfer *higher* vibrations in the same way. During a Transmission Meditation at which I am present, I am overshadowed by Maitreya Who is Himself overshadowed by the Spirit of Peace and is transmitting the energy of the Avatar of Synthesis (or the Shamballa Force) and that of the Buddha. Through me, and by the group holding hands, this becomes a group overshadowing (the group is spiritually 'nourished' by Maitreya). In my experience, those people most afraid of 'lower vibrations'—always from other people—leave something to be desired in their own.

What is overshadowing exactly and how does it work? (Mar. '83)

Overshadowing is part of the Science of Impression, a complex science in which the Masters are adept. It is a process whereby a more advanced Being can manifest some (or all) of his consciousness through a Being of lesser degree. A clear example is the overshadowing of the disciple, Jesus, by the Christ. The Christ remained in the Himalayas while His consciousness worked through the body of Jesus. This is the classical method for the manifestation of Avatars or Teachers.

The overshadowing can be partial and temporary or more or less total and long term. When used by the Spiritual Hierarchy of this (and other) planets, it is always done with the conscious co-operation and acceptance of the disciple. His free will is never infringed. (With the Black Lodge this is not the case and a method of total obsession is often used.)

The overshadowing takes place either at the Monadic level or at the soul level in the case of a disciple. Maitreya, the Christ, is overshadowed at the Monadic level by a Cosmic Avatar called the Spirit of Peace or Equilibrium (in much the same way as He, Maitreya, overshadowed Jesus).

All of this spiritual overshadowing, which is an extension of the principle of telepathy, is of quite another order than the 'overshadowing' of a medium by some discarnate entity as in spiritualism.

In order to be overshadowed must one's consciousness be centred at the causal level? (Sept. '85)

I assume the questioner means overshadowed by Maitreya or even a Master, in which case the answer is yes. This is something quite different, of course, from the usual, spiritualistic overshadowing of trance mediums which takes place from the astral planes.

What, if any, is the difference between ordinary telepathy (such as ESP and psychic sensitivity) and the mental telepathy between you and your Master or between Alice Bailey and the Master D.K.? (Sept. '85)

Telepathy is a natural human faculty but is as yet largely undeveloped. Most telepathic contacts take place instinctively, haphazardly, as a result of astral action and sensitivity, whereas true telepathy is a mental—mind to mind—process and requires mental polarization to function in a controlled, purposeful fashion.

There is this major difference between true, mental (spiritual or soul) telepathy and the more common psychic sensitivity: the latter receives its information (its channelling) from some level of the astral planes. The information or teaching received is, therefore, subject to the illusory nature of those planes (the planes of illusion) and is always more or less a distortion of reality. True mental telepathy, on the other hand, is the direct communication between two fully conscious, focused minds, using the plane of "mind" as the medium through which to make contact. It is really the demonstration of a soul faculty. It is deliberate, instantaneous, and infallible.

The Masters work only from the soul level and use this form of contact between Themselves and those disciples whose mental polarization is sufficiently developed to allow it. There are various degrees of contact and types of relationship between Masters and disciples: this can run all the way from infrequent (and, on the part of the disciple, unconscious) impression, to a moment-to-moment spiritual overshadowing which stops just short of obsession. In this way the disciple's free will is not infringed. Obsession (as in the case of Hitler, for example) is the method used by the lords of materiality. The Disciple Jesus was deeply overshadowed—but not obsessed—by Maitreya the Christ.

Why is the overshadowing at the end of your lectures more intense than at the beginning? (June '86)

Because I have the lecture still to give! After I have given the lecture and answered the questions it does not matter if Maitreya brings up His big guns!

The force or quality of the energies transmitted during the public lectures, and the overshadowing, are much less dynamic now than in years past. What is the reason for this? (Nov. '84)

This question strikes me as extraordinary and strange considering that the very opposite is taking place. Far from being less dynamic now than before, each few months sees an increase in the potency of the energies released throughout each meeting. This becomes possible as I—simply through use—am able to 'take' or support an ever increasing potency of these spiritual forces. If you could draw a graph of the heightening of the voltage, so to speak, you would find a steady line of ascent at an angle of about 45 degrees over the years. Also, over the last few years, the overshadowing by Sai Baba has become more and more frequent at these meetings. This hardly suggests a reduction of energy.

Of course, those working regularly in a Transmission group or engaged in other powerful meditation forms will be gradually attuning themselves to the impact of higher energies. The overshadowing, therefore, may not seem so overwhelming as at the initial experience of it.

Another explanation might be this: the energies are felt (when felt physically, which is by no means always the case) in the etheric body and in the chakras (force centres in the spine). But this represents only the lower end of the potencies. As the potency is gradually increased, this could raise them (the higher levels) above the point of awareness, or sensitivity, of different individuals, thus giving them the impression that the energies were less strong. I know, too, of many people who do not 'feel' the energies in a physical sense at all but who nevertheless know when they start and stop, or they may actually see them as emanations of brilliant light.

It could be, also, that the questioner is losing some of his/her sensitivity to spiritual potencies. In that case may I suggest more meditation—especially Transmission Meditation—to re-sharpen the senses?

Can you give me your opinion on all these people who say they are channelling the Masters? (July/Aug. '86)

A large number of the questions submitted to me refer to teachings of various kinds and seek to elucidate my opinion—positive or negative—about these teachings. While of course I have my opinion about these various teachings and groups (if I have come in contact with them), I really do not see it as my role to act as an authority in relation to them, nor as a guide to individuals or groups seeking to avoid unnecessary work in reading or evaluation of these teachings. No one will develop the necessary discrimination and intuition who leans so heavily on others as many do on me. I do understand that being in touch with a Master I am in a privileged position and I can understand the tendency of individuals to look to me for guidance in reading, study, etc. But everyone must make their own choices, judgements and, if necessary, mistakes. I do not see my job as that of guiding people through the minefield of the astral plane communications so prevalent today.

When I took your book (*The Reappearance of the Christ and the Masters of Wisdom*) in a brown paper bag to a Sahaja Yoga meeting and asked about seven members of the group (who have had their kundalini raised to the crown chakra and thus use the 'cool-wind' or the 'life-force energy' to determine the status of their and others' health, the truth in books, etc.) to focus their attention on the book, they all felt 'catches,' which they felt indicated untruth in your book. Would you explain why this happened, please? (Apr. '86)

Without seeking to claim infallibility, I must say, with respect, that your experience with this group who "have had their kundalini raised to the crown chakra" does not cause me to blush with too much shame, nor would I be too happy in allowing them to determine the state of my health by these methods. I would rather trust the most hidebound, allopathic doctor! I wonder how many 'catches' (of the breath?) they would have felt had they been divining the 'truth' of the Christian Bible, the Bhagavad Gita, the Koran, Upanishads, etc. The point is, had they 'felt' no 'catches' this would not prove that my book contains only 'truth' any more than their feeling them indicates the opposite. If it indicates anything at all (which, you will have gathered, I very much doubt) perhaps it indicates their sensing of ideas with which they are unfamiliar and would tend to reject.

Suggested Reading

I have started and organized a Transmission group with about 9-10 young people, who meet weekly and have questions which need an immediate answer. I am troubled by the fact that I know so little. I would like to know much more about energy, for instance. Of course, I have got the book *Transmission - A Meditation for the New Age*, and I also subscribe to *Share International*. I am reading it but now I have the feeling of knowing even less than before. It's all just bits and pieces, nothing whole. Somebody asks about a ray, and I don't know what he means. They ask about initiation and degrees of Masterhood. I don't know anything about this either. What, for example, are Monads? The only thing I understand is your statement that the Christ is again in the world, in a human body. I believe it and pass on this message. That is all. Is that enough to guide a group of intelligent young people? I don't think so. Could you recommend me a book maybe? (Apr. '85)

Your problem of lack of knowledge is not an unusual one; so few people have studied the esoteric teachings. But really, to be in a Transmission group it is not necessary to know or understand everything. It is an act of service requiring only patience and the desire to serve. Of course, there are many books which may be studied which will help you to answer the young people's questions, but why should they not study the books themselves, since it is they who are asking the questions? The *Alice Bailey Teachings*, given by the Tibetan Master, D.K., contain answers to all the questions which your group are likely to ask. The first book of the series, *Initiation Human and Solar*, gives much information on initiation, the Masters, etc.. *Esoteric Psychology*, Vols. 1 and 2, give a vast range of information on the rays, while the compilation, *Ponder on This*, covers many subjects in an easily accessible manner. My own book, *The Reappearance of the Christ and the Masters of Wisdom*, answers questions asked during the course of my lectures on a wide range of subjects. But the young people should be encouraged to make the necessary study and research for themselves and not to rely on a teacher. It takes a very long time to become reasonably competent in esoteric matters.

For people who lead a busy life what books would you recommend as essential reading for students of esoteric teaching?

At the end of my book, *The Reappearance of the Christ and the Masters of Wisdom*, I give a list of books as suggested further reading. Among the most valuable books for those with very limited time for reading are *Ponder on This* and *Serving Humanity*, both compilations, from the books of Alice A. Bailey, by Aart Jurriaanse whose articles on esotericism are a regular feature of *Share International Magazine*.

The Role of Service in the Evolution of the Disciple

[The following article is an edited transcription of a talk given by Benjamin Creme at the Tara Center Network Conference held in San Francisco, California, U.S.A. in July 1986. The relevant questions and answers raised during the Conference are also included in this section.]

The basic impulse behind all evolution is that activity of the soul which we call service. Service is nothing less than the demonstration in relationship of the law of love. It is the love of God for Its creation which impels the Logos Itself to take incarnation and to demonstrate Itself through a planetary form. We are part of that planetary form. We are thoughtforms in the mind of the Logos. As the Christ so beautifully put it, "we are His dreams." He brought us into manifestation, and in the same way can take us out of manifestation. We owe our whole existence and conscious awareness to His act of service on behalf of the solar Logos. He, in His turn, has created His body of manifestation, the solar system, in relation to His awareness of the Plan of "the One about whom naught may be said" at the centre of our galaxy. We are related to that same impulse every time we serve. Every impulse of the soul leading to service is a demonstration at our own quite small level of an impulse initiated many countless light-years away and light-years back in time by the Logos at the heart of our galaxy.

That is how important and how unimportant we are: how unimportant we are as individual personalities, and how important we are as active exponents of our soul's nature. As we serve, we grow in service and we grow in love. As we grow in love, we grow into more service and into more love. It is the nature of God to love and to serve. We are living in a 2nd ray solar system (this is an esoteric truism). That means that in this solar system God is love. The 2nd ray of love-wisdom is the basic, synthesizing ray of the whole system. Whatever other ray may be demonstrating, whatever other ray quality might be ours either as souls or as personalities, standing behind them all is the 2nd ray of love-wisdom. Every other ray, including the 1st and 3rd, is a sub-ray of the 2nd ray. We are made in the image of God as love, and the nature of God as love is to serve. There is only one impulse in the whole of cosmos, demonstrating in multi-faceted ways: the impulse to serve. Hence the importance of service in the evolution of the individual, and, specifically, of the disciple.

The disciple has, at some level, dedicated himself to serve the Plan of evolution of the planet insofar as he has made himself aware of that Plan. At any given moment he can be aware only of a tiny fragment of the Plan but his purpose in incarnation is to demonstrate his knowledge of that fragment to the best of his soul's ability.

The aim of all disciples, therefore, should be to see above and beyond the limited view of the personality to the broader, more inclusive view of the soul and to work from the soul level. Our difficulty in working together and relating to each other is to do with the differences of our ray structures. It is that which keeps us apart. So long as our personality, which has a limited sense of the whole, is dominating and potent, we will find resistance from other equally dominant personalities governed by different rays. It is this which creates the friction in every group and every international conference.

Humanity today is so disparate, so proud of its differences, so proud of its individuality. This is a direct result of the influence of the last two thousand years of Pisces. So successful has been that influence that a large section of humanity is now demonstrating a powerful, self-assertive individuality. This is a necessary preliminary step—in order to give it up. You cannot give up what you do not already have. To give up your individuality you must have individuality. Humanity is beginning to demonstrate the potency of Leo. Leo is the sign of the potent, self-loving, self-oriented, egotistical personality. all of which is necessary in order to move into Aquarius and demonstrate the server.

From Leo, the Self-Server to Aquarius, the World Server

Leo and Aquarius are polar opposites. Leo is in the bottom half of the zodiacal chart and Aquarius is at the top. They are absolutely, diametrically opposed. You move, eventually, from Leo into Aquarius; from the man or woman dedicated to serving his/her own separate personality, to the world server.

It is necessary, first of all, to serve your own separate personality to become potent in personality expression. Because if you are not potent in personality expression, the soul has nothing to use. You are the vehicle for your soul and the soul needs an integrated, potent personality through which it can pour its energy and carry out its plans and purposes. The difficulty for the soul is that it tries to do it through inadequate material.

That is what the process of evolution is about. It is, first of all, about evolving an instrument, a personality apparatus with a powerful, focused mental body, a purified astral body and a strong and healthy physical body. With that threefold personality the soul eventually creates a vehicle through which its own nature can powerfully be expressed. Leo serves his own personality. Aquarius serves the world. That is the movement from the potent, self-loving, self-serving personality to the world server.

Let me quote the Master D.K. quoting from the *Old Commentary* (Leo, the self-server, is the lion, of course):

> "The lion begins to roar. He rushes forth, and in his urge to live, he wields destruction. And then again he roars and, rushing to the stream of life, drinks deep. Then, having drunk, the magic of the waters works. He stands transformed. The lion disappears, and he who bears the water pot stands forth and starts upon his mission."

The lion, Leo, the self-serving, potent personality, changes and becomes Aquarius. He becomes the 'water carrier.' The destruction which the lion wields is precisely the destructiveness of the self-loving, self-serving, potent individual. If you are not potent as a personality, you neither destroy nor create very much. One has to become potent in the personality sense. By that I do not mean become a domineering, dominating personality, but an effective, potent one.

The aim of the evolutionary process then is, first of all, to create the integrated personality, the Leo characteristic, to demonstrate an effective, active personality expression in which the physical, the astral, and the mental processes are integrated, synchronous in their vibration. It is all to do with synchronicity of vibration.

Under the law of love, like attracts like. It is the magnetic, cohesive, attractive force of love which brings together the atoms of matter to create the building bricks of life. That is the function of the energy which we call love, the 2nd ray of love-wisdom. By its action we come into being. By its action the creative process develops, the forms are built. Without that action there would be no forms. The Christ Principle, the energy of evolution per se, governs the creation of the matter aspect. The little building-bricks of matter are formed by the cohesive energy which we call love, holding together the tiny particles of substance to create all that we see, and of course all that we do not see as well. That cohesive force works through synchronicity of vibration.

Service is the key. Eventually, the soul (which really brings us to the first initiation—it is the first Master) looks down and sees its vehicle ready for the first time in thousands of incarnations, and brings its instrument, ourselves, into meditation of some kind. It repeats this in every subsequent incarnation until you may have a whole life dedicated in a really powerful way to some meditation process.

So the soul works, gradually 'gripping' its vehicle. Meanwhile, the Masters watch this process. They work co-operatively with the soul and give various stimuli to the disciple as he approaches initiation. They stimulate energetically the vehicles and higher chakras of the individual. They may stimulate the heart centre, seeking to evoke the energy of love, to awaken the heart or love nature of the individual. (The heart is almost always the first of the chakras to be opened.) They work by stimulus and by testing, and most importantly of all by the provision of a field of service to the individual.

This is itself a test. The soul wants to serve. The Master helps this process along by providing a field of service. If he is not in direct touch with his Master, the Master does it through the person's out-of-body experience. The aspirant will want to serve in some way (he might want to serve for a few incarnations and do nothing about it, but he will *want* to serve.). It is the soul who is demanding service because that is its nature. The Masters call Their work "the Great Service." Their existence on this planet is to do with Their desire to serve. They are not here for any other reason than to serve the plan of evolution of all the kingdoms.

As you serve, you change. A most extraordinary thing happens. The aim of the disciple is to shift from the integrated, self-serving Leo to the world server in Aquarius. The lion of the *Old Commentary* disappears and "he who bears the water pot stands forth and starts upon his mission." The self-serving, separative, potent individual in Leo becomes the integrated disciple, the world server, the water-carrier in Aquarius.

The Christ comes today to serve the world, to act as the Agent of God, the Avatar, the World Teacher for this age. He says, "I am the Water Carrier." He brings the *Waters of Life*, the new livingness which He releases on all planes. He brings a new potency to our life, on the physical, the emotional and on the mental and spiritual planes. We are entering into an entirely new kind of livingness such as only the very advanced initiates can possibly be aware of up until now. This will become the reality for the vast majority of people. The race as a whole will make this tremendous step forward into becoming the world disciple.

The paths of the individual disciple and the world disciple are parallel. You move through service. Coming out of the herd as the separate and potent self-serving personality in Leo, and, in Aquarius, sacrificing that hard-won separate individuality, one places it at the service of the soul and therefore of the world. That is the Law governing the evolution of disciples.

Steadfastness, Service and Sacrifice

Three very important principles govern the evolution of disciples. They are *steadfastness*, determination to keep to it utterly, without moving and never backsliding, steadfastness to the Plan, to the pledge of the disciple; *service* and *sacrifice*. These are governing principles. Of course they are inter-related. You cannot serve in fits and starts. True soul service is a steadfast expression. The soul never has desire for rest, for change (except for a change of vehicle when the old one runs out of steam). The disciple, to progress at all, must show steadfastness; he cannot become a disciple if he does not.

He must not just *desire* to serve, but must actually serve. Otherwise no progress can be made. I am approached by many people who say, "I'm longing to serve! For years and years I have longed to serve. I have a deep feeling that I was born to play a very important role in helping the starving millions of the world. Can you tell me how to start?" I have actually received that kind of request not once, but many times. I am always meeting people who say, "I am working on myself in order better to serve—of course I can't serve until I get myself really together and healthy." And they mean it. I do not say this in any cynical way—they believe it. They really feel that if they had a better body they would obviously be able to serve better. Which is true, but it does not mean that they would serve better but simply that they would have a better capacity.

Some of the best servers I know of have been ill all their lives. We have instances in the past of great disciples like Helena Blavatsky and Alice Bailey who were ill for many years. Alice Bailey was ill for goodness knows how many years. Only the continuous activity of her Master kept Madame Blavatsky in the body for the last thirteen or so years of her life. She had a number of illnesses which would have killed off any other entity; but she had a will and demonstrated that will in service. The will to serve, the sacrificial will of the soul, is the power which impels these great disciples, notwithstanding the limitations of the physical body, the tiredness, the fatigue, the fools with which they must have been surrounded if history can be believed—notwithstanding all of that, the drain on their attention, their energy, their goodwill, their patience—they served as few serve in the world. That is true of all the great ones.

As you serve, you change. Why do you change? Because service works in you to perform a miracle. It is literally a miracle; a transforming process takes place. Your soul makes you serve, and you begin to serve in whatever small, limited capacity. The nearer you are to the field of service, the quicker you get on with it. It need not be at the other side of the world, although that might be your calling. You can start right where you are now. The aim is to shift out of a totally self-serving, centralized situation. We are all centralized; we are all living as the centre of our world. That is the psychic experience of all of us, if you think about it. That is the action of the desire principle. And of course it is a stage. It is not something wrong or evil, but it is a necessary stage to get out of. As you serve you shift your point of focus. You identify with what you serve. You identify more and more with that which you serve, until, without your even being aware of it, you lose consciousness of yourself, you forget yourself, and as you forget yourself you get healthier, more potent, more energetic.

The process is one of decentralization. As you relate to those whom you serve, you become more and more decentralized. You identify with a wider and wider sphere of life, until you can, if you become a Master, identify with all of life.

The Master has no sense of Himself as a separate individuality at all. He has no personality feeling. He has no sense of "I." There is no sense in the Master's consciousness of a separate being. He has only group consciousness. We do not know what it is, we cannot even imagine it, but it is what inevitably will be developed over this coming Age of Aquarius, as we move from the Leo into the Aquarian experience; as we move from the self-server in Leo, to the world server in Aquarius, and become the water-carrier.

The Christ works through us. He brings the Waters of Life "in abundance," as He says. And He says "I seek to channel these Waters of Life through you." As we become the water-carriers, the world servers, we act as channels for these Waters of Life, and through us the Christ transforms the world. Through us He builds the forms, the structures, the consciousness of the new age.

The role of service in the evolution of the disciple is the nature of God working through the disciple. Hence its importance and hence, of course, its effectiveness. It is not like a tool which might or might not work. It will work, it is inevitable that it will work, because it is the nature of God Itself. And as we demonstrate the nature of God through service, we become gods. We actually become gods. From being human beings, men and women, we become living, creative divine beings.

Service is the key to that whole process and provides the disciple with the lever for his evolution. Service is the lever of the evolutionary process.

You mentioned sacrifice as one of the three elements crucial to the whole question of this service activity. When I hear that word, sacrifice, I think of the Christian term of sacrifice which is to limit oneself, deny one's needs, therefore feeling like a martyr. I believe sacrifice and denial is a

function of the ego, and our mortal selves, leading to pain and suffering. Please clarify service.

You say, "Sacrifice and denial is a function of the ego." I wonder if it is. To my mind, sacrifice is the motivating spiritual instinct which brings the soul of the individual man or woman into incarnation in the first place. There is no coming into incarnation without the self-sacrificial will of the soul. The soul incarnates in co-operative response to the Will of God, to its knowledge of the Plan which brings groups of souls into incarnation at any particular time, governed by certain rays which makes them peculiarly suitable at that time. It is an opportunity for service. They will be presented with an opportunity for service, either individually or as part of a group, a small group, or a very wide group. So the initial impulse to incarnate is to serve. It is self-sacrifice.

Self-sacrifice is not denial, doing without, it really has nothing to do with that at all. That is a church interpretation of the Christian message, a denial of life. If sacrifice is a denial of life, then it is evil. Anything which denies life is evil.

There are various grades of life. In the case of the self-sacrifice of the soul and the world server, sacrifice really comes into relation with service, world service. The self- sacrifice of the server is not self-denial. It is the very opposite, actually. It is the sacrifice only of time, of energy, of attention to other things; in other words, it is a sacrifice of the lower for the higher, which is not really a sacrifice at all. Seen as such it is the lever of evolution itself. Hence the stressing of service as crucial in the evolution of the disciple.

Every disciple who comes into relationship with Hierarchy is immediately presented with some task, some role of service which entails sacrifice. Not the sacrifice of his livingness. On the contrary, it is to bring about the manifestation of a greater, a higher livingness. All he is asked to sacrifice are these things which we all have and which we misuse totally, time, energy, and the like. So in taking up some service and going through the small bits and pieces of sacrifice of the personality in order to better serve, you are not sacrificing anything at all. You are gaining that which you think you might be losing, because all you are losing is that sense of yourself as a separate entity. And when you lose that sense of yourself as a separate entity, you become what you essentially are, a soul.

I prefer to use the word "surrender" instead of "sacrifice," to surrender our being to the soul's guidance.

Yes, surrender is part of it. A better word than surrender, I think, is "renunciation." The path of the disciple is really the path of renunciation, again, of the lesser for the greater. It culminates in the Great Renunciation, the fourth initiation, when the Arhat, as He then is—not quite the perfected Master and Adept, but the fourth degree initiate divine man—severs the knots, the final ties which keep him bound to the physical plane. He has to renounce everything, all that might lure him back into matter.

It is sacrifice, it is renunciation, but of course it does not feel like that at the time. It is a demonstration of his true inner reality as a Son of God and entails the renunciation of that which holds him back from its complete demonstration. That is the Crucifixion Initiation or the Great Renunciation. It is not a sacrifice at all, it is a surrender, if you like, but better, a renunciation of that which no longer works for him, is not needed any more.

Sai Baba uses the term "detachment." He is talking about the same thing, right?

There are two kinds of detachment. There is detaching yourself in the sense of renouncing the lower for the higher; you are detaching yourself from that which holds you to the lower aspect of yourself, the personality, service to the personality. You can only grow out of service to the personality by detaching yourself from your own personality. That is what getting out of Leo and into Aquarius is about. From self-service to world service. It is done through detachment. But there is the detachment from your emotions which is part of that process, and then there is the detachment from the result of the work which you do in service.

There is also detachment from life which is not the same thing. There are many people who detach themselves from the impact on themselves of their own emotions, their own highly disturbing astral nature, by isolating themselves from any circumstances which could invoke that nature. So they go into monasteries, convents, they isolate themselves, they surround themselves with people who will never evoke, never draw it from them. That is a self protective device which is really a trap, and in no way brings about the detachment which can be arrived at only through the hurly-burly and interaction of life.

You talked about sacrifice and service, and the other thing that you talked about, was steadfastness. Could you go into that in more detail?

Steadfastness is the result of spiritual discipline. It is not necessarily the result of physical plane discipline, or mental discipline, the discipline of an ordered life, ordered work, starting at nine and finishing at five, everyday.

Steadfastness is living from the spirit level of yourself, holding the soul aspect of yourself in the forefront. I do not mean you go around all the time saying, "I am a soul, I am a soul, I must remember, I am a soul." Not at all. Steadfastness is the continuous concentration of everything you have on the highest light of truth that you have. For what you believe in, rightly or wrongly, but what you believe in from wherever you are coming; the focusing of all your attention and all your aspiration, and bringing the whole of your available will power to bear on the furthering of that idea or ideal or purpose or whatever it is.

I was aware, when I began this work years and years ago, way back in the fifties, of a great aspiration from time to time. I would have sacrificed myself for the world. I remember, when I came into contact with the Space Brothers and I knew there was a world to be saved, that I was perfectly ready to die, I thought. I was never challenged, so I do not know, but I had a total readiness to sacrifice myself if by doing so it would save the world from war. I had a great aspiration to serve and to sacrifice myself. It came out of a kind of misunderstanding, really, of what the whole thing was about. It is quite obvious that my dying would not save the world at all. It was a colossal arrogance for one thing, to imagine that just by my dying, the world could be saved. It was like Christians thinking that Jesus died and saved the world. Well he did not. He could not. No one can. My dying would not have perform the same function, but something of my higher self or soul-aspiration manifested, and I was moved and uplifted and ready to die if it would save the world.

I do not have that kind of aspiration anymore. I suppose I do have aspiration, but I find it very difficult to see it, to recognize it, because it has shifted totally. Most of my best coworkers are working under that high, uplifting, specifically aspiring quality. Fiery aspiration, that is what makes the whole activity in which we are engaged function. But I myself do not feel, that aspiration. I recognize something quite different. I have, I suppose, the steadfastness. What I do, I do because it has got to be done. I simply bring my will to bear to do the things that I do. What I do have now, I think, is the kind of steadfastness that comes from the will, the continuous application to go on, and on, and on, so long as it is needed. That is steadfastness. That is necessary; you have to have that to produce anything.

Could you give advice to us, as we go back to our respective groups or jobs after the conference, how to keep your sense of steadfastness?

I think it is very easy to be caught up, as I then was, lifted up by the ideal of sacrifice, and the great cause. You are thrilled with the very idea that this is where it is all happening, and you are a part of it. You are so uplifted that service is a joy. But after you have done it for a few years, the joy, well, the joy does not go but the pleasure principle no longer works. The joy may be there, but joy and pleasure are not the same at all.

Joy is not an emotional thing. While it is emotional, it will go down. The people who do not continue, who are not steadfast, are those who have a wonderful, thrilling emotional response to the message, and have a wonderful, thrilling desire to serve, for a time, while their emotion carries them forward. But if it does not go higher than the emotions, if their mental body is not involved, if their soul is not involved, and if from the soul their will is not involved, then they are not going to be steadfast. They are not going to carry on when nobody responds, when the media do nothing, when nothing happens, when Maitreya does not reveal Himself, day after day, week after week, year after year. You have got to go on, and on, just plugging away. Do you think when Oxfam began the people involved knew, could know, that it would be one of the major aid agencies in the world? No, they just addressed the problem where it was, with a tiny income, and a tiny office, and then gradually expanded throughout the world.

You have to start small, with a small image of yourself, but plugging away at that need, what you have to do. Get it above the emotional level. Bring in the soul, the purpose and will of the soul, and galvanize it from the soul level. When you do that, it does not matter if you like it or not. You do all the boring things because they have to be done. The discipline of the spirit is steadfastness itself. That is where the will and purpose of the soul keeps you steadfast, because it is nothing to do with you, you are simply addressing world need.

Could you comment on what people in new age circles often say, I am "meant to be" here, or "meant to do" that? Is there really a 'meant'?

The Master D.K. wrote about service: "True service is being in the right place and staying there." That means being in the right position to serve, wherever you are called to. That might be at home, or at the farthest corner of the earth. But being in the right situation vis-a-vis your soul's purpose. And staying there, being steadfast. That is what is meant by staying there. Being steadfast.

People say: "Where am I meant to be? Am I where I am meant to be? Am I doing what I am meant to do?" That question irritates me. Of course, I understand where it is coming from. It is the knowledge that the soul has its purpose, and that people are meant to respond to soul purpose. But it does not mean that they are meant to be in California or Ohio or New York or wherever. It is not that specific.

Nor is it that there is only one possible field of service for any individual. The soul knows best where your field of service is. But unless you are in touch with the soul, *you* do not know. So the thing is to just get going at what draws you, attracts you, and if you are sufficiently responsive to your soul, you can be sure your soul will guide you to the right field of service. That is being in the right place. And the steadfastness is staying there. The rest is glamour.

As I understand it, people see themselves as manipulated, like puppets on strings, by the Masters. Master Morya has put this one here. The Master Koot Hoomi this one here. The one they know best, the Master D.K., is manipulating them into this or that, depending on what they like. If they like art, it is always the Master Serapis. If they like mysticism or meditation, it is the Master Koot Hoomi, or Maitreya Himself. If they feel themselves pretty strong-minded individuals, powerfully dominant types, it is sure to be the Master Morya who is manipulating them and putting them in the right place at the right time.

You would be surprised how little of that actually happens. These Masters, the Masters Morya, Koot Hoomi, Serapis, Jesus, the Master R (the one they call St. Germain), are very advanced, sixth degree initiates, Chohans, and They have nothing to do with the bulk of 'new age' people, who are either on the verge of the first initiation, or, at most, at some point between the first and second initiation. None of the Chohans have anything to do with people at that stage. That is all glamour.

There is a 'meant' in the sense that there is soul purpose and if you are carrying out your soul purpose, you will be in the right place vis-a-vis the needs of the time, vis-a-vis the aim of your service. And if you are steadfast, you will stay there.

I'd like to defend the 'new age' groups. They are trying to work on themselves to clear the emotional blockage, to have better understanding of themselves.

I am sure that is true. The thing is that people spend so much time doing that, clearing the way in order to serve, to do the soul's work in service, that they never actually find time to get around to the service. There is no reason why people should not serve while they are getting on with clearing away the rubbish of the personality, but people do not. They say, "I will serve when I am ready, and I will be ready when I am clear, and I will be clear when I do this and that, when I meditate for the next 50 years, or when I go through this rebirthing and that releasing ìand go to this guru and that group, and so on." They do not get around to serving. That is what I am talking about.

I am putting the emphasis on the role of service in the evolution of the *disciple*. You may be talking about the activity of the aspirant. I am talking about disciples. Probationary disciples also are tested and called upon to serve. It is their proven capacity to serve which makes them full fledged disciples. The *need* of the disciple is to serve. The beauty of the disciple is his service. Because the disciple is already in touch with his soul, if he does not use in service the energy which comes to him from the soul, he becomes neurotic, it turns bad on him. The neuroses of disciples are the outcome of their wrong use, or non-use, of soul energy. Then they go to all these other things.

Since I cannot be a leader in the political or economic groups, I feel somewhat inadequate, if it is only through the political or economic groups that the major changes in the world can take place.

Why do you have to be a leader? You are a citizen of the United States, a more or less democratic society with a Constitution which grants you the power of voting for a form of government to organize the communal life of the United States. That gives you enormous power. You can use that power in different ways. You can just go along mechanically and vote the way your mother and father voted, or your friends vote, or you can vote the way that you really want to vote. That has a crucial effect on the life of this country. Everybody living in the United States is responsible for the present administration of the United States. Just as everyone in Britain is responsible for the present administration in Britain. In France, or West Germany, or wherever, the same applies. Wherever you have that right to vote, you have responsibility. You are responsible for the activity of your country, at home and abroad. That is enormous power.

Over the last two thousand years, we have demonstrated the knowledge aspect of God culminating in our present-day science and technology. We are now on the point, on a mass scale, of demonstrating the love nature of God, the inner spiritual reality which Man is, through the action and stimulus of the Christ and the Masters of Hierarchy. What the Masters call "the Crisis of Love,"—demonstration of the Love principle through humanity—that spiritual crisis is focused today through the political and the economic field. It is the political and economic problems which divide the world today; they provide the two major divisions, East and West, North and South. That is why the Christ, you will find, when He makes His appeal to the world, will place them at the very centre of His concerns. He will call for the transformation, in the first place, of our political and economic structures.

That is something which all of us have the power to affect. It is the millions of ordinary little men and women everywhere in the world who will force the governments to implement the principle of sharing, the solution to the world's problems. That is the power of the masses today. The masses, educated by the Christ, inspired by the Christ, whose aspiration is focused by the Christ, will force the governments to act. World public opinion, energized, inspired, focused, and educated, is a force against which no government on earth can stand. Do you see how important you are, as individuals?

APPENDIX

THE LIST OF INITIATES
Their Rays And Stage Of Evolution

The figures in brackets refer to the initiate's exact point of development attained during that life. The initiatory degree has been omitted in the case of Avatars.

Five figures follow the brackets;the rays relate to the soul, personality, mental apparatus, astral vehicle and physical body. Also is indicated the dates of birth and death, and the field of endeavour in which the initiate became known. Many of the people on the list were so versatile that it was virtually impossible to classify them in one category. However, the limits of space available left no option. In a few cases, unfortunately, it was impossible to find all the relevant data; such omissions are denoted by a question mark.

Arthur Adamov (1.6)	2-3-5-6-3	(1908-70)	Dramatist
Konrad Adenauer (1.7)	1-3-1-6-3	(1876-1967)	Statesman
Alfred Adler (2.0)	2-1-1-2-7	(1870-1937)	Psychiatrist
Jankel Adler (2.0)	2-4-1-6-3	(1895-1949)	Painter
Aeschylus (1.7)	4-1-3-4-7	(524-455 BC)	Dramatist
Akbar the Great (1.45)	1-1-3-6-3	(1542-1605)	Emperor
Akhnaton (1.5)	2-6-1-6-7	(1372-1354 BC)	King
Alexander the Great (1.5)	1-1-3-6-1	(356-323 BC)	King
Hans C. Anderson (1.6)	6-4-2-6-7	(1805-75)	Author
Fra Angelico (2.5)	6-4-6-2-7	(1387-1455)	Painter
Apelles (1.6)	2-4-4-6-3	(fl. 325 BC)	Painter
Guillaume Apollinaire (1.6)	2-3-4-6-7	(1880-1918)	Poet
Apollonius of Tyana (5.0)	6-1-1-2-7	(16-c.97 AD)	Philosopher
St. Thomas Aquinas (2.0)	6-6-7-2-3	(1225-74)	Theologian
Archimedes (2.2)	5-2-1-2-1	(c. 287-212 BC)	Mathematician
Aristophanes (1.6)	2-4-1-4-7	(448-385 BC)	Comic dramatist
Aristotle (2.4)	7-5-1-6-3	(384-322 BC)	Philosopher
Sir Richard Arkwright (1.6)	2-1-5-4-5	(1732-92)	Inventor
Matthew Arnold (2.2)	2-4-6-4-3	(1822-88)	Poet
Raymond Aron (2.0)	3-7-6-6-3	(1905-83)	Historian/sociologist
Antonin Artaud (1.6)	3-4-4-6-3	(1896-1948)	Dramatist

Asoka (3.0)	2-4-1-4-3	(265-238 BC)	Emperor
Roberto Assagioli (2.0)	2-2-3-6-3	(1888-1974)	Psychiatrist
Mustafa Kemal Atatürk (2.2)	1-1-5-2-7	(1881-1938)	Statesman
St Augustine (2.3)	6-6-1-4-7	(354-430)	Theologian
Emperor Augustus (1.75)	1-1-6-6-1	(63-14 BC)	Emperor
Marcus Aurelius (1.4)	2-6-6-2-7	(121-180)	Emperor
Sri Aurobindo Ghose (3.7)	2-6-1-6-3	(1872-1950)	Mystic
Jane Austin (1.75)	2-4-6-6-3	(1831-94)	Novelist
J S Bach (3.1)	2-4-7-6-3	(1685-1750)	Composer
Francis Bacon (3.7)	7-4-4-6-3	(1561-1626)	Statesman
Roger Bacon (2.6)	7-4-1-6-3	(1220-92)	Philosopher
Baha'u'llah (3.0)	6-6-6-4-7	(1817-92)	Bahaism founder
Alice A Bailey (3.2)	2-1-1-2-3	(1880-1949)	Occultist
John Logie Baird (1.7)	2-5-3-6-7	(1888-1946)	Inventor
Honoré de Balzac (2.0)	3-7-6-6-3	(1799-1850)	Writer
Béla Bartók (1.8)	2-7-4-4-3	(1881-1945)	Composer
Charles P. Baudelaire (1.7)	2-4-1-6-3	(1821-67)	Poet
Pierre de Beaumarchais (1.7)	2-7-6-2-1	(1732-99)	Comic dramatist
Thomas à Becket (1.75)	6-2-4-6-3	(1118-70)	Archbishop/martyr
The Venerable Bede (2.0)	6-6-2-6-1	(c. 673-735)	Historian/scholar
Ludwig van Beethoven (3.1)	4-4-1-2-7	(1770-1827)	Composer
Brendan Behan (1.0)	2-4-1-6-3	(1923-64)	Writer
Aphra Behn (2.0)	2-1-5-2-3	(1640-89)	Writer
Belisarius (1.7)	5-1-1-4-3	(505-565)	General
Alexander Graham Bell (1.75)	3-2-1-2-3	(1847-1922)	Inventor
Giovanni Bellini (3.0)	7-6-1-4-7	(c. 1430-1516)	Painter
Vincenzo Bellini (1.8)	2-2-4-4-3	(1801-35)	Composer
David Ben-Gurion (1.7)	3-1-1-6-3	(1886-1973)	Statesman
Eduard Benes (2.0)	1-6-3-2-1	(1884-1948)	Statesman
Karl Friedrich Benz (1.7)	3-1-5-4-3	(1844-1929)	Engineer
Alban Berg (2.0)	2-4-7-6-7	(1885-1935)	Composer
Henri Bergson (1.75)	3-1-3-2-3	(1859-1941)	Philosopher
Hector Berlioz (2.3)	4-4-4-6-3	(1803-69)	Composer
Sarah Bernhardt (1.65)	2-4-4-6-3	(1844-1923)	Actress
Annie Besant (2.15)	7-1-4-6-7	(1847-1933)	Theosophist
Otto von Bismarck (2.0)	1-1-1-6-3	(1815-96)	Statesman
William Blake (2.2)	2-4-1-6-3	(1757-1827)	Poet/painter
H P Blavatsky (4.0)	1-2-1-6-3	(1831-91)	Occultist
Louis Blériot (1.6)	3-5-7-2-3	(1872-1936)	Aviator

Boadicea (1.6)	4-1-1-6-3	(1st cent. AD)	Warrior-queen
Giotto di Bondone (2.4)	6-4-6-2-7	(1266?-1337)	Painter/architect
William Booth (1.65)	2-6-6-2-7	(1829-1912)	Salvation Army founder
Lucrezia Borgia (1.6)	1-4-7-2-5	(1480-1519)	Patroness
Hieronymus Bosch (1.8)	6-4-7-6-3	(1450-1516)	Painter
Don Giovanni Bosco (1.7)	1-6-1-2-7	(1815-88)	Preacher
Louis Botha (1.6)	1-3-1-4-1	(1862-1919)	Statesman/soldier
Sandro Botticelli (2.7)	2-6-7-4-7	(1445-1510)	Painter
Robert Boyle (2.4)	1-1-3-2-3	(1627-91)	Scientist
Tycho Brahe (1.8)	2-1-7-6-3	(1546-1601)	Astronomer
Prajapita Brahma (1.7)	2-4-6-6-4	(1875-1969)	Founder of Brahma Kumaris sect
Johannes Brahms (2.5)	2-4-4-6-3	(1833-97)	Composer
Louis Braille (1.6)	3-6-3-2-3	(1809-52)	Teacher of the blind
Bertholt Brecht (1.6)	1-4-1-6-3	(1898-1956)	Dramatist
Pieter Breughel (1.9)	4-4-1-6-7	(c. 1520-69)	Painter
Leonid Brezhnev (2.0)	1-7-6-6-7	(1906-82)	Politician
Benjamin Britten (1.8)	2-4-4-6-3	(1913-76)	Composer
Louis César Broglie (1.6)	1-3-1-4-3	(1875-1960)	Physicist
Emily Brontë (1.4)	2-4-4-6-3	(1818-48)	Writer
Henry Brougham (1.7)	1-1-7-2-3	(1778-1868)	Politician
Anton Bruckner (2.2)	4-6-4-2-3	(1824-96)	Composer
Isambard Kingdom Brunel (1.7)	2-5-1-6-5	(1806-59)	Engineer
Giordano Bruno (2.3)	1-1-7-6-7	(1548-1600)	Philosopher
Paul Brunton (1.8)	2-4-6-6-7	(1898-1981)	Spiritual writer
Georg Büchner (1.6)	4-1-1-4-7	(1813-37)	Poet
Gautama Buddha	2-2-1-2-7	(c. 563- c.483 BC)	Avatar
Luther Burbank (1.6)	2-2-4-6-3	(1849-1926)	Horticulturalist
William Byrd (2.0)	4-6-4-6-7	(1543-1623)	Composer
Julius Caesar (1.3)	1-3-1-6-3	(c. 100-44 BC)	Statesman
Count Cagliostro (3.2)	1-4-7-6-1	(1743-95)	Occultist
Pedro Calderón (1.8)	6-4-1-2-1	(1600-81)	Dramatist
Caligula (1.2)	1-6-6-6-1	(AD 12-41)	Emperor
Maria Callas (2.0)	3-1-1-4-3	(1923-77)	Singer
John Calvin (1.8)	6-1-6-6-3	(1509-64)	Theologian
Albert Camus (1.6)	3-4-3-4-3	(1913-60)	Writer
José Raúl Capablanca (2.0)	2-3-7-2-7	(1888-1942)	Chess-master

Michel Angelo da Caravaggio (2.6)	7-1-4-2-1	(1569-1609)	Painter
Thomas Carlyle (1.7)	6-6-1-2-1	(1795-1881)	Writer
Enrico Caruso (1.2)	2-4-1-4-3	(1873-1921)	Singer
Pablo Casals (2.0)	2-4-7-6-3	(1876-1973)	Musician
Catherine the Great (1.6)	1-6-1-4-1	(1729-96)	Empress
St Catharine of Alexandria (2.6)	6-6-6-6-7	(d. AD 307)	Martyr
William Caxton (1.6)	2-5-1-6-5	(c. 1422- c.1491)	Printer
Edgar Cayce (1.7)	2-2-4-6-7	(1877-1945)	Clairvoyant
Miguel Cervantes (1.7)	6-4-3-6-7	(1547-1616)	Writer
Paul Cézanne (2.6)	3-4-7-6-3	(1839-1906)	Painter
Marc Chagall (1.9)	2-4-4-6-7	(1887-1985)	Painter
Neville Chamberlain (1.6)	3-7-1-6-7	(1869-1940)	Politician
Charles Chaplin (1.6)	2-4-1-4-4	(1889-1977)	Film actor/director
Charlemagne (2.2)	1-1-1-6-7	(742-814)	Emperor
Vicomte de Chateaubriand (1.6)	3-6-1-4-7	(1768-1848)	Writer/politician
Geoffrey Chaucer (1.6)	2-4-6-2-3	(1342-1400)	Poet
Anton Chekov (1.8)	2-4-2-4-3	(1860-1904)	Author
Frederick Chopin (2.0)	4-4-1-6-2	(1810-49)	Composer
Chou En-lai (2.3)	1-3-1-4-3	(1898-1976)	Politician
Queen Christina (1.5)	2-6-6-4-7	(1626-89)	Queen of Sweden
Winston Churchill (3.0)	2-1-1-4-1	(1874-1965)	Statesman
Marcus Tullius Cicero (1.7)	3-3-1-4-5	(106-43 BC)	Orator/statesman
Giovanni Cimabue (2.35)	6-6-4-6-7	(1240-1302)	Painter
Georges Clemenceau (1.6)	3-1-1-6-7	(1841-1929)	Statesman
James Clerk-Maxwell (1.7)	2-1-1-2-5	(1831-79)	Physicist
Jean Cocteau (1.7)	3-4-4-2-3	(1889-1963)	Poet/playwright
Christopher Columbus (2.0)	6-6-1-2-3	(1451-1506)	Explorer
Auguste Comte (1.7)	3-4-1-6-3	(1798-1857)	Philosopher
Confucius (5.0)	3-7-2-6-1	(551-479 BC)	Philosopher
Joseph Conrad (1.75)	4-4-6-6-7	(1857-1924)	Writer
Constantine I (the Great) (1.8)	1-6-6-2-7	(c. 274-337)	Emperor
Captain James Cook (1.7)	3-7-1-6-7	(1728-79)	Explorer
Nicolas Copernicus (2.3)	2-3-5-2-3	(1473-1543)	Astronomer
Le Corbusier (2.0)	3-7-7-4-7	(1887-1965)	Architect
Pierre Corneille (1.7)	3-2-1-6-3	(1606-84)	Dramatist
Jean Baptiste Corot (1.8)	3-2-4-6-7	(1796-1875)	Painter

Hernando Cortés (1.7)	6-1-7-6-7	(1485-1547)	Explorer
Alfred Cortot (1.6)	4-2-4-2-3	(1877-1962)	Musician
Francois Couperin (2.3)	4-4-4-6-7	(1668-1733)	Composer
Miles Coverdale (1.6)	6-6-7-6-3	(1488-1569)	Biblical scholar
Noel Coward (1.3)	2-4-3-4-3	(1899-1973)	Actor/dramatist
Oliver Cromwell (2.1)	1-1-6-6-3	(1599-1658)	Statesman
Aleister Crowley (1.6)	6-1-7-6-1	(1875-1947)	Occultist
Mme Curie (2.0)	3-3-5-4-7	(1867-1934)	Physicist/chemist
Gottlieb Daimler (1.6)	3-5-1-4-3	(1834-99)	Engineer
John Dalton (2.0)	2-5-5-4-3	(1766-1844)	Chemist
Dante Alighieri (2.0)	1-4-1-6-7	(1265-1321)	Poet
Georges Jacques Danton (1.7)	3-4-1-6-3	(1759-94)	Politician
Darius the Great (1.6)	1-1-6-4-7	(548-486 BC)	King
Charles Darwin (2.0)	2-7-5-2-5	(1809-82)	Scientist
King David (1.7)	6-1-1-6-7	(1000-960 BC)	King
Claude Debussy (1.7)	3-4-4-6-3	(1862-1918)	Composer
Charles de Gaulle (2.4)	3-1-1-4-1	(1890-1970)	General/statesman
Eugène Delacroix (2.3)	3-4-1-4-7	(1798-1863)	Painter
Demosthenes (1.7)	6-1-3-6-1	(383-322 BC)	Orator/politician
René Descartes (2.3)	5-5-1-4-3	(1596-1650)	Philosopher/ mathematician
Jan de Witt (1.7)	3-1-7-6-1	(1625-72)	Politician
Sergei Diaghilev (1.6)	4-4-1-6-3	(1872-1929)	Impresario
Grantly Dick-Read (1.6)	2-6-4-2-3	(1890-1959)	Gynaecologist
Charles Dickens (1.9)	2-4-2-4-3	(1812-70)	Writer
Emily Dickinson (1.8)	2-6-6-4-7	(1830-86)	Poet
Denis Diderot (1.7)	3-6-4-2-3	(1713-84)	Writer
Rudolph Diesel (1.6)	6-7-1-4-5	(1858-1913)	Engineer
Diogenes (1.6)	1-6-1-4-7	(412-323 BC)	Philosopher
Benjamin Disraeli (1.7)	2-3-1-4-7	(1804-81)	Statesman
Gaetano Donizetti (1.8)	4-4-4-2-7	(1797-1848)	Composer
John Donne (1.8)	2-4-7-4-3	(1572-1631)	Poet
Fyodor Dostoevsky (2.0)	6-7-4-6-3	(1821-81)	Writer
Arthur Conan Doyle (1.7)	2-6-4-6-1	(1859-1930)	Writer
Sir Francis Drake (1.7)	1-4-1-6-1	(c. 1540-96)	Admiral
Hans Driesch (1.7)	3-3-7-6-3	(1867-1941)	Scientist
Henri Dunant (1.8)	3-6-1-4-3	(1828-1910)	Philanthropist
Albrecht Dürer (2.4)	1-7-7-4-1	(1471-1528)	Painter
Antonin Dvorak (2.1)	2-4-7-2-3	(1841-1904)	Composer

Meister Eckhart (2.2)	6-6-1-6-3	(c. 1260-1327)	Mystic/philosopher
Mary Baker Eddy (2.0)	2-6-1-6-3	(1821-1910)	Christian Science founder
Thomas Edison (1.7)	3-1-1-2-5	(1847-1931)	Inventor
Frederik van Eeden (1.6)	3-3-1-4-7	(1860-1932)	Writer
Albert Einstein (2.2)	2-2-4-2-3	(1879-1955)	Physicist
Dwight Eisenhower (1.5)	3-1-1-2-3	(1890-1969)	General/president
Elijah (2.5)	2-1-1-6-1	(fl. c. 900 BC)	Prophet
George Eliot (1.6)	2-4-1-6-3	(1819-80)	Writer
T S Eliot (2.0)	2-3-1-6-7	(1888-1965)	Poet
Queen Elizabeth I (1.6)	2-3-1-6-7	(1533-1603)	Queen
Ralph Waldo Emerson (2.2)	2-3-7-6-3	(1803-82)	Poet
Friedrich Engels (1.7)	3-4-7-2-7	(1820-95)	Political philosopher
Epicurus (1.6)	6-4-6-4-3	(c. 341-270 BC)	Philosopher
Desiderius Erasmus (2.2)	2-2-1-6-3	(1466-1536)	Humanist
Euclid (2.3)	3-5-3-6-7	(fl. 300 BC)	Mathematician
Euripedes (1.8)	3-4-1-6-3	(c. 480-406 BC)	Dramatist
Max Euwe (2.0)	1-5-3-6-7	(1901-83)	Chess-master
George Farquhar (1.8)	6-4-1-6-7	(1678-1707)	Dramatist
Ferdinand II of Aragon (1.7)	3-7-7-6-7	(1452-1516)	King
Georges Feydeau (1.7)	4-2-7-2-3	(1862-1921)	Dramatist
Johann Gottlieb Fichte (1.7)	2-6-7-6-3	(1762-1814)	Philosopher
Alexander Fleming (2.0)	2-5-5-2-3	(1881-1955)	Bacteriologist
Henry Ford (1.7)	5-7-7-6-3	(1863-1947)	Engineer
St Francis of Assisi (3.5)	6-6-6-2-3	(1182-1226)	Founder of Franciscan Order
General Franco (1.7)	1-1-1-6-7	(1892-1975)	Dictator
Benjamin Franklin (2.5)	4-5-1-6-3	(1706-90)	Statesman/scientist
Frederick II, the Great (1.7)	5-7-7-2-7	(1712-86)	King
Sigmund Freud (2.0)	2-7-1-6-3	(1856-1939)	Founder of psychoanalysis
Friedrich Froebel (1.6)	2-5-1-4-3	(1782-1852)	Educator
Erich Fromm (1.6)	6-2-4-6-7	(1900-1980)	Psychoanalyst
Buckminster Fuller (2.0)	2-1-7-4-7	(1896-1983)	Architect/engineer
Galileo Galilei (2.2)	1-4-1-6-5	(1564-1642)	Astronomer
Leon Michel Gambetta (1.6)	3-1-1-4-1	(1838-82)	Statesman
Indira Gandhi (2.0)	1-1-7-6-3	(1917-1984)	Indian prime minister
Mahatma Gandhi (2.0)	2-2-6-2-3	(1869-1948)	Indian leader

Giuseppe Garibaldi (2.0)	1-4-7-6-3	(1807-82)	Patriot
Elizabeth Gaskell (2.0)	2-2-1-4-6	(1810-65)	Writer
Paul Gauguin (2.0)	5-4-1-6-7	(1848-1903)	Painter
Johann Karl Friedrich Gauss (1.7)	3-4-1-6-3	(1777-1855)	Mathematician
Genghis Khan (1.5)	1-7-6-6-1	(1162-1227)	Conqueror/ruler
George Gershwin (1.6)	2-4-3-6-3	(1898-1937)	Composer
Edward Gibbon (1.6)	2-4-1-2-7	(1737-94)	Historian
Giorgione (2.3)	4-4-7-6-2	(c. 1478-1511)	Painter
Jean Giraudoux (1.7)	2-4-1-6-3	(1882-1944)	Writer/diplomat
William Gladstone (1.7)	2-6-1-6-3	(1808-98)	Statesman
Christoph W. Gluck (1.8)	2-4-4-4-3	(1714-87)	Composer
Johann von Goethe (2.2)	2-1-4-4-7	(1749-1832)	Poet
Nikolai Gogol (1.7)	2-4-1-6-7	(1809-52)	Dramatist
Carlo Goldoni (1.7)	2-2-4-6-7	(1707-93)	Dramatist
Oliver Goldsmith (1.7)	6-2-6-6-3	(1728-74)	Writer
Charles George Gordon (1.6)	1-6-1-2-1	(1833-85)	General
Francisco José de Goya (2.4)	1-4-1-4-1	(1746-1828)	Painter
El Greco (3.0)	1-4-7-6-1	(1541-1614)	Painter
Pope Gregory I (2.0)	1-6-1-6-7	(c. 540-604)	Pope
Edvard Grieg (1.7)	2-4-2-6-3	(1843-1907)	Composer
Franz Grillparzer (1.6)	4-4-7-6-7	(1791-1872)	Poet
Hugo Grotius (2.0)	1-3-1-2-3	(1583-1645)	Jurist/theologian
Ernesto (Che) Guevara (1.7)	7-1-1-2-3	(1928-67)	Revolutionary leader
Georges I. Gurdjieff (2.2)	4-4-1-6-3	(1872-1949)	Occultist/teacher
Hazel Hunkins Hallinan (2.0)	3-4-1-6-7	(1890-1982)	Suffragette
Frans Hals (2.3)	3-4-1-4-3	(c. 1580-1666)	Painter
Dag Hammarskjöld (2.0)	2-6-1-6-3	(1905-61)	Diplomat
George Frederick Handel (2.4)	4-6-1-4-7	(1685-1759)	Composer
Hannibal (1.7)	1-1-6-6-3	(247-182 BC)	Soldier
James Keir Hardie (1.7)	2-6-1-2-3	(1856-1915)	Politician
Gerhart Hauptmann (1.6)	2-4-3-6-7	(1862-1946)	Dramatist
Franz Joseph Haydn (2.4)	3-4-4-2-7	(1732-1809)	Composer
Friedrich Hebbel (1.5)	2-4-1-4-7	(1813-63)	Dramatist
Georg Hegel (2.0)	4-2-5-4-3	(1770-1831)	Philosopher
Heinrich Heine (2.0)	4-4-1-2-7	(1797-1856)	Poet
W K Heisenberg (1.6)	2-6-3-4-1	(1901-76)	Physicist
Ernest Hemingway (1.6)	2-1-1-6-1	(1899-1961)	Writer

King Henry VIII (1.6)	1-1-1-4-1	(1491-1547)	King
Heraclitus (2.0)	3-4-1-2-3	(c.. 535-475 BC)	Philosopher
Hercules (2.2)	1-6-1-6-1	(c. 8000 BC)	Avatar
Hermes (4.0)	5-1-1-6-3	(c. 7000 BC)	Avatar
Herodotus (1.7)	5-1-7-6-7	(c. 485-425 BC)	Historian
William Herschel (2.0)	2-2-1-6-1	(1738-1822)	Astronomer
Heinrich Hertz (1.7)	3-7-5-6-3	(1857-94)	Physicist
Theodor Herzl (1.7)	3-7-7-2-3	(1860-1904)	Zionist leader
Hermann Hesse (2.1)	4-4-3-6-3	(1877-1962)	Writer
Paul Hindemith (1.7)	4-4-1-2-3	(1895-1963)	Composer
Paul von Hindenburg (1.7)	1-1-1-6-7	(1847-1934)	General/president
Hippocrates (2.0)	2-4-5-6-7	(c. 460- c.370 BC)	Physician
Iwasa Hiroshige (2.0)	4-4-7-6-7	(1797-1858)	Painter
Adolf Hitler (2.0)	2-4-1-4-3	(1889-1945)	Dictator
Ho Chi-Minh (1.7)	1-5-1-6-3	(1892-1969)	Chief of state
Geoffrey Hodson (1.6)	2-4-6-6-3	(1892-1983)	Theosophist
Hugo von Hofmannsthal (1.7)	2-4-6-6-3	(1874-1929)	Poet/dramatist
Katsushika Hokusai (2.0)	4-7-7-6-5	(1760-1849)	Painter/ woodblock artist
Hans Holbein (2.3)	4-1-4-6-5	(1497-1543)	Painter
Homer (1.7)	4-2-6-2-4	(9th cent. BC)	Poet
Herbert Clark Hoover (2.0)	2-3-3-1-7	(1874-1964)	President
Gerard Manley Hopkins (2.2)	4-6-4-2-7	(1844-89)	Poet
L. Ron Hubbard (1.8)	3-7-1-6-3	(1911-86)	Founder of Scientology
Victor Hugo (2.0)	3-4-5-6-3	(1802-85)	Writer
David Hume (1.7)	3-6-1-6-3	(1711-76)	Philosopher
Aldous Huxley (1.7)	2-4-4-2-3	(1894-1963)	Writer
Henrik Ibsen (2.0)	2-4-1-6-5	(1828-1906)	Dramatist
Jean Auguste Ingres (2.2)	4-7-7-4-7	(1780-1867)	Painter
Arletta Jacobs (2.0)	5-1-3-6-1	(1849-1929)	Suffragette
Alfred Jarry (1.6)	3-4-4-6-7	(1873-1907)	Writer
Thomas Jefferson (2.0)	2-6-1-4-7	(1743-1826)	President
Jesus of Nazareth (4.0)	6-1-1-2-1	(24 BC-9 AD)	Avatar
Jezebel (1.5)	1-6-3-6-3	(d. 846 BC)	Phoenician princess
Mohammed Ali Jinnah (1.8)	3-1-2-4-7	(1876-1948)	First governor of Pakistan
St Joan of Arc (3.3)	5-1-3-6-6	(c. 1412-31)	Martyr
Pope John XXIII (2.0)	6-2-4-6-3	(1881-1963)	Pope

St John the Baptist (3.3)	2-6-1-6-1	(b.c. 27 BC)	Prophet
St John the Beloved (3.0)	2-2-6-2-1	(d. c. 100 AD)	Disciple/apostle
Samuel Johnson (1.6)	2-1-1-6-7	(1709-84)	Writer
Ben Jonson (2.0)	2-4-1-6-3	(1572-1637)	Dramatist
St Joseph (2.2)	6-2-3-4-2	(1st cent. AD)	Carpenter
Joseph of Arimathea (2.0)	2-6-1-2-4	(1st cent. AD)	Councillor
Joshua, son of Nun (2.3)	6-7-6-1-1	(fl. 1500 BC)	Isrealite leader
James Joyce (1.7)	2-4-1-4-3	(1882-1941)	Writer
Judas Iscariot (1.7)	6-6-3-4-3	(1st cent. AD)	Disciple
William Q Judge (2.0)	6-2-1-6-3	(1851-96)	Theosophist
Carl Jung (2.2)	2-6-4-4-3	(1875-1961)	Psychiatrist
Kabir (4.2)	2-2-4-4-7	(c. 1450-1518)	Poet
Franz Kafka (1.7)	2-4-4-6-3	(1883-1924)	Writer
Theodor Kaluza (1.5)	3-5-1-4-7	(____-____?)	Physicist
Aminu Kano (1.5)	2-6-1-2-3	(1920-__?)	Revolutionary
Immanuel Kant (2.2)	6-4-1-2-5	(1724-1804)	Philosopher
Edvard Kardelj (2.5)	7-6-7-6-1	(1910-79)	Yugoslav leader/ diplomat
John Keats (1.7)	4-6-2-2-2	(1795-1821)	Poet
Helen Adams Keller (1.7)	1-1-4-2-5	(1880-1968)	Writer/scholar
Frank Billings Kellogg (2.1)	2-3-1-6-7	(1856-1937)	Statesman
J F Kennedy (2.4)	2-1-7-6-1	(1917-63)	President
Jomo Kenyatta (1.5)	2-6-1-2-1	(1894-1978)	Politician
Johann Kepler (1.7)	3-5-1-2-5	(1571-1630)	Astronomer
John Maynard Keynes (1.8)	5-2-1-2-3	(1883-1946)	Economist
Inayat Khan (2.1)	6-2-6-6-3	(1882-1927)	Sufi teacher
Nikita Khrushchev (2.0)	1-1-6-2-3	(1894-1971)	Soviet premier
Sören Aaby Kierkegaard (2.0)	2-4-6-2-3	(1813-55)	Philosopher
Martin Luther King (2.0)	2-2-1-6-3	(1929-68)	Civil rights leader
Mary Kingsley (2.0)	2-1-7-2-7	(1862-1900)	Traveler/writer
Rudyard Kipling (1.8)	6-6-4-4-3	(1865-1936)	Writer
Richard Kirwan (2.0)	5-5-7-4-3	(1733-1812)	Chemist
Shibasaburo Kitasato (2.0)	3-5-5-6-7	(1852-1931)	Bacteriologist
Lord Kitchener (1.7)	6-7-1-6-7	(1850-1916)	Soldier/statesman
Paul Klee (2.0)	4-2-4-6-3	(1879-1940)	Painter
Melanie Klein (1.8)	2-1-1-4-3	(1882-1960)	Psychoanalyst
Heinrich von Kleist (1.6)	2-1-4-6-3	(1777-1811)	Dramatist/poet
Otto Klemperer (1.7)	4-4-1-6-7	(1885-1973)	Conductor
John Knox (2.0)	6-6-1-6-3	(1505-72)	Reformer

Arthur Koestler (1.7)	2-4-1-6-3	(1905-83)	Writer
Fritz Kreisler (1.6)	4-2-2-4-3	(1875-1962)	Musician
Sri Krishna (5.0)	2-6-4-6-3	(c. 3000 BC)	Avatar
Krishnamurti (4.0)	2-2-4-6-7	(1895-1986)	Teacher
Paul Kruger (2.0)	1-1-1-6-7	(1825-1904)	Politician
Eugène Labiche (1.7)	2-4-3-6-7	(1815-88)	Comic dramatist
Charles Lamb (1.7)	2-4-4-6-3	(1775-1834)	Writer
Lao-tse (4.2)	2-4-4-2-3	(570-490 BC)	Philosopher
Pierre Simon Laplace (2.0)	3-3-1-2-3	(1749-1827)	Mathematician/ astronomer
Hugh Latimer (1.7)	6-6-6-2-3	(c. 1485-1555)	Martyr
Antoine Lavoisier (1.7)	3-5-5-6-3	(1743-94)	Chemist
D H Lawrence (1.7)	2-2-4-4-3	(1885-1930)	Writer
T E Lawrence (1.6)	2-6-6-6-3	(1888-1935)	Soldier
C W Leadbeater (2.4)	7-3-5-6-7	(1847-1934)	Theosophist
Anton van Leeuwenhoek (1.7)	3-5-5-2-7	(1632-1723)	Scientist
Gottfried Leibniz (1.7)	5-7-5-6-1	(1646-1716)	Philosopher/ mathematician
Vladimir Ilyich Lenin (2.2)	5-7-1-6-3	(1870-1924)	Soviet leader
John Lennon (1.6)	3-7-4-4-3	(1940-80)	Musician
Pope Leo X (2.0)	6-3-7-6-3	(1475-1521)	Pope
Leonardo da Vinci (4.4)	4-7-7-4-7	(1452-1519)	Painter
Gotthold E. Lessing (1.7)	3-4-4-2-3	(1729-81)	Writer
C S Lewis (1.7)	2-6-6-6-3	(1898-1963)	Writer
Abraham Lincoln (3.3)	1-2-1-2-1	(1809-65)	President
Carl Linnaeus (1.6)	2-4-3-2-3	(1707-78)	Botanist
Franz Liszt (2.2)	4-6-3-6-7	(1811-86)	Composer
Dr David Livingstone (1.6)	2-6-1-6-7	(1813-73)	Explorer/missionary
David Lloyd-George (1.8)	4-6-1-6-3	(1863-1945)	Statesman
John Locke (2.3)	4-7-1-2-7	(1632-1704)	Philosopher
Frederigo Garcia Lorca (2.3)	7-4-1-6-3	(1899-1936)	Poet
Hendrik Antoon Lorentz (2.2)	3-5-5-6-3	(1853-1928)	Physicist
Ignatius de Loyola (1.7)	6-6-1-2-7	(1491-1556)	Soldier/ecclesiastic
St Luke (2.4)	6-6-2-6-3	(1st cent. AD)	Disciple/apostle
Martin Luther (2.3)	6-6-1-2-3	(1483-1546)	Religious reformer
Rosa Luxemburg (1.7)	6-3-1-6-3	(1871-1919)	Revolutionary
Douglas MacArthur (1.7)	1-3-1-6-1	(1880-1964)	General
Niccolo Machiavelli (1.6)	3-3-6-6-3	(1469-1527)	Statesman

Count Maurice Maeterlinck (1.7)	4-4-7-6-3	(1862-1949)	Dramatist
Ferdinand Magellan (2.0)	1-1-5-6-3	(c. 1480-1521)	Navigator
Gustav Mahler (1.9)	4-4-4-6-3	(1860-1911)	Composer
Maimonides (Moses ben Maimon) (2.3)	2-1-1-4-3	(1135-1204)	Philosopher
Archbishop Makarios III (1.7)	3-3-3-6-7	(1913-1977)	Ecclesiastic/ politician
Thomas Mann (2.0)	4-4-7-2-3	(1875-1955)	Writer
Andrea Mantegna (2.2)	2-4-6-6-1	(1431-1506)	Painter
Mao Tse-tung (3.2)	1-1-1-2-1	(1893-1976)	Chief of state
Jean Paul Marat (1.7)	3-1-1-6-3	(1743-93)	Politician
Guglielmo Marconi (2.0)	2-3-5-6-3	(1874-1937)	Inventor
Pierre de Marivaux (1.6)	2-4-6-2-7	(1688-1763)	Comic dramatist
St Mark (2.3)	6-4-6-6-3	(1st cent. AD)	Disciple/apostle
Christopher Marlowe (1.8)	2-4-1-4-1	(1564-93)	Dramatist
Marpa (4.5)	6-4-4-6-3	(11th cent. AD)	Yogi
Simone Martini (2.5)	6-4-1-2-7	(c. 1284-1344)	Painter
Karl Marx (2.2)	6-2-5-6-3	(1818-83)	Political philosopher
St Mary (2.2)	6-6-2-2-3	(d. c. 63 AD)	Mother of Jesus
Masaccio (2.7)	4-4-7-6-3	(1401-28)	Painter
Henri Matisse (2.4)	3-6-1-4-7	(1869-1954)	Painter
St Matthew (2.4)	6-7-4-6-3	(1st cent. AD)	Disciple/apostle
William Somerset Maugham (1.7)	2-2-4-2-7	(1874-1965)	Writer
Guy de Maupassant (2.2)	3-4-4-2-1	(1850-93)	Writer
Damodar K Mavalankar (1.7)	2-6-3-6-3	(1857-____?)	Theosophist
Vladimir Mayakovsky (1.7)	4-4-1-6-7	(1894-1930)	Poet
Lorenzo Medici (1.8)	4-1-3-4-3	(1449-92)	Ruler
Meher Baba (2.4)	2-3-5-6-7	(1894-1969)	Spiritual teacher
Golda Meir (1.7)	3-1-1-6-3	(1898-1978)	Prime minister
Herman Melville (1.6)	6-4-4-6-3	(1819-91)	Writer
Felix Mendelssohn-Bartholdy (2.4)	4-4-1-6-3	(1809-47)	Composer
Friedrich Mesmer (1.6)	3-7-1-6-3	(1734-1815)	Physician
Prince Metternich (1.6)	1-1-1-6-7	(1773-1859)	Statesman
Michelangelo (3.3)	1-4-4-6-1	(1475-1564)	Sculptor/painter
Milarepa (3.5)	6-4-4-4-3	(1052-1135)	Poet
Darius Milhaud (1.8)	2-4-4-4-7	(1892-1974)	Composer

John Milton (1.8)	2-6-4-6-7	(1608-74)	Poet
Amedeo Modigliani (1.7)	6-4-4-4-7	(1884-1920)	Painter/sculptor
Mohammed (3.4)	2-3-1-6-3	(570-632)	Prophet
Molière (2.2)	3-3-1-6-3	(1622-73)	Dramatist
Tirso de Molina (1.6)	2-4-3-6-3	(1584-1648)	Dramatist
Michel Eyquem de Montaigne (1.7)	3-6-3-6-5	(1533-92)	Writer
Charles de Montesquieu (2.0)	3-6-4-6-3	(1689-1755)	Philosopher
Claudio Monteverdi (2.4)	4-4-7-6-7	(1567-1643)	Composer
Montezuma II (1.6)	6-1-6-6-3	(1466-1520)	Emperor
Henry Moore (1.8)	2-4-7-6-7	(1898-1986)	Sculptor
Moses (2.3)	6-6-1-4-1	(12th cent. BC)	Prophet
W A Mozart (3.0)	4-4-4-4-3	(1756-91)	Composer
Swami Muktananda (4.0)	4-4-2-4-3	(1908-1982)	Spiritual teacher
Kaj Munk (1.7)	3-4-6-4-3	(1898-1944)	Dramatist/priest
Bartolomé Murillo (2.2)	4-6-1-6-3	(1618-82)	Painter
Alfred de Musset (1.7)	3-4-5-6-3	(1810-57)	Poet/dramatist
Benito Mussolini (2.2)	2-1-1-6-1	(1883-1945)	Dictator
Guru Nanak (3.0)	6-6-1-2-3	(1469-1538)	Founder of Sikhism
Napoleon I (2.2)	3-1-1-4-5	(1769-1821)	General/emperor
Gamal Abdel Nasser (1.7)	2-1-1-6-1	(1918-70)	Egyptian president
Jawaharlal Nehru (2.0)	1-2-1-6-3	(1889-1964)	Indian statesman
A S Neill (1.7)	2-6-1-4-3	(1883-1973)	Educator
Horatio Nelson (1.6)	1-1-5-2-7	(1758-1805)	Naval commander
Nero (1.4)	1-1-4-6-3	(37-68 AD)	Emperor
Barnett Newman (1.7)	4-7-7-6-7	(1905-70)	Painter/ mathematician
Isaac Newton (2.2)	3-3-1-6-5	(1642-1727)	Scientist
Ben Nicholson (1.7)	2-4-4-6-3	(1894-1982)	Painter
Friedrich Nietzsche (1.9)	1-4-1-6-3	(1844-1900)	Philosopher
Florence Nightingale (1.6)	2-2-4-6-6	(1820-1910)	Nurse/ hospital reformer
Alfred Nobel (1.7)	2-6-3-6-1	(1833-96)	Inventor/ manufacturer
Nostradamus (1.7)	3-3-6-6-3	(1503-66)	Astrologer
Yoshikazu Okada (2.1)	6-6-6-4-3	(1901-1974)	Spiritual teacher
Colonel H S Olcott (2.2)	2-1-7-6-7	(1832-1907)	Theosophist
Omar Khayyam (1.6)	6-4-6-2-7	(c. 1050-c. 1123)	Astronomer/poet
Eugene O'Neill (1.6)	2-6-1-4-3	(1888-1953)	Dramatist

J Robert Oppenheimer (2.0)	5-3-7-6-3	(1904-67)	Physicist
Origen (4.3)	2-1-1-6-7	(185-254)	Theologian/ philosopher
Ouspensky (2.0)	2-4-6-6-3	(1878-1947)	Writer
Ovid (Publius Ovidius Naso) (1.7)	1-4-7-6-3	(43 BC-17 AD)	Poet
Ignace Jan Paderewski (2.0)	6-4-7-4-7	(1860-1941)	Musician/statesman
Nicolo Paganini (1.7)	4-4-1-4-7	(1782-1840)	Musician
G P da Palestrina (2.0)	4-6-4-6-3	(1525-94)	Composer
Olof Palme (2.1)	3-6-7-4-7	(1927-1986)	Prime minister
Panini (1.8)	2-5-5-6-7	(6th-7th cent. BC)	Sanskrit grammarian
Emmeline Pankhurst (1.7)	6-6-1-2-3	(1857-1928)	Suffragette
Paracelsus (2.3)	1-4-5-6-7	(1493-1541)	Physician
Vilfredo Pareto (2.0)	2-3-3-6-3	(1848-1923)	Economist/ sociologist
Charles Parnell (1.7)	6-6-1-4-3	(1846-91)	Politician
Blaise Pascal (2.4)	5-3-1-2-3	(1623-62)	Scientist
Boris Pasternak (1.7)	3-4-3-6-7	(1890-1960)	Writer
Louis Pasteur (2.2)	5-7-7-2-3	(1822-95)	Chemist
Patanjali (4.3)	2-6-1-4-3	(1st cent. BC)	Philosopher
George S. Patton (1.7)	1-6-1-2-1	(1885-1945)	General
St Patrick (2.2)	6-1-4-4-1	(c. 385-c. 461)	Bishop
St Paul (3.0)	5-1-1-6-1	(1st cent. AD)	Apostle
Pericles (1.8)	1-7-1-2-1	(495-429 BC)	Statesman
Evita Perón (1.6)	1-3-4-6-3	(1919-52)	Actress/politician
Juan Perón (1.7)	1-1-1-6-7	(1895-1974)	Soldier/statesman
Johann H. Pestalozzi (1.7)	2-6-7-6-3	(1746-1827)	Educator
Peter the Great (1.7)	6-7-1-6-3	(1672-1725)	Emperor
St Peter (3.5)	1-4-1-2-7	(1st cent. AD)	Disciple/apostle
Francesco Petrarch (1.7)	2-7-1-4-7	(1304-74)	Poet/scholar
Phidias (2.2)	4-7-7-6-7	(5th cent. BC)	Sculptor
Pablo Picasso (2.4)	7-4-1-6-3	(1881-1973)	Painter
Pindar (Pindaros) (1.7)	3-7-7-2-3	(c. 522-c. 440 BC)	Poet
Father Pio da Pietrelcina (2.3)	6-2-6-2-3	(1887-1969)	Healer/stigmatist
Pontius Pilate (1.4)	2-6-3-6-7	(26 BC)	Roman procurator
William Pitt (the Younger) (2.3)	1-1-1-2-3	(1759-1806)	Statesman
Max Planck (2.2)	2-7-1-4-5	(1858-1947)	Physicist
Plato (2.4)	2-4-7-6-7	(c. 427-c. 347 BC)	Philosopher

Marco Polo (1.6)	3-3-6-6-3	(1254-1324)	Explorer
Ezra Pound (2.0)	7-1-1-4-7	(1885-1972)	Poet
Nicolas Poussin (2.4)	7-7-6-4-3	(1594-1665)	Painter
Praxiteles (1.6)	4-4-4-6-1	(fl. 4th cent. BC)	Sculptor
Dr Joseph Priestley (2.0)	3-7-5-6-3	(1733-1804)	Churchman/chemist
Sergei Prokofiev (1.8)	4-7-1-4-3	(1891-1955)	Composer
Marcel Proust (1.7)	2-4-4-6-7	(1871-1922)	Writer
Giacomo Puccini (1.7)	4-4-4-6-7	(1858-1924)	Composer
Alexandr Pushkin (2.0)	4-4-1-6-3	(1799-1837)	Poet
Pythagoras (2.2)	2-6-5-6-3	(fl. 6th cent. BC)	Philosopher/ mathematician
Jean Racine (2.2)	3-1-7-4-7	(1639-99)	Poet
Sir Walter Raleigh (1.7)	1-4-3-4-7	(1552-1618)	Courtier/navigator/ writer
Rama (4.0)	1-6-1-2-1	(c. 6000 BC)	Avatar
Ramakrishna	2-6-6-4-7	(1836-86)	Avatar
Ramana Maharshi	2-6-4-2-3	(1879-1950)	Avatar
Jean Philippe Rameau (2.2)	3-4-4-6-7	(1683-1764)	Composer
Rameses II (2.0)	1-1-7-2-5	(1292-1225 BC)	King
Raphael (3.0)	2-4-7-6-7	(1483-1520)	Painter
Grigori Efimovich Rasputin (1.6)	6-6-3-6-7	(c. 1871-1916)	Monk
Maurice Ravel (2.0)	4-7-3-4-7	(1875-1937)	Composer
Max Reger (1.7)	2-2-4-4-3	(1873-1916)	Composer
Wilhelm Reich (2.0)	2-1-7-6-3	(1897-1957)	Psychoanalyst
Rembrandt (3.0)	2-4-3-4-7	(1606-69)	Painter
Auguste Renoir (2.0)	4-2-3-2-3	(1841-1919)	Painter
Ottorino Respighi (1.65)	4-4-3-6-3	(1879-1936)	Composer
Cecil Rhodes (1.6)	6-1-7-6-3	(1853-1902)	Statesman
Sir Ralph Richardson (1.7)	2-4-7-2-3	(1902-83)	Actor
Cardinal Richelieu (1.7)	3-3-1-4-7	(1585-1642)	Statesman/cleric
Rainer Maria Rilke (1.7)	2-4-4-6-3	(1875-1926)	Poet
Arthur Rimbaud (1.7)	3-4-1-2-3	(1854-91)	Poet
Paul Robeson (1.6)	2-4-1-6-3	(1898-1976)	Singer/actor
Robespierre (1.7)	1-3-1-4-3	(1758-94)	Revolutionary
Auguste Rodin (1.9)	3-4-4-2-7	(1840-1917)	Sculptor
Helena Roerich (4.0)	1-2-1-6-3	(1879-1955)	Occultist
Nicholas Roerich (2.1)	7-7-7-6-7	(1874-1947)	Painter

Archbishop Romero (1.7)	2-2-3-6-1	(1917-80)	Human rights spokesman
Pierre de Ronsard (1.6)	2-4-4-6-3	(1524-85)	Poet
Wilhelm von Röntgen (1.7)	5-7-5-2-3	(1845-1923)	Physicist
Anna Eleanor Roosevelt (2.0)	7-6-1-2-1	(1884-1962)	Humanitarian
Franklin D. Roosevelt (2.2)	2-4-1-2-1	(1884-1945)	President
Mark Rothko (1.8)	2-4-4-6-3	(1903-70)	Painter
Jean Jacques Rousseau (2.2)	2-6-7-4-7	(1712-78)	Political philosopher
T Subba Row (1.7)	2-1-7-6-7	(1856-90)	Theosophist
Peter Paul Rubens (3.0)	4-7-1-4-7	(1577-1640)	Painter
Bertrand Russell (1.7)	3-3-1-6-3	(1872-1970)	Philosopher
Charles Taze Russell (1.6)	6-2-1-6-3	(1852-1916)	Jehovah's Witness founder
Ernest Rutherford (2.0)	2-7-7-2-5	(1871-1937)	Physicist
Michiel de Ruyter (2.0)	1-7-1-6-7	(1607-76)	Naval leader
Anwar Sadat (1.9)	2-6-6-2-3	(1918-81)	Egyptian president
Sai Baba of Shirdi	2-4-1-4-3	(1840-1918)	Avatar
Claude de Saint-Simon (1.7)	7-2-6-6-3	(1760-1825)	Political philosopher
George Sand (1.6)	2-4-4-6-3	(1804-76)	Writer
Sappho (1.6)	4-4-4-6-3	(b.c. 650 BC)	Poet
Jean Paul Sartre (1.7)	3-2-3-6-3	(1905-80)	Philosopher/writer
Erik Satie (1.5)	3-5-7-2-4	(1866-1925)	Composer
Girolamo Savonarola (1.7)	6-4-1-6-1	(1452-98)	Religious reformer
Friedrich von Schiller (1.7)	2-4-6-2-7	(1759-1805)	Dramatist/poet
Domenico Scarlatti (2.4)	2-3-4-4-7	(1685-1757)	Composer
Heinrich Schliemann (1.7)	7-1-7-4-7	(1822-90)	Archaeologist
Arnold Schönberg (1.9)	6-4-1-4-7	(1874-1951)	Composer
Artur Schopenhauer (2.2)	6-6-1-2-7	(1788-1860)	Philosopher
Franz Schubert (2.4)	4-2-2-4-2	(1797-1828)	Composer
Robert Schumann (2.3)	6-4-4-6-5	(1810-56)	Composer
Albert Schweitzer (2.4)	2-2-1-4-3	(1875-1965)	Medical missionary
Seneca (the Younger) (1.7)	3-7-6-2-7	(c. 5 BC-65 AD)	Philosopher
William Shakespeare (3.5)	2-4-1-4-3	(1564-1616)	Dramatist/poet
Shankaracharya	2-1-1-6-3	(788-820)	Avatar
George Bernard Shaw (2.0)	2-3-1-2-7	(1856-1950)	Dramatist/writer
Dmitri Shostakovich (2.0)	7-4-4-6-7	(1906-75)	Composer
Sir James Young Simpson (1.7)	5-1-5-4-3	(1811-70)	Physician
Alfred Percy Sinnett (2.2)	2-6-1-6-3	(1840-1921)	Theosophist

Adam Smith (1.7)	3-3-5-4-3	(1723-90)	Economist/ philosopher
Joseph Smith (1.7)	6-6-6-2-7	(1805-44)	Founder of Mormons
Jan Christiaan Smuts (2.0)	2-7-1-6-7	(1870-1950)	Statesman
Socrates (2.4)	6-2-1-6-3	(c. 469-399 BC)	Philosopher
King Solomon (1.7)	2-1-4-2-3	(c. 1015-977 BC)	King
Sophocles (1.7)	3-6-1-4-7	(c. 496-c. 405 BC)	Dramatist
Baird Spalding (1.6)	2-3-5-6-7	(1857-1953)	Traveler/writer
Spartacus (1.5)	1-1-2-2-1	(d. 71 BC)	Rebel
Baruch Spinoza (2.4)	2-3-3-4-3	(1632-77)	Philosopher
Nicolas de Stael (1.8)	4-4-4-6-7	(1914-55)	Painter
Joseph Stalin (2.0)	1-7-7-2-1	(1879-1953)	Chief of state
John Steinbeck (1.6)	7-4-4-6-7	(1902-68)	Writer
Rudolph Steiner (2.2)	2-4-1-6-3	(1861-1925)	Philosopher
Antonio Stradivari (1.65)	2-4-2-4-7	(c. 1644-1737)	Violin maker
David Friedrich Strauss (2.0)	6-1-1-2-7	(1808-74)	Theologian
Richard Strauss (1.8)	1-6-4-4-7	(1864-1949)	Composer
Igor Stravinsky (2.3)	7-4-1-6-7	(1882-1971)	Composer
Johan August Strindberg (1.7)	4-1-7-4-3	(1849-1912)	Dramatist
Peter Stuyvesant (1.7)	6-7-7-2-7	(1592-1672)	Administrator
Achmad Sukarno (1.7)	6-1-3-4-3	(1902-70)	President of Indonesia
Anne Mansfield Sullivan (1.75)	2-2-7-6-3	(1866-1936)	Teacher
President Svoboda (1.7)	5-6-1-6-3	(1895-1979)	Statesman
Emanuel Swedenborg (2.3)	2-4-4-6-3	(1688-1772)	Mystic
Jonathan Swift (1.7)	6-4-1-4-3	(1667-1745)	Writer
Rabindranath Tagore (2.2)	2-4-1-4-7	(1861-1941)	Poet/philosopher
Charles de Talleyrand (1.7)	3-1-3-2-3	(1754-1838)	Statesman
Thomas Tallis (1.7)	4-6-6-6-3	(c. 1505-85)	Composer
Piotr Ilyich Tchaikovsky (1.8)	4-4-3-6-7	(1840-93)	Composer
Pierre Teilhard de Chardin (2.35)	2-6-3-2-3	(1881-1955)	Scientist/philosopher
Alfred Tennyson (2.0)	6-1-4-4-7	(1809-92)	Poet
St Teresa of Avila (3.1)	6-6-3-4-3	(1515-82)	Saint/mystic
Nikola Tesla (2.0)	2-3-1-6-5	(1856-1943)	Inventor
U Thant (1.7)	2-2-1-6-2	(1909-74)	Diplomat
Jacques Thibaud (1.6)	2-2-4-4-3	(1880-1953)	Musician
Dylan Thomas (1.5)	2-4-1-4-3	(1914-53)	Poet

Henry Thoreau (1.6)	2-3-3-6-3	(1817-62)	Writer
Thucydides (1.6)	5-3-1-2-7	(c. 460-c. 400 BC)	Historian
Tintoretto (2.5)	4-7-1-6-7	(1518-94)	Painter
Titian (3.0)	4-4-7-6-7	(c. 1490-1576)	Painter
Marshal Tito (2.5)	1-1-1-4-1	(1892-1980)	Yugoslav premier
J R Tolkien (1.7)	4-6-4-4-3	(1892-1973)	Writer
Leo Tolstoy (2.2)	2-4-6-6-3	(1828-1910)	Writer
Arturo Toscanini (2.0)	3-1-4-4-3	(1867-1957)	Conductor
Leon Trotsky (2.2)	7-1-7-6-3	(1879-1940)	Revolutionary
Wellesley Tudor Pole (2.0)	2-7-7-6-3	(1884-1968)	Mystic
J M W Turner (2.5)	4-4-1-2-3	(1775-1851)	Painter
Mark Twain (1.7)	6-2-4-6-7	(1835-1910)	Writer
William Tyndale (1.7)	6-6-7-6-3	(c. 1492-1536)	Biblical scholar
Paolo Uccello (2.6)	2-4-4-6-7	(1396-1475)	Painter
St Ursula (2.5)	6-6-6-6-7	(4th cent. AD)	Martyr
Anthony van Dyck (2)	4-4-7-6-7	(1599-1641)	Painter
Vincent van Gogh (1.9)	2-6-1-4-7	(1853-90)	Painter
Diego de Silva y Velasquez (2.4)	4-7-1-4-7	(1599-1660)	Painter
Giuseppe Verdi (1.9)	4-4-4-6-7	(1813-1901)	Composer
Jan Vermeer of Delft (2.4)	3-7-4-2-7	(1632-75)	Painter
Paolo Veronese (3.0)	7-4-7-6-7	(1528-88)	Painter
Pancho Villa (1.7)	1-1-3-6-7	(1877-1923)	Revolutionary
Antonio Vivaldi (2.2)	3-4-3-6-7	(1678-1741)	Composer
Vivekananda	2-1-1-6-1	(1862-1902)	Avatar
Francois de Voltaire (2.0)	2-4-1-6-3	(1694-1778)	Writer/philosopher
Joost van den Vondel (2.0)	3-1-7-6-5	(1587-1679)	Poet
Richard Wagner (2.1)	1-1-4-4-7	(1813-83)	Composer
Dame Barbara Ward (2.0)	3-3-5-6-3	(1914-81)	Economist/author
George Washington (2.3)	2-3-1-6-3	(1732-99)	Soldier/president
James Watt (1.7)	2-5-5-4-3	(1736-1819)	Inventor
Anton von Webern (2.0)	4-7-7-6-3	(1883-1945)	Composer
Wang Wei (1.7)	2-7-2-2-3	(699-759)	Buddhist poet/ painter
Kurt Weill (1.7)	6-4-7-6-7	(1900-50)	Composer
Peter Weiss (1.6)	2-3-5-6-7	(1916-82)	Dramatist
Duke of Wellington (1.7)	3-1-1-2-7	(1769-1852)	General/statesman
H G Wells (1.7)	2-2-1-4-3	(1866-1946)	Writer

John Wesley (1.6)	6-6-2-6-3	(1703-91)	Founder of Methodism
Walt Whitman (1.7)	3-6-1-4-7	(1819-91)	Poet
William Wilberforce (1.7)	3-1-1-6-3	(1759-1833)	Political reformer
Tennessee Williams (1.6)	2-4-6-4-3	(1912-82)	Dramatist
George Wishart (2.0)	1-6-6-6-7	(c. 1513-46)	Reformer/martyr
Ludwig Wittgenstein (1.8)	2-7-6-6-7	(1889-1951)	Philosopher
William Wordsworth (1.7)	6-6-4-6-7	(1770-1850)	Poet
Christopher Wren (1.7)	1-1-4-6-7	(1632-1723)	Architect
John Wycliffe (1.7)	2-6-6-2-3	(c. 1329-84)	Religious reformer
Xerxes (1.7)	1-1-3-6-1	(c. 519-465 BC)	King
W B Yeats (1.8)	2-4-4-6-3	(1865-1939)	Poet/dramatist
Yogananda	2-4-6-6-3	(1893-1952)	Avatar
Ossip Zadkine (1.6)	2-4-3-4-3	(1890-1967)	Sculptor
Emiliano Zapata (1.6)	1-1-1-6-3	(c. 1877-1919)	Revolutionary
Emile Zola (2.3)	3-4-1-4-7	(1840-1902)	Writer
Zoroaster (4.5)	4-1-4-6-7	(628-551 BC)	Teacher
Francisco Zurbaran (2.0)	6-7-7-4-7	(1598-1662)	Painter
Huldreich Zwingli (1.7)	6-6-1-2-3	(1484-1531)	Religious reformer

THE GREAT INVOCATION

From the point of Light within the Mind of God
Let light stream forth into the minds of men.
Let Light descend on Earth.

From the point of Love within the Heart of God
Let love stream forth into the hearts of men.
May Christ return to Earth.

From the centre where the Will of God is known
Let purpose guide the little wills of men --
The Purpose which the Masters know and serve.

From the centre which we call the race of men
Let the Plan of Love and Light work out,
and may it seal the door where evil dwells.

Let Light and Love and Power restore the Plan
on Earth.

REFERENCES CITED BY THE AUTHOR

Alice A. Bailey, *Destiny of the Nations* (London: Lucis Press, 1949)

———, *Discipleship in the New Age,* Vol. I & II (London: Lucis Press, 1944)

———, *Education in the New Age* (London: Lucis Press, (1954)

———, *Esoteric Healing* (London: Lucis Press, 1953)

———, *Esoteric Psychology* (London: Lucis Press, 1936)

———, *Externalisation of the Hierarchy,* (London: Lucis Press, 1955)

———, *Letters on Occult Meditation* (London: Lucis Press, 1922)

———, *The Reappearance of the Christ* (London: Lucis Press, 1948)

H. P. Blavatsky, *The Secret Doctrine* (London: Theosophical Publishing House, 1888)

Brandt Commission, *North-South: a Programme for Survival* (Cambridge, MA: MIT Press, 1980)

Helena Roerich, *Leaves of Moria's Garden, Vol. I : The Call,* (New York: Agni Yoga Society, 1924)

———, *Leaves of Morya's Garden, Vol. II: Illumination,* (New York: Agni Yoga Society, 1925)

Benjamin Creme, *The Reappearance of the Christ and the Masters of Wisdom* (1980)

———, *Transmission—A Meditation for the New Age* (1983)

Messages from Maitreya the Christ ,
Volume One — One Hundred Messages (1980)
Volume Two — Messages 101-140 (1982)
(Cassette tapes of these messages are available.)

A Master Speaks (1985)
(Compilation of articles by the Master written for *Share International Magazine)*

Share Internation Magazine

The above books and tapes, including this book, are available from the following:

For North and South America:
TARA CENTER, P.O. Box 6001, North Hollywood, CA 91603, USA

For the U.K.:
TARA PRESS, 59 Dartmouth Park Road, London NW5 1SL, London, U.K.

For the rest of the world:
SHARE NETHERLANDS, P.O. Box 41877, 1009 DB Amsterdam, Holland